CREATING BREAKTHROUGH IDEAS

The Collaboration of Anthropologists and Designers in the Product Development Industry

Edited by
Susan Squires and Bryan Byrne

Foreword by John F. Sherry, Jr.

Bergin & Garvey
Westport, Connecticut • London

Library of Congress Cataloging-in-Publication Data

Creating breakthrough ideas : the collaboration of anthropologists and designers in the product development industry / edited by Susan Squires and Bryan Byrne ; foreword by John F. Sherry, Jr.
    p. cm.
    Includes bibliographical references and index.
    ISBN 0–89789–682–3 (alk. paper)
    1. Manufacturing processes. 2. Design, Industrial. I. Squires, Susan. II. Byrne, Bryan, 1963–
    TS183.C73 2002
    658.5'75—dc21   2001037914

British Library Cataloguing in Publication Data is available.

Library of Congress Catalog Card Number: 2001037914
ISBN: 0–89789–682–3

First published in 2002

Bergin & Garvey, 88 Post Road West, Westport, CT 06881
An imprint of Greenwood Publishing Group, Inc.
www.greenwood.com

Printed in the United States of America

The paper used in this book complies with the Permanent Paper Standard issued by the National Information Standards Organization (Z39.48–1984).

10 9 8 7 6 5 4 3 2 1

Contents

Foreword: Ethnography, Design, and Customer Experience: An Anthropologist's Sense of It All

John F. Sherry, Jr.

Management pundits (Pine and Gilmore 1999; Schmitt 1999; Underhill 1999; Wolf 1999) have finally awakened to a notion that anthropologists have always held as foundational: we are living in an experience economy. This awakening is akin to M. Jourdain's discovery that he had been speaking prose his entire life. Marketers in general, and advertisers in particular (Levy 1978; Randazzo 1993; Williamson 1978) have long realized that their principal mission is to shape the experience of others. What is especially intriguing about our own era—whether you construe the period as hyperindustrial or postmodern—is the apparent supermediation (Real 1989) of experience. From the French philosophers (Baudrillard 1994; Debord 1983) to the American cultural critics (Berman 2000; Frank 1997; Postman 1986), from the lit-crit ad analysts (Twitchell 1996) to the ethnographers of consumption (Appadurai 1986; Gottdiener 1996; McCracken 1988; Sherry 1995), we hear a common warning. The technologies of influence that undergird consumer culture have grown so pervasive and so transparent that they come to resemble a total institution. Soon marketers will not merely shape our experience, they will determine it, providing it to us prepackaged and, effectively, preconsumed.

Although well intentioned (one hopes), this warning is usually declaimed *ex cathedra*, ostensibly by cultural guardians concerned with the erosion of plebian integrity encouraged by those "hucksters of the symbol" (Sahlins 1976) that our culture so outrageously rewards. Ironically, anthropologists have paid surprisingly little attention to the empirics of consumer behavior until (with a few notable exceptions) relatively recently, favoring superstructural critique to infrastructural investigation. Because of a confluence of historical factors—intellectual, ethical, financial—this reflexively uncritical criticism is being balanced by a wave of ethnographic research into the behaviors consumers actually evince, and into some of the motivations underlying those behaviors.

What ethnographers are discovering is that consumption is an active process, literally produced by consumers-cum-*bricoleurs*, in as nonmonolithic a fashion as one might care to imagine. Or, to qualify more precisely this process, consumption is cocreated by marketers and consumers. Marketers provide the tesserae from which consumers compose the mosaics of lifestyles, although in a postmodern climate of multiphrenic selves (Gergen 1991) and marketing cyberscapes (Sherry 1998) the colored stone metaphor—even recognizing consumers' penchant for recutting and altering the hues of these very stones—grows increasingly anachronistic. As rapidly as selves morph, so does the stuff of marketplace behavior. Marketers introduce artifacts and meanings into the environment, which consumers appropriate, transmute, and nativize to suit local desires. Marketers in turn reappropriate and countertransmute these local adaptations and resistances, sending the wheel spinning once again. For better and for worse, marketing and consumption are among the most potent forces of cultural change and cultural stability at work in the world today.

If consumption drives culture, who better than anthropologists to study the driving? If marketing profoundly affects the quality of the drive, who better than anthropologists to advise marketers? Some of us have been making this argument for decades, from inside business schools, advertising agencies, consulting firms, and sundry corporations. Practitioners have been much quicker to recognize the contribution that anthropology stands to make than have our academic colleagues. If applied anthropology has always been the bastard stepchild of the four fields, then certainly "business" anthropology has been the Rosemary's baby of this aspiring fifth subdiscipline. If we demonize ethnographers for consorting with practitioners, then perhaps this book is a useful tool with which to begin an exorcism. The inevitability of "development" has proven a compelling moral mandate for anthropological intervention. So also must the inexorable commingling of desire and stuff demand enlightened anthropological guidance.

A successful marketer purports to give consumers not what they say they want, but what they really want (Levitt 1984). The determination of this deep underlying motivation is generally left to methodologists who have never encountered a consumer in a naturalistic setting, nor practiced systematic subjective personal introspection (Holbrook 1995; Sherry 1995). Further, concern for unanticipated or unintended consequences of marketing decisions does not seem to fall within the purview of these researchers. Even among forward-thinking firms that seat consumer advocates on their boards of directors, it is rare to find a consumerist attitude in the research function. It seems to me that an anthropological habit of mind is a ready remedy for these particular grievances. An ethically engaged ethnographer can penetrate the heart of consumer experience, and render it accessible to intervention in a way that not only minimizes potential harm, but also optimizes the potential benefit consumers are likely to derive. This is a prosocial use of proprietary inquiry.

Before the anthropologist may speak to marketers effectively, the power base of engineering must be breached. Most firms have an engineering ethos, and a product orientation shapes their view of marketing. This is true of as many industries as you care to examine. Engineering (or product development) and marketing are distinct and hostile subcultures speaking mutually unintelligible languages, despite their ostensible devotion to a common cause (Workman 1993). Engineers pursue features and benefits; they seek solutions to problems. They have a concrete, particularistic view of product development. Although marketers are more attuned to consumer experience and grasp the wisdom of seeking emic understanding, their intuitions have been honed in an engineering environment. Marketers are too quick to sacrifice qualitative understanding to exigent rollout, to reduce meanings to metrics—but not quick enough to suit most engineers. Since consumers don't know what they want (maintain the engineers), how can marketers presume to know? Enter the anthropologist.

The history of our discipline suggests that engineers can become exemplary anthropologists. I believe marketers hold similar promise. The key to conversion lies in construing consumer behavior in terms of contexts and systems, and demonstrating the insights of cultural phenomenology as they emerge in focused field immersion. In an era of interdisciplinary teams and cross-functional task forces, it is easier to get marketers, designers, and developers into a field setting. Getting inquirers grounded in the methods of ethnography and the analytics of ethnology is a more difficult proposition, but certainly not insurmountable, especially when an anthropologist becomes part of the task force. When an ethnographer helps the marketers and the engineers see the "familiar" as "strange," new product development leaps to an entirely different plane. The chapters of this volume couldn't illustrate this principle more clearly.

The contribution of ethnography does not end with an interpretation of the ecology of consumer behavior, although frequently this is the case.

Nor does it end when the product produced has all the functional and ergonomic properties to compete favorably in the category. We live in a world of functional parity, where optimal features and benefits are the ante to get into the game. If ethnography contributes merely to the addition of bells and whistles, it falls far short of its promise. A well-designed product is increasingly evaluated on its esthetic dimension, for the experience it helps the consumer enjoy. Ethnography lays bare the cultural erotics that consumers employ to animate the world of goods, and renders those principles accessible to creatives (designers, advertisers, and other visionaries) whose job it is to translate them into artifacts and relationships.

Ecology, ergonomics, esthetics, and erotics—these are the building blocks of what we are calling "design ethnography." End-user studies are the tip of this disciplinary iceberg, and this is where media and corporate interest are currently fastened. Knowing *what* consumers do is simply the prelude to knowing what consumers *are*. And consumer behavior is far more complex than any of our disciplines, applied or not, have even begun to imagine. Practical, creative, humane interveners into our lives require the kind of nuanced insight and sensitive counsel that only anthropologists can provide, if only as a projective field, as grist for their vocational mills. The contributors to this volume demonstrate that the unpacking of customer experience is a challenging enterprise, but one not best left to untrained professionals or to lone researchers, for that matter.

I invite the reader to complement these chapters with a tacking between observation of and introspection into the role of design in his or her own everyday life. Put the reading to work in the service of apprehending your built environment. See how the legibility of the world of goods improves with an ethnographic lens. I commend the authors for placing such powerful tools at our disposal, and challenge the designers of products, services, brands, and markets to use the fruits of improved understanding of customer experience to exalt consumers everywhere.

REFERENCES

Appadurai, A. 1986. *The Social Life of Things*. New York: Cambridge University Press.

Baudrillard, J. 1994. *Simulacra and Simulation*. Ann Arbor: University of Michigan Press.

Berman, M. 2000. *The Twilight of American Culture*. New York: Norton.

Debord, G. 1983. *The Society of the Spectacle*. Detroit: Black and Red.

Frank, T. 1997. *The Conquest of Cool*. Chicago: University of Chicago Press.

Gergen, K. 1991. *The Saturated Self*. New York: Basic Books.

Gottdiener, M. 1996. *The Theming of America*. Boulder: Westview.

Holbrook, M. 1995. *Consumer Research: Introspective Essays on the Study of Consumption*. Thousand Oaks, CA: Sage.

Levitt, T. 1984. *The Marketing Imagination*. New York: Free Press.

Levy, S. 1978. *Marketplace Behavior: Its Meaning for Management*. New York: MACOM.

McCracken, G. 1988. *Culture and Consumption*. Bloomington: Indiana University Press.

Pine, J., and J. Gilmore. 1999. *The Experience Economy*. Boston: Harvard Business School Press.

Postman, N. 1986. *Amusing Ourselves to Death*. New York: Viking.

Randazzo, S. 1993. *Mythmaking on Madison Avenue*. Chicago: Probus.

Real, M. 1989. *Super Media: A Cultural Studies Approach*. Thousand Oaks, CA: Sage.

Sahlins, M. 1976. *Culture and Practical Reason*. Chicago: University of Chicago Press.

Schmitt, B. 1999. *Experiential Marketing*. New York: Free Press.

Sherry, J.F., Jr. 1995. *Contemporary Marketing and Consumer Behavior: An Anthropological Sourcebook*. Thousand Oaks, CA: Sage.

———. 1998. *Servicescapes: The Concept of Place in Contemporary Markets*. Lincolnwood, IL: NTC Business Books.

Twitchell, J. 1996. *Adcult, USA: The Triumph of American Advertising*. New York: Columbia University Press.

Underhill, P. 1999. *Why They Buy: The Science of Shopping*. New York: Simon and Schuster.

Williamson, J. 1978. *Decoding Advertisements*. New York: Boyars.

Wolf, M. 1999. *The Entertainment Economy*. New York: Random House.

Workman, J. 1993. The Nature of the Marketing/R & D Interface in a Range of Organizational Settings, in *AMA Winter Educators' Conference Proceedings*, Vol. 4, edited by R. Varadaragan and B. Jaworski. Chicago: American Marketing Association.

Introduction: The Growing Partnership between Research and Design

Susan Squires and Bryan Byrne

Open any business journal such as the *Harvard Business Review, Journal of Product Development Management, Wired*, or *@issue*. There is bound to be an article that stresses the need for businesses to understand customers by observing what customers do, getting inside their heads, or discovering what they want. Occasionally business gurus' phrases describe these activities as part of more general processes they call human-centered innovation, user-centered design, user research, user-experience modeling, design ethnography, strategic design, or thinking "outside the box."

Whatever the name, the goal is the same: discover and use *cultural* knowledge to help companies create, implement, and evaluate their products and services. The outcomes themselves may be called "breakthroughs" for two reasons. First, in keeping with business definitions of breakthroughs, they may represent new ways of thinking whether this refers to objects, activities, images, organizations, or perceptions. Second, even if these new ways of thinking are variations on existing themes, they may provoke action.

Ultimately, from our vantage point, consumer-driven innovation is a way to hedge business risks. Globalization is forcing businesses to keep pace with ever more dynamic, contradictory, and unpredictable technological and sociocultural processes. They must cope with severe international competition, mercurial financial markets, malleable public policies, and quick shifts in consumer demographics and consumption preferences. Despite those business risks, companies have to manufacture the *right* commodities and deliver them in the *right* way to the *right* consumers at least four out of ten times every year—just to stay solvent. For many executives, the risks are so daunting they are willing to spend more on multidisciplinary product development and leverage cultural knowledge and design as integral elements of their business strategy.

The shift in managerial tactics has pushed designers into closer working relationships with social scientists, notably anthropologists, sociologists, and psychologists. Although designers may not always use the word "culture," they have been paying an ever-increasing amount of attention to the "context" of the people for whom they create objects. Designers often use the term "context" as a proxy term for both the physical and social features and processes that affect individual behavior, perceptions, and preferences. Over the past century our understanding of the links between the cultural context of consumers and design has become increasingly sophisticated. Today many design and business professionals recognize that cultural trends, and the principles that underlie them, can best be discovered through some form of rapid ethnographic analysis. Designers and social scientists can use those ethnographic insights in a generative manner. They become particularly effective when united in a process that includes rapid ideation and prototype development (Kelley 2001).

Ethnography is typically defined as the description and explanation of the culture of a group of people. The professionals who are most likely to conduct these ethnographies are trained in anthropology, psychology, sociology, and design. An anthropological definition of culture must include consideration of the interrelated ways that people behave, think, communicate, organize, and interact with their surroundings, objects, and each other. Although the most famous published ethnographies have focused on community groups and took years of prolonged fieldwork to complete, most of these ethnographies are done within weeks and are never published. They are conducted for public and private organizations that need to learn and act quickly.

Unlike academic investigations, applied ethnographic analyses cannot end with descriptions or explanations. They must draw out the implications of the cultural insights and offer practicable guidelines for future ideas, plans, policies, organizations, activities, products, services, and images.

Of course, applied cultural innovation is easier said than done. Participants must become aware of, and be capable of, challenging their own cultural assumptions. In essence, the people who create these breakthrough ideas must be able to break through their own cultural limitations and set new ones, for both themselves and those for whom they are creating. No single group of professionals can operate alone in such an ambitious effort. Cultural researchers must work with other professionals such as engineers, business managers, and designers. They have to forge more or less predictable collaborative processes that leverage the skills of very different people to constantly break free from their most cherished individual, professional, and cultural perceptions. Ideally, those processes will enable them to create and use cultural insights as tools to bridge that uncertain gap between what exists and what might yet exist. The individuals themselves must enjoy open-ended mandates, short-term deadlines, high-risk projects, and chaotic working conditions.

WHY EDIT THIS BOOK?

There are plenty of books on innovation. Academic and corporate institutions have been experimenting with interdisciplinary innovative processes for years. Universities such as MIT, Harvard, and Stanford serve as subsidized catalysts for technological and corporate innovation. Huge manufacturers such as Intel, Hewlett-Packard, and IBM work closely with global research and development and managerial consulting groups such as SRI Consulting, Ernst and Young, and Accenture to create collaborative processes and products, services, and business practices that resonate with and change sociocultural systems. Nonprofit associations such as the Product Development Management Association (PDMA) and the Industrial Design Society of America (IDSA) keep their well-placed members updated through newsletters, journals, seminars, and conferences. People throughout this complex network author articles and books that discuss the processes involved in product development (see for example, Cooper and Kleinschmidt 1990; Foote 1996; Dougherty 1998; Kerzner 1998; Trott 1998; Kelley 2001; Rothstein 2000).

We edited this book as part of our continuing effort to understand and improve on our own working processes. When we started working at GVO, a design firm, back in 1997, neither of us could find useful guides to collaborative ethnographic and design innovation. We had to improvise in unfamiliar situations when others were looking to us for guidance. Knowing that social scientists were largely uninformed of product development, we wanted social scientists from academia and business to share insights, provide state-of the-art lessons, and prepare students.

We took a more interdisciplinary approach after our closest business and design colleagues asked if they could use the volume as a platform to speak to our colleagues. We agreed. As they began writing, the theme and tenor of the book changed. It became obvious that the primary challenge was creating collaborative multidisciplinary teams, not merely applying anthropological concepts or methods.

The term "collaboration" deserves comment. Following Robert Freeman (1993), we define collaboration as a work process

that occurs when two or more people or organizations join forces over a long period of time to produce something neither can achieve alone. In the process, each participant contributes something significant and different, derives something of personal and/or organizational benefit, and acknowledges the mutual dependence on the other required to achieve the mutual desired results. (Uhl and Squires 1995)

Although we focus on the collaboration of designers and social scientists (especially sociocultural anthropologists) the authors all delve into principles, advantages, and challenges involved in fostering any kind of collaborative organization and process. As such, anybody interested in creating multidisciplinary teams must forge shared working concepts and processes; they will inevitably challenge professional assumptions about corporate organizations, communication, projects, professional development, and the very act of consumption. The first step for mavericks is to compare their professional positions. The second step is to use the lessons to design collaborative work cultures. Their subsequent experiments require patience, negotiation, dedication, experimentation, and evaluation. Those experiences may not create consensus, but they will be informative and productive.

All of the authors who contributed to this volume have gone through their own collaborative experiments, sometimes in league with one another. They have forged their own opinions. Thus, if you consider this book as a whole, our disagreements are just as interesting as our agreements. We agree that culture is important to product development because it can reduce business risk. We agree that collaborative work organizations and processes can be achieved only through experimentation across projects. We offer examples of what works and what does not. We agree that science, commerce, humanities, and the arts all have their place in the creation of breakthrough ideas. And, we agree that we must lobby academic institutions to develop educational programs that create skilled workers.

There is plenty to disagree about, too. Nobody knows what to call the type of work we do. Nor is there consensus about what collaborative work organizations and processes can or should be institutionalized in consultancies, research institutes, and corporations. Odds are that the processes and organizations are contingent on other things that still must be investigated. Just as important, we certainly have not settled the great debates about how to embrace both scientific and interpretive/artistic modes of investigation and creativity.

In the end, we believe that our opinions vary enough to provide you with a more balanced and informative view of our work than if we had simply published a pap propaganda piece or safely limited our conversation to like-minded professionals.

ACKNOWLEDGMENTS

We would like to acknowledge those who have helped us over the past three years. First, we wish to thank our authors who contributed in either the book or who presented their papers at a panel we organized at the American Anthropological Association meetings in November 1999. They are Eric Arnould (University of Nebraska), Mark Dawson (Eastman Kodak), Rita Denny (B/S/R), Will Reese (Design Science), Inga Treitler (Terranova), and Christina Wasson (DePaul University) who all are anthropologists. Tony Salvador (Intel) is a psychologist. Heiko Sacher (GVO) is an interaction designer.

We would also like to thank those who contributed to the volume but did not offer their own papers at the AAA panel. John Sherry (Northwestern University) is an anthropologist and professor of marketing. Ed Sands (S-D Media) and George Walls (formerly of Laerdal Medical Corp.) are both entrepreneurs with strong backgrounds and training in business administration and new product development. Sally Ann Applin (Kinematic) is a talented and independent designer. Chuck Leinbach (University of California, Long Beach) is an industrial designer, business administrator, intellectual property lawyer, and professor. Ken Friedman is an experienced designer who teaches at the Department of Knowledge Management, Norwegian School of Management.

Many more of our colleagues contributed in other ways. We wish especially to thank the members of GVO, particularly Michael Barry, Robert Hall, Nolan Vogt, Gary Waymire, Tom Williams and Steve Portigal, and Sherry Rosario for inspiring and supporting our research and editorial work. We have also benefited from discussions with Curtis J. Bailey (Sundberg Ferar), Vicki Baharam (Hauser Design), H. Russell Bernard (University of Florida), Janette Blomberg (Sapient), Peter Brandenburg (Motorola), Burton James Brown (University of Florida), Jean Canavan (Motorola), Ron Curedale (Frog), Steve Hauser (Hauser Design), Tom Hirsh (Insearch), Tom Kelley (IDEO), Alison Myers (University of South Florida), Ron Pierce (Hauser Design), Steve Portigal (GVO), Rick Robinson (E-Lab and, now, Sapient), Elizabeth Saunders (SonicRim), Nermal Sethia (California State Polytechnic University), Clive Stevens (Laerdal Medical Corp.), Bonlynne Walls, and Steve Wilcox (Design Science).

Last, we owe a debt of gratitude to our editors. Carmen Garcia Ruiz helped us edit some of the first drafts. And Jane Garry, our publisher from Greenwood Publishing Group, wisely let us go through our paces before taking over.

REFERENCES

Cooper, R. and E. Kleinschmidt. 1990. *New Products: The Key Factors in Success.* Chicago: American Marketing Association.

Dougherty, D. 1998. *Organizational Capacities for Sustained Product Innovation.* Commentary Report No. 98–118. Cambridge: Marketing Science Institute.

Foote, C. 1996. *The Business Side of Creativity.* New York: W.W. Norton & Co. Freeman, R.E. 1993. Collaboration, Global Perspectives, and Teacher Education. *Theory into Practice* 32 (1): 33–39.

Kelley, T. 2001. *The Art of Innovation: Lessons in Creativity from Ideo, America's Leading Design Firm.* New York: Doubleday.

Kerzner, H. 1998. *Project Management.* New York: John Wiley & Sons.

Rothstein, P.D. 2000. *The "Re-emergence" of Ethnography in Industrial Design Today.* IDSA Chicago Design Education Conference Proceedings. http//www.idsa.org/whatsnew/99ed_proceed/paper019.htm

Trott, P. 1998. *Innovation Management and New Product Development.* London: Pitman Books.

Uhl, S.C., and S.E. Squires. 1995. *Enhancing Systemic Change Through Effective Collaboration: A Formative Perspective and Approach.* Paper presented to the American Anthropological Association. Washington, DC.

PART I

CONVERGING PROFESSIONS

Part I examines the historical motivation for the collaboration of social scientists and designers.

The first chapter is by Dr. Chuck Leinbach. An intellectual property lawyer turned designer, Leinbach uses his work with psychologist Ron Sears to explain how and why product development benefits from the partnership of social scientists and designers. He argues that we must modify our organizations, professional assumptions, and managerial processes to support this collaborative work.

Anthropologist William Reese provides firsthand accounts from some of the first social scientists who brought their discipline's concepts and methods to product development. His case studies make it clear that many of the things we take for granted (automotive vehicles, clothing, financial transactions, weapons, transportation systems, furniture, etc.) are the result of early collaboration among social researchers, engineers, and designers.

Managing for Breakthroughs: A View from Industrial Design

Charles Leinbach

> At Sony, we assume all products of our competitors will have basically the same technology, price, performance, and features. Design is the only thing that differentiates one product from another in the marketplace. (Norio Ohga quoted in T. Peters 1997: 436)

All other things being equal, consumers tend to purchase the products they feel are better designed. Norio Ohga, chairman and CEO of Sony, learned this a long time ago. In an era in which state-of-the-art technologies grant us a great degree of latitude and prices can easily be set, culturally appropriate product design provides a competitive edge. It's no longer enough to think of design as styling or art. Design must embody meaningful features, functions, and user interfaces that consumers will understand and benefit from. Designers cannot assume to know what lies in the hearts and minds of the people for whom they design. Nor can they assume to be utopian visionaries who can act upon their individual insights into the human condition or upon their skills as artisans and artists. Instead, as I will argue, product developers, including designers, would do well to adopt theories and practices that

1. treat creativity as both a psychological and sociocultural process;
2. define products using a synthetic approach to culturally-insightful design that incorporates technology, art, and business; and
3. aspire to create intellectual property rather than tangible products.

My careers as an intellectual property lawyer, industrial designer, consumer researcher, businessperson, and professor have all led me to this conclusion. This chapter is my first effort to spell out my reasoning. I hope to establish a conceptual basis for future collaborative work between designers, social scientists, business scholars, and jurists. To understand why we should implement these changes, we must confront several partially understood topics. Psychologists have a great deal to say about creativity in the abstract, and about design, innovation, and management, but virtually nothing to say about business strategy and intellectual property. Although anthropologists define humanness with respect to creativity, they have paid less attention to the process of creativity, innovation, and design than they have to the evolutionary patterns of consumer and corporate culture and, recently, to intellectual property. Designers have a lot to say about the individual process of creativity, form, and innovation, but relatively little about the evolution of culture artifacts, business management, and intellectual property. Business administrators talk constantly about management, corporate culture, innovation, and property but have very little understanding of user cultures or the social circumstances in which innovation happens. And lawyers concentrate on invention and property rights. They have little to add about corporate and/or consumer culture. However, all of their perspectives are of great use—especially when set against each other.

DESIGNING FOR THE RV TRIBE

Let me ground my discussion of these topics in an example of my own work. As you read, think about this case. It will help you gain insight into why we have to rethink our positions on creativity, innovation, intellectual property, management, and design. Back in the 1980s, I teamed up with Ron Sears (see Will Reese's chapter in this book) and a West Coast design firm to redesign recreational vehicles (RVs) for a major manufacturer. The project was particularly interesting because RV enthusiasts form a distinct nomadic cultural group that largely relies on a huge variety of highly valued special products. I've always found Bryson's (1989) humorous description of RV enthusiasts a good way to introduce them:

[A]stronauts go to the moon with less backup. RV people are another breed—and a largely demented one at that. They become obsessed with trying to equip their vehicles with gadgets to deal with every possible contingency. Their lives become ruled by the dread thought that one day they may find themselves in a situation in which they are not entirely self-sufficient. You can see these people at campgrounds all over the country, standing around their vehicles comparing gadgets: methane-powered ice cube makers, portable tennis courts, anti-insect flame throwers, inflatable lawns. They are a strange and dangerous people and on no account should be approached. (Bryson 1989: 94)

Understanding the risks, Ron and I persuaded the RV manufacturer to let us perform the first strategic human factors and industrial design overhaul of motor homes. The premise of our project was simple. The primary but oft forgotten rule of both applied human sciences (e.g., psychology, anthropology) and design is that products ought to be designed around the behavior of users, not the reverse. All too often, manufacturers and designers approach design as the outgrowth of technological possibilities. They expect users to adjust to the products they design. We took a contrary view. We told our clients that we would draw on the combined strengths of ethnographic research and design to generate new ideas about products. The client gambled by providing us with a mother vehicle, a wallet full of gasoline credit cards, and six months to do our work. During that time, we acted as participants, observers, analysts, and designers while following the migration of a group that is part of an authentic American subculture.

For the better part of a year we traveled, connecting "Good Sam dots" with "KOA dots" on America's blue highways. At each point we first observed the ongoing activities for a day and then followed up for another day or two by watching, videotaping, and recording the behaviors and practices of these nomadic Americans. Between gizmo demos and bad coffee, we conducted hundreds of casual conversations and formal interviews, collected thousands of photographic stills, hundreds of pages of notes, and about seven and four-tenths miles of videotape. We converted each image and note to a necessarily brief yellow sticky note.

We eventually analyzed every service and mechanical feature of our vehicle and seven competitive products. We speculated about the design implications of all the things we were learning. I made thousands of tiny sketches as Ron scribbled a nearly infinite number of key words on Post-it notes and posted them on large 4' × 8' foam-core boards. Eventually we created coherent conceptual categories and arrays of our sketches and Post-it notes. The combination of sketches and Post-it notes was especially valuable because they were easily replaceable, allowing us to cluster them according to recurring content themes and patterns of ideas.

We discovered that RVers go on excursions, not so much to escape the people they live with in their fixed domicile as to join their kindred. RVers tend to be successful, healthy, married, and adventurous retirees who have friends scattered around the country. Physical stamina and their quest for their kind went a long way toward explaining their driving patterns and their perceptions and use of their RVs. We learned that RVers don't like to drive long distances, partly because their own kidneys determine a shorter interval distance than a tank full of gas will take them. They commune in the evening and until late in the morning, leave in early afternoon, drive a few hours, and set up at the next RV spot.

In part, the design of their RVs and the kinds of things that they keep determine where and how frequently they stop. For example, more people store extra satellite dishes in the RV's shower than actually shower there. They like to take showers in the camps because the facilities actually have water pressure, and doing so extends the life of their RV's freshwater supply while gaining (for some) more hanging storage (in the shower-now-closet). We also learned that the design of their gas tanks affect how they perceive the cost of their journey and the frequency with which they must fill their tanks.

Their entire pattern of cultural behavior and perceptions of their own RVs began to affect our thinking about what future products we might create. For example, we noticed that the gas tanks on these behemoths were taking up space and adding lots of weight that must have affected fuel mileage. One suggestion, only partially facetious, was to redesign the fuel gauge, making it about half as wide, so that the driver *would not actually see* the gauge needle move toward empty as he climbed a long hill in second gear. Second, we suggested that the manufacturer reduce the size of the gas tanks because people hate spending upward of $200 to fill up the tank. Furthermore, RVers typically don't need that much gas. Since they stop frequently, they don't need to haul gas that, ironically, reduces their mileage efficiency. These kinds of insights would not normally occur to office-bound designers, product engineers, salespeople, and corporate officers.

At the end of our research phase, Ron and I joined Bally Design and the San Diego–based McCulley Group to further analyze and act on the implications of the research. Confident that we could outgimmick pocket meat grinders, we reimmersed ourselves in yellow Post-it notes, this time consulting with our teammates. We created hundreds of ideas, took the best, fabricated dozens of scale models, and tested them among users throughout the United States. Eventually we built a full-sized, working prototype motor home. Then we brought in fresh observers to give us their opinions. The resulting space plans and subsystem features stimulated demand for the new vehicle so quickly and unexpectedly, that the manufacturer reduced the production of other lines to meet the backlog for its new model.

According to client insiders, our SlideSuite reversed the company's fortunes. Even more flattering, the space plan and feature package has become one of the most copied in the history of the industry. The project was extensive and expensive, but few have challenged its value (there will always be critics). In my opinion, we succeeded because we combined our ethnographic and design studies with the client's business mission, strategy, and project objectives.

Our success can best be understood by addressing the growing interrelationships between creativity, invention, innovation, consumer research, design, and management. Our goal was to innovate, that is to supplement, enrich, and/or replace a client's product line. Our ideas and recommendations arose from the insight and knowledge we developed in the field. We worked with consumers to discover things about themselves they did not necessarily notice. We evaluated the competitors' products in ways that would not have been considered from corporate headquarters. Our client wisely allowed Ron and I to collaborate with other subcontractors of creative services in a collective, open, and reassuring work environment to foster the creation of new and patentable product concepts.

THE PSYCHOLOGICAL AND SOCIAL BASIS OF CREATIVITY AND INNOVATION

As I mentioned at the outset and suggest in the case study, any understanding of innovation demands that we consider both the psychological and sociocultural aspects of creativity. Most dictionaries define creativity as the ability to conceive and bring into being something that does not yet exist. For example, it is the ability to create new genres of art as well as exemplars of each. Amabile presents creativity as the intersection of (1) expertise, (2) thinking skills, and (3) motivation. Expertise "is, in a word, knowledge—technical, procedural, and intellectual." Creative thinking skills, Amabile says, "determine how flexibly and imaginatively people approach problems. Do their solutions upend the status quo? Do they persevere through dry spells?" Motivation is either extrinsic (provided from outside the doer) or intrinsic, "an inner passion to solve the problem at hand that leads to solutions far more creative than do external rewards such as money" (Amabile 1998: 70).

To supplement Amabile's definition of creativity, I would add a Gardner-like concept of interpersonal knowledge, as an aspect of something Goleman (1995) calls emotional intelligence and what R. Peters (1987) names practical intelligence. Creativity is in some respects the consequence of intelligence. Quinn, Baruch, and Zien (1997: 3) define intellect as the capacity to create and apply information. Intellect includes five factors, in ascending order of importance:

1. *cognitive knowledge*, the rules and facts of a discipline,
2. *skills*, the capacity to perform a task,
3. *systemic understanding*, understanding interrelationships among key variables,
4. *motivation*, the drive to discover or invent, and
5. *intuition and synthesis*, the capacity to predict relationships that are not directly measurable.

Together, these intellectual abilities make it possible for people to raise questions, make associations, and decide. However, intelligence does not have to be used creatively. One might use one's systemic knowledge and practical skills in circumstances in which nothing new is formulated. They might enjoy applying formulas or protocols but never be motivated to change them.

Creativity requires a change in the status quo. One must not only be aware of existing circumstances, but should also be able to modify them. Creative outcomes satisfy one or more of the following conditions (Couger 1995: 14, 365–385):

1. novelty,
2. modifies or rejects accepted ideas,
3. motivated, and
4. formulates or reformulates the conceptual issue itself.

The results of the creative process are normally unanticipated, novel conclusions. They are often reached by asking questions, reformulating conceptual issues, challenging assumptions, and acquiring knowledge.

The definitions of both creativity and intelligence suggest that internal and external processes are operating. Some of the leading scholars and business leaders consider both. For example, MIT's Nicholas Negroponte (T. Peters 1997: 376) points to external aspects that foster creativity that "comes from unlikely juxtapositions. The best way to maximize differences is to maximize ages, cultures, and disciplines." Others feel it comes from "cross-pollination" (Hargadon and Sutton 2000: 161). Von Hipple (1994) asserts that the biggest overlooked source of new product ideas is "lead users." Peter Drucker (1993: 30–107) lists seven broad sources of innovation: the unexpected; incongruities; process need; industry and market structures; demographics; changes in perception; and new knowledge. And although Drucker teaches that lone wizards rarely succeed, he describes the individual as the depository of essential (tacit) knowledge.

Once we think of creativity as an *individual* biological and cognitive process that occurs within sociocultural processes operating at the level of human *groups*, we move from psychology to anthropology. Like psychology, contemporary anthropological theory rests on the premise that human intellectual and creative capacity distinguishes us from other primates; to a certain extent, creativity defines us as human beings. It sets us apart from other species that face more stringent biological limits to cognition, communication, and physical dexterity. However, anthropology takes into account population and group phenomena that psychologists tend to exclude. As Boas stated the case clearly long ago,

The psychologist may try to investigate the process of artistic creation. Although the process may be fundamentally the same everywhere, the very act of creation implies that we are not dealing with the artist alone but also with his reactions to the culture in which he lives and that of his fellows to the work he has created. ... When we are discussing the reactions of the individual to his fellows, we are compelled to concentrate our attention upon the society in which he lives. We cannot treat the individual as an isolated unit. (Boas 1962: 15)

When thought of in historical terms, it becomes self-evident that creativity is almost always aimed at some real external condition or process that exists apart from the inventor. In the case of product design, we must consider not only the conditions in which we create, but also the living conditions, knowledge, and goals of those for whom we create. The information that product developers need to learn about many of these activities, skills, structures, and perceptions is usually unavailable in handbooks or journals. If it has been reduced to print, it often loses its potential to connect ideas in new ways. Product developers usually have to discover tacit knowledge for themselves, by fostering the right environment. Davenport and Pruzak (1998: 70) remind us that "tacit, complex knowledge, developed and internalized by the knower over a long period of time is almost impossible to reproduce in a document or database." Gardner explains that

creativity is a facet of broad human intelligence in which competence must entail a set of skills of problem-solving enabling the individual to resolve generic problems or difficulties that he or she encounters and, when appropriate, to create an effective product—and must also entail the potential for finding or creating problems—thereby laying the groundwork for acquisition of new knowledge. These prerequisites represent my effort to focus on those intellectual strengths that prove of some importance within a cultural context. (Gardner 1993)

The RV case study demonstrates the point. Ron and I used our own personal and professional training to reexamine the cultural systems that RVers took for granted. We learned about RVers and about their perceptions and handling of the products they used (and didn't use) on the road. We made observations and associations, asked questions, challenged our own assumptions, asked new questions, and slowly began ordering the cultural domains that RVers lived by but could not simply express. In the process, we posed problems for specific products and subsystems, reexamined them, and came up with new ones.

The cultural contexts provided Ron and me with a wealth of tacit cultural knowledge and experiences that we could systematically and a-systematically juxtapose in ways we had not anticipated. By using videotape, sketches, and Post-it notes, we quickly mixed and matched observations, themes, statements, problems, and potential creative solutions. Then we did it again the following day. By stepping out of our own cultural contexts into one where others don't even question their environment, and by drawing on powerful research and design methods, we eventually came up with ideas that led to novel, creative ideas for products that could be patented, and thus owned, by our clients.

RESEARCH AND DESIGN

Clearly, Ron and I operated within the cultural contexts of both the RVers and our corporate partners. I have found that businesses tend to limit their own ability to innovate by relying too heavily on either creative individuals apart from external influences or an almost exclusive and wholly uninspired survey approach. Designers tend to stress the importance of individual psychological talents. Marketing researchers tend to minimize individual creativity and stress scientific, literalist, and a-cultural research. They tend to conceive of product development in terms of "problem solving" and present highly quantitative demographic and opinion surveys that assume that they are talking with the right consumers and getting accurate information. Nadler and Hibino (1990: 77) express the frustration with this approach clearly: "[C]urrent, excessive reliance on scientific mechanisms has clearly failed, failed in the attempt to convert knowledge to effective systems that have been and are still impoverished because of the excessive demand for and reliance upon scientism in their formulation." Fortunately, our client allowed us to guide them through an unfamiliar creative process. We, and many other product developers, favor a combination of grounded, interpretive, and scientific research to discover recurrent themes and opportunities that consumers themselves may not be aware of. Leonard and Rayport (1997: 13), two prominent scholars who advocate consumer-based design, call the emerging approach "empathic design." They write that empathic design enables researchers to figure out what consumers cannot ask for:

A common criticism of the kinds of innovative ideas arising out of empathic design is "but users haven't asked for that." Precisely. By the time they do, your competitors will have the same new product ideas you have—and you will be in the "me-too" game of copying and improving their ideas. Empathic design techniques involve a twist on the idea that users should guide new product development. In this approach, they still do—they just don't know it. Developing a deep, empathetic understanding of users' unarticulated needs can challenge industry assumptions and lead to a shift in corporate strategy. (Leonard and Rayport 1997: 13)

The work that researchers and designers such as Ron and I are doing together is far more akin to the rapid ethnographic process and must involve a mixture of scientific and interpretive methods. In general,

the development effort is better understood as an open-ended process rather than as a project in which a specific problem is solved. The role of the design organization is not so much one of analysis or problem solving as it is of *interpreting* the new situation—listening to and talking with customers and technical experts and discerning the new possibilities that open up during those interactions. Interpretation, no less than invention, is a highly creative process. (Lester, Piore, and Malek 1998: 89)

This same process is forcing designers to move away from their own conception of the ideal design professional. The emerging profile of a good designer is moving

from individualistic notions of creativity, from "isolated genius" theories of innovation, and toward an understanding of creativity as a social process. It suggests a way of thinking about the creativity of organizations—of communities—rather than the creativity of individuals. (Lester, Piore, and Malek 1998: 90)

If, indeed, their creative environment and methods can be "replicated anywhere," innovative groups may be considered representative of John Seely Brown's "communities of practice" that are by definition communities of professionals who work across corporate boundaries and whose allegiance belongs first to their colleagues and only secondarily with their employers (Brown and Duguid 2000: 142). Thus, as Hargadon and Sutton explain,

the best innovators aren't lone geniuses. They're people who can take an idea that's obvious in one context and apply it in not-so-obvious ways to a different context. . . . The best of these innovators (as groups) have systematized the generation and testing of new ideas—the systems they've devised can be replicated anywhere because it has everything to do with organization and attitude, and very little to do with nurturing the solitary genius. (Hargadon and Sutton 2000: 157)

By focusing on the working processes rather than adhering to a specific corporate culture, these communities of professionals are becoming more mobile and willing to find people they can work with.

EMPATHIC DESIGN AND RAPID PROTOTYPING

The approach that Ron and I took involved people who represent virtually every stage in product development processes. After we returned from our field excursion, we worked with designers, modelers, marketers, and businesspeople. We reviewed our findings and created product categories and alternative designs. Our team selected the most promising concept sketches and refined them. The industrial designers, engineers, and prototype modelers worked with sketches, CAD drawings, and detailed foam and plastic models to get a better sense of how the products would look, feel, and operate.

Empathic design can be especially exasperating to engineers and modelers because they are normally told to figure out how to make something rather than to decide what to make. For example, a skilled product molder in a different project once interrupted an innovation session by yelling, "This is a waste of my time. Just tell us what to make!" He had other things to do and was rewarded for modeling extant ideas, not for generating them.

In an era of empathic design, the real strengths of designers lie in their crossover skills—moving from verbal to visual to verbal modes, or from technical to artistic to technical modes of knowledge embodiment and communication. Thus, designers are ultimately in the knowledge transfer business. Industrial designers perform knowledge transfer mostly in the form of drawings and prototypes—prototypes in potentially infinite series, each iteration of which represents a learning experience for the prototyper and stimulates observers to ask further questions, leading to the next iteration, and yet further learning. If thought of in terms of knowledge transfer, then it becomes clear that clients are not or should not be particularly interested in the prototype itself. It is merely a device that helps better determine how the client will reap profits coming from the sale of the service or entertainment provided by the eventual product itself (Leinbach 1992: 48). Designers provide a *service* that includes temporary prototypes that help determine *what* to make as well as *how* to make it. Clients should expect that abandoned prototypes narrow the range of possible wrong solutions. Most management is substantially knowledge management—managing the large virtual portfolios of all possible answers, narrowing the field, heading-off big mistakes for the client. Trial and error, failing early and often, rapid prototyping—all are about more effectively and efficiently generating something new. But if the political environment is not receptive to experimentation, if management insists upon making its job easier through stasis, or excess control, little innovation is likely to occur. The worldviews we harbor are important to success in innovative activities.

DESIGN AND THE CREATION OF INTELLECTUAL PROPERTY

Design is a service that generates and transfers knowledge. Therefore, design management is ultimately knowledge management. Intellectual *capital*, defined as the totality of human brainpower assets of an organization, suggests that the knowledge gained from research, sketching and rapid prototyping has future value. Companies such as Sony are most interested in creating concepts and designs that distinguish them from their competitors. It follows that they are most interested in intellectual capital and innovative designs that help them differentiate and protect themselves from competitors. As such, clients and designers must understand that they are creating intellectual capital, not simply products with cool designs.

Still, to be useful, the process of empathic design must extend beyond the studio into patent offices where intellectual capital is transformed into intellectual property. Consequently, teams conducting empathic design have to consider the nontangible, business-oriented aspects of their work. The implication for teams taking the empathic design approach is that the odds that their real contribution lies in business modeling and whole operational processes rather than a single tangible object are rising every day.

Texas Instruments and Xerox provide good examples. Over the past few years, Texas Instruments "has earned a larger portion of its $200 million in annual profits from licensing patents and winning infringement cases than from selling products" (Shulman 1999: 5). Some years ago, Xerox began calling itself the document company, de-emphasizing copier hardware in its ads. Kevin Rivette quotes a Xerox officer as recently saying,

[I]t's not enough to make or do things you can sell. Nor is it necessarily even enough to make or do or sell things in innovative ways. . . . It's *what you do* with innovation—*how you manage and utilize your intellectual property assets* in conjunction with all the other assets of your company to grow, fix, or sell your business— that determines whether you win or lose. (Rivette and Kline 2000)

As I mentioned in the case study of the RV design project, we learned a great deal about the cultural norms (contested and uncontested) among RVers. Such learning included their perceptions, activities, relationships, and possessions. The value that the project team added for the client corporation went beyond the redesign of physical objects to the enhancement of knowledge (applied and unapplied) and intellectual property that enabled the client to modify its product lines, change its corporate strategy, and apply the learning (as capital) to future product lines. To succeed, we had to step outside of the client's normal corporate operations. Our client re-aimed its intellectual property toward the design and manufacture of a product line that better fit the lifestyles of the RVers.

CONCLUSION

I have argued that under the current business circumstances, it is incumbent on businesses and all professionals dealing with new product development to consider the strategic role that design plays. Traditionally design has helped differentiate one's products and corporate image. It is becoming more concerned with the creation of intellectual capital and intellectual property. Clients must issue marketable product services, products, and images in highly dynamic markets. The market is a moving target; the development teams have to think ahead, discover what their consumers and companies may not know, and then act on that knowledge by creating useful and valuable new property.

Obviously, it's a challenge to explain the growing ties between creativity, invention, innovation, intellectual property, cultural research, industrial design, and knowledge management. Each subject attracts a great deal of scholarly attention, but they typically are not dealt with collectively. I'm endeavoring to understand and integrate these ideas. Designers and managers who are thinking about doing empathic design might consider the following set of guidelines before they make the cultural transformation.

- Decide if you want to be in business.
- Understand that "being innovative" is the ante for "being in business."
- Accept constant change as normal.
- Recognize innovation as a set of *survival tools* that take the form of new knowledge, whether tacit discoveries or tangible items.
- Understand that innovation requires effort, observation, analysis, collaboration, and risk.
- Treat innovation as problem seeking and formulating rather than problem solving or calculation.
- Hire or assign people who embrace the kind of uncertainty and work that innovation requires.
- Reward collaboration, the sharing of tacit knowledge, passion, and tenacity.
- Reassign those who whine to routine jobs (if in a creative organization there are such jobs).
- Delegate roughly formulated problems to the appropriate people and give them room for experimentation within constraints, and move on to the next ill-formulated questions.

- Share knowledge with managers, but limit their ability to control and dictate working processes.
- Patent, protect, and commercialize (where appropriate).

The emerging innovation process rests on the consonance and clash of perspectives; it emerges from the perceptions, measurements, juxtapositions, and talents of product development professionals and consumers. Perhaps the philosopher Hegel best articulated the nineteenth-century understanding about the evolution of ideas with his thesis-antithesis-synthesis model; new ideas are based on the union of what already exists and elements that conflict with or negate them. Contemporary interpretations of Hegel in the workplace include Pascale's (1990) "vectors of contention" and various spins on "managing chaos" (Brown and Eisenhardt 1998). On a very practical level, these ideas are akin to conversations between professional scholars, researchers, designers, managers, and lawyers who have different approaches and interests. That is exactly the kind of environment, often contentious, in which much of contemporary empathic design is performed. Managers of any creative undertaking must now find and hire those people who understand and value both stable and dynamic views of the world. They must actually prefer the murky middle, seeing ambiguity as the most likely condition for the creation of something new. The entire organization must pursue a "kind of" balance but not stasis. As Waldrop (1992) suggests, "this balance point, often called the *edge of chaos*, is where the components of a system never quite lock into place, and yet never quite dissolve into turbulence either. The edge of chaos is where life has enough stability to sustain itself and enough creativity to deserve the name of life."

REFERENCES

Amabile, T. 1998. How to Kill Creativity. *Harvard Business Review* (Sept.–Oct.).

Boas, F. 1962. *Anthropology in Modern Life*. New York: Dover.

Brown, J., and P. Duguid. 2000. *The Social Life of Information*. Boston: Harvard University Press.

Brown, S., and K. Eisenhardt. 1998. *Competing on the Edge: Strategy as Structured Chaos*. Boston: Harvard University Press.

Bryson, B. 1989. *The Lost Continent; Travels in Small Town America*. New York: HarperCollins.

Couger, J. 1995. *Creative Problem Solving and Opportunity Finding*. Danvers, MA: Boyd and Fraser.

Davenport, T., and L. Pruzak. 1998. *Working Knowledge*. Boston: Harvard University Press.

Drucker, P. 1985. *Innovation and Entrepreneurship: Principles and Practices*. New York: Harper and Row.
————. 1993. *Post-Capitalist Society*. New York: HarperCollins.
Gardner, H. 1993. *Frames of Mind*. New York: Basic Books.
Goleman, D. 1995. *Emotional Intelligence*. New York: Bantam Books.
Hargadon, A., and R. Sutton. 2000. Building an Innovation Factory. *Harvard Business Review* (May–June).
Leinbach, C. 1992. Purchasing the Design of Service. *Design Management Journal* (Winter).
Leonard, D., and J. Rayport. 1997. Spark Innovation Through Empathetic Design. *Harvard Business Review* (Nov.–Dec.): 102–113.
Lester, R., J. Piore, and K. Malek. 1998. Interpretive Management: What General Managers Can Learn from Design. *Harvard Business Review*, (March–April): 86–96.
Nadler, G., and H. Hibino. 1990. *Breakthrough Thinking*. Rocklin, CA: Prima.
————. 1999. *Creative Solution Finding*. Rocklin, CA: Prima.
Pascale, R. 1990. *Managing on the Edge*. New York: Simon and Schuster.
Peters, R. 1987. *Practical Intelligence*. New York: Harper and Row.
Peters, T. 1997. *Circle of Innovation*. New York: Vintage Books.
Quinn, J. 1992. *Intelligent Enterprise*. New York: Free Press.
Quinn, J., J. Baruch, and K. Zien. 1997. *The Innovation Explosion*. New York: Free Press.
Rivette, K., and D. Kline. 2000. *Rembrandts in the Attic*. Boston: Harvard University Press.
Shulman, S. 1999. *Owning the Future*. New York: Houghton Mifflin.
Von Hipple, E. 1994. *The Sources of Innovation*. New York: Oxford University Press.
Waldrop, M. 1992. *Complexity: The Emerging Science at the Edge of Order and Chaos*. New York: Touchstone.

2

Behavioral Scientists Enter Design: Seven Critical Histories

William Reese

> The relationship between man and the cultural dimension is one in which both man and his environment participate in molding each other. Man is now in the position of creating the total world in which he lives. . . . In creating this world he is actually determining what kind of an organism he will be. This is a frightening thought in view of how very little is known about man. (Hall 1969)

The anthropologist who wrote those words, Edward Hall, is still right. We know frighteningly little about ourselves in comparison to the enormous impact we exert on the world around us. But we do seem slowly to be arriving at a new point of convergence among the technologies that are available for learning more. Leaders in product development have come increasingly to realize that we know too little about people to be able to design and redesign for customers effectively. The work of social scientists, especially over the last four decades, has contributed importantly both to heightening that awareness, and to answering the questions to which it has given rise.

The following account describes the experiences of behavioral scientists during a key moment in this history, as they moved into positions at a number of noted design consulting firms in the United States. The account is not exhaustive. Given the site of its production—the center of a noisy, open office in a busy East Coast design research firm—it couldn't be. Compiling such a history in such circumstances would require a kind of miracle (or short of that, many more months to write). Instead, my approach has been to interview fellow behavioral researchers, and to employ their voices to delineate strands in the current traditions that are producing and supporting behavioral scientists in design. Though the discussion begins by addressing general developments from the early 1900s through the 1960s, the real meat of it consists of seven case histories deriving from interviews with key players, starting from the early 1970s.

The behavioral scientists I interviewed are for the most part Ph.D.'s with scientific training in the social sciences. Design consulting is a small, highly specialized segment of the product development industry. Long before social scientists began to work for consulting firms (much less start companies of their own), psychologists and anthropologists had taken jobs as employees of major corporations and as independent contractors for government projects in industrial design. Yet their recent history culminates, in a certain sense, in design consulting. Today, the relative independence of user research from any single product, product line, or industry testifies to its emergence as a self-sustaining service in the market.

The contributions made by social scientists to design began to achieve notoriety in the 1970s, when a psychologically minded designer named Charles Mauro, who had worked for leading design firms such as Henry Dreyfuss Associates and Raymond Loewy Associates, began to work on design projects for the U.S. State Department. This was also around the time that psychologists such as Jane Fulton Suri (now of IDEO) and Ron Sears (of the Design Consortium) found opportunities to apply their observational skills to problems of behavioral context in various industries. Lucy Suchman, generally acknowledged as one of the first anthropologists to become a prominent figure in the design industry, began work then, too, at the Xerox Palo Alto Research Center (PARC). But to understand these developments, it is necessary to backtrack briefly to the 1920s, when psychologists, anthropologists, and sociologists first found a way to apply their insights to product development.

THE FIRST 50 YEARS

At the turn of the century, according to German-trained engineer and ergonomist Karl Kroemer, there were basically two different approaches to the study of work and design. One approach concerned itself with human anatomical and physiological traits, and was essentially European. In contrast, the American approach concerned itself with human psychological and social traits (Kroemer and Kroemer-Elbert 1994). What both approaches shared, intermittently, was that wartime efforts drove projects that required a synthesis of their individual strong points. In England, Scandinavia, Germany, and Italy, the work focused on minimal nutrition requirements, optimal body postures at work, and other capacities and limitations of the body and mind. In America, the earliest studies dealt with ways to improve work efficiency through task ordering. Among the latter were, for example, the studies (now somewhat infamous) by Frederick Taylor in 1898, and later by his student Frank Gilbreth, on how day laborers could more expediently carry quantities of steel ingots and bricks (Moroney 1995: 2). During World War I, American psychologists developed something called "intelligence testing" to screen aviators and specialized military personnel. Later on, industrialists adopted the same approach under the rubric "industrial psychology" (Kroemer and Kroemer-Elbert 1994: 5–6).

Throughout the next decades (1920s and 1930s), the increasing use of the automobile stimulated a certain degree of curiosity among psychologists. Researchers at Ohio State and Iowa State universities, for instance, studied the behavioral characteristics of drivers thought to be accident-prone, and the perceptual abilities of people moving at high speed (Moroney 1995: 3).

It was at about this time that anthropologists began to work in industrial settings. Although inspired by the same interests in worker productivity as the psychologists, their work led to different results. The main practitioners in this early period were the psychiatrist Elton Mayo and the anthropologist Lloyd Warner. The two of them collaborated with staff from Harvard University and the Western Electric Company in a study on the effects of a given physical environment on worker productivity (i.e., the Hawthorne Studies, named after Western Electric's Hawthorne Works in Chicago). Mayo and Warner demonstrated for the first time that social processes, such as informal work groups, influenced overall output (Baba 1986: 4–5). Anthropologists C.M. Arensberg, E.D. Chapple, F.L.W. Richardson, L.R. Sayles, and W.F. Whyte all built on these studies through the 1940s and early 1950s, developing them methodologically and extending their theoretical implications.

Industrial anthropologists of the 1940s and 1950s also developed interaction analysis, a technique to predict discrete components of human interpersonal behavior. In the course of their work, they consulted with private firms and conducted ethnographic analyses (e.g., studies by B.B. Gardner and W.F. Whyte, and L.R. Sayles, *inter alia*, for machine and materials companies in 1945 [Baba 1986]). Lloyd Warner and B.B. Gardner founded the first known consulting firm that specialized in social research. Social Research, Inc., essentially was a spin-off organization formed from their work with the Committee on Human Relations in Industry at the University of Chicago. The firm's methodological tool kit included ethnographic observation and intensive interviewing. In keeping with the tenor of the era, Social Research focused on business management, not product design.

The American scholars most willing to engage in some degree of product design tended to be linguists and biological anthropologists. Benjamin Lee Whorf, originally an inspector for a fire insurance company, would become one of the leading figures in sociolinguistics. Lurking around factories, Whorf discovered that a great many hazards had a linguistic foundation. Factory workers smoked and tossed cigarette butts more often around signs saying EMPTY GASOLINE TANKS than they did around signs that read GASOLINE TANKS even though the vapors in the empty tanks made them more hazardous (Whorf 1941). Similarly, Edward Hall's pioneering work during the 1960s and 1970s strengthened anthropological interests in public spaces, body language, and architecture.

But it was during World War II, and after it, that social scientists became involved in product development intensively. In America, in particular, the needs of the U.S. military created a special new field and area of expertise, which came to be called engineering psychology or human factors analysis. The classic example is the remedy it offered to military aviation during the Korean War. More American pilots were dying in training exercises, the story goes, than in the war itself. So officials of the U.S. Defense Department summoned behavioral experts to assist them in the design of more intelligible and easy-to-use machinery and cockpit controls (Helander 1997: 5). "War," after all, "is a situation with high penalties for system failure, in terms of both human and equipment losses," say Segal and Fulton Suri matter-of-factly (forthcoming: 166). Indeed, most human factors work through the 1950s was meant to remediate such system failures—to save lives and to preserve expensive military machinery. A review of various projects of the time shows a consistent emphasis on gaining better control of automobiles, airplanes, and rockets. An interesting exception is the work by Bell Labs, however, which in 1946 hired physiological specialists to help develop telephone handsets and push-button layouts (Moroney 1995: 6). Today, the U.S. government, including agencies such as the Federal Highway Administration, the National Bureau of Standards, and the Federal Aviation Administration, continues to sponsor much work in human factors research.

Over the same period in Europe, the earlier emphasis on worker physiology became assimilated to issues of occupational safety and health. Here, strong labor unions shaped a certain social consciousness, particularly in Scandinavia and Germany (Helander 1997). "Ergonomics" came to imply accident prevention. British experts founded the Ergonomics Society in Cambridge, in 1950. American specialists formed the Human Factors Society in 1956.

EARLY LEADERS

At first, the social scientists who began to work specifically in the design field came out of the human factors tradition, and they tended to come from the fields of behavioral and experimental psychology. Indeed, one of the first, Ron Sears, wrote a doctoral dissertation on persistent behavior in rats. Yet these early entrants all cultivated a broader vision, many of them a specifically sociocultural one. Jane Fulton Suri, head of human factors research at IDEO, drew inspiration and direction from the anthropologist Edward Hall. Liz Sanders (SonicRim), once a college major in both psychology and anthropology, has called her observational methods applied anthropology. Steve Wilcox (Design Science), who devoted an issue of a premier design journal to the importance of anthropology in product development, also has a bachelor's degree in anthropology. Similarly, Rick Robinson (E-lab, and now, Sapient Corporation), and Lucy Suchman (Xerox PARC) also work within anthropological and ethnographic traditions.

The sympathy toward anthropology is interesting not in itself, but for what it shows of a shared orientation to professional problem solving. To one extent or another, all of the individuals discussed here found that making a truly powerful contribution to practical design problems depended on their abandoning a fragmented, mentalistic model of behavior in favor of a more holistic, broadly contextual approach. As Chuck Mauro put it recently in conversation with me about his redesign of the NASA shuttle control room, "It's not a choice. You *have* to be interested in this contextual stuff. Or you just can't solve the problem." The launch facility floor, with its distinctive patterns of job sharing and its special workload variations (panic-sleep-panic) presents an especially robust example of the importance of applying such a contextually sensitive approach. But it is far from the only one. To some degree, all of the practitioners found that an intimate knowledge of a person's behavioral environment (Hallowell 1955) was a prerequisite to getting the job done right.

MAURO

I start with Chuck Mauro, whose main contribution is to have broken the barrier between design and human factors traditions. Human factors expertise did not emerge strongly enough to be marketed as a design criterion until the early 1980s. But Mauro was ahead of that curve, partly because of his work for the U.S. government, as well as for private industry. A designer and student of key human factors disciplines—physiology, psychology, and anatomy—Mauro is perhaps the first person to have applied human factors analysis to both public and private projects.

He did this, moreover, in the context of unusually high-profile work beginning in the late 1970s.

In 1976, Mauro worked with one of the most famous of American industrial designers, Raymond Loewy, the creator of such great American icons as the Coca-Cola bottle. But the project that Loewy assigned to Mauro was a far cry from consumer product work. It was a U.S. State Department project on agricultural equipment, including combines and planting machines, for the USSR during the period of détente. According to Mauro, the Soviets required that one member of the prospective design team have expertise in ergonomics or human factors. Mauro had studied psychology and physiology at the NYU School of Medicine as part of his own, idiosyncratically devised graduate program under an OSHA fellowship in 1971. And he had just come off a three-year stint working on John Deere tractors and combines under Niels Diffrient at the design firm of Henry Dreyfuss Associates. So he fit the criteria well. In Russia, he was to gain not only a unique design experience, but also an appreciation for how a national ideology can influence technological design:

There is a big difference between the American and Soviet approaches to agriculture. In the US, each farming function is optimized in an individual machine, say, "the wheat combine," "the corn combine," "the potato harvester," and so forth. The Soviet approach, on the other hand, was to design a single big machine as the sole power source. It was basically an engine, with lots of different drive train connections. And on this one power source they would hang everything: combines, plows, planters, pickers.

The net effect [in the Soviet case] was an engineering nightmare. The Soviet machine did nothing well. It sacrificed function for versatility. Yet we were prohibited from changing its design. The reason the Soviets gave us was that [the configurations] we recommended were "antithetical" to the way in which they and their allies in the Third World worked. "Our culture and that of our allies drives this design," they said.

Now when it came to the automobile, of course, they told us they wanted an Italian-style sports car.

With some help from Raymond Loewy, Mauro in 1978 founded his own firm, Mauro Associates, which aimed to apply human factors, broadly construed, to all manner of design problems.

The NASA project, for which Mauro is best known, fell to him in the late 1980s. A friend of his at NASA brought him the work, which started as a cleanup job. Mauro had to figure out the possible design implications of a thousand-page human factors study, which had been done by a Washington, D.C., firm specializing in military work. The study aimed to determine the optimal layout of the master control room for the U.S. space shuttle. The really grievous shortcoming of the previous group's study, in Mauro's view, was that it had failed to notice how the special behavioral habits and organization of the control room significantly affected human functional capacities. "Basically, a space flight is complete panic for 18 minutes at launch, people sleeping for the next four days, and then complete panic again when everybody comes down. So the control room configuration has to accommodate under- and over-staffing, cross training, and workload variations. They would be stuck with operations problems until they tackled this contextual stuff."

Mauro's team picked up the project at an especially volatile time: a year after the *Challenger* disaster. The explosion shortly after liftoff of the space shuttle *Challenger*, in January 1986, had resulted in the death of all seven of its crewmembers, including a schoolteacher who was supposed to have been the first civilian in space. "So as you can guess, I was on everybody's radar screen. My project was on the critical path to the launch of the redesigned space shuttle, and if you were on the critical path, you got a lot of attention. Every morning at 9:00 A.M. the operations manager called me to inquire as to the project's status."

The origin of the *Challenger* disaster lay, according to Mauro, largely in the lack of a centralized view of the shuttle's differentiated main systems. Redesign work to facilitate the integration of these systems was needed. Thus one important development that eventually came out of his team's efforts was the outline of a new user interface that would be better capable of conveying the thousands of data points coordinating the various components of the system than the one used during the *Challenger* disaster.

The bulk of the work, however, concerned the functional architecture of the control room floor itself. NASA gave Mauro an empty room and put him in charge of developing its entire physical layout, from the workstations and conference rooms to the reference areas and emergency monitor storage rooms. His team's mandate even included such secondary, tedious issues as the security requirements of secure or "red" cabling, which had to be kept a minimum distance from the low-security or "black" lines.

Since then, Mauro has trimmed his team down to a lean group of helpers, and renamed the firm Mauro New Media. Over the years, the team's specialty has continued to be large-scale systems integration. Its most significant project in the 1990s was the redesign of the trading system used on the floor of the New York Stock Exchange (NYSE).

In 1992, the Exchange was seriously considering abandoning the open-outcry system for an automated market. Our recommendation was definitely to not do that. The floor of the New York Stock Exchange works only because of its culture, not in spite of it. The relationships among the people on the floor determine the system's effectiveness. All you have to do is look at a typical function allocation profile to see that there is no way someone can map all that over. We did an extensive analysis in the first six months of the trading functions of the specialist, the broker, the clerk, and the reporter. Trying to re-create that on a computer interface was virtually impossible.

Now that the NYSE has outgrown its floor, it is again considering how to develop a fully automated system. Mauro is hoping that they will be able to view the tasks confronting them as "more than a hardware problem."

When the NYSE does a billion-share day, I know it does it because of decisions I made—not from my design background, nor from my marketing knowledge, but on the strength of my psychology and physiology background, and because of my willingness to examine another subculture in order to make decisions affecting all those systems.

Mauro had arrived on the scene in the early 1970s, while working with Loewy on the Soviet project. The next folks to appear arrived later in that decade. In 1979, Jane Fulton Suri (IDEO) was working at the Institute for Consumer Ergonomics (ICE) in the United Kingdom. And Ron Sears (Richardson/Smith) was just about to join the National Cash Register Company (NCR). Though they were working on different continents, Fulton Suri and Sears were cutting new paths in the two cousin traditions of American human factors and European ergonomics.

FULTON SURI

Jane Fulton Suri of IDEO, in San Francisco, has been a principal champion of discovery research, as it has come to be called in the design field. She has been a prominent and articulate advocate of steering design questions self-consciously back toward the front end of projects in established design consulting firms (ID TWO, IDEO). Traditionally, design concepts were worked out early on. The concepts then underwent some conceptual development and were passed off to engineering for implementation well after the direction had been established. Her studio at ID TWO, however, had by 1987 developed a new kind of practice and specialization. A client would arrive with a new technology, an embryonic idea for its use, and the merest outline of a project brief. Fulton Suri would then "discover what we could learn about people and behavior, and their needs and priorities, in ways that could inform the development of those early concepts."

Our work on the H.P. Heartstream defibrillator, a couple of years ago, is perhaps a good example of this. Now this was something along the lines of a fire extinguisher, which could be kept handy and used by nonexperts in emergencies to resuscitate a victim of cardiac arrest. We performed contextual research, and a whole range of iterative testing through early prototypes, trying to create emotionally stressed circumstances, so that we could see what was working. As it turned out, even trained professionals kind of go to pieces in times of emergency and panic. So a nonexpert must have absolutely unambiguously explicit cues, in order to use the defibrillator successfully. The client was disappointed, at first, because our team didn't immediately produce the answer about the best configuration, even with a psychologist onboard. But subsequently, the client has not only understood, but has actually embodied into the company's own development process the ideas of early prototyping and of rapid cycling of testing ideas—of focusing right away on what's really working.

If there was a precedent for someone like Jane Fulton Suri at ID TWO, it may have been partly the firm's values. "The company possessed a clearly articulated philosophy," she says, "about the purpose of design as answering to human needs." But the natural arc of her own intellectual trajectory had a lot to do with this, too.

Fulton Suri began at ICE Ergonomics in England in 1979. She was trained in experimental psychology, which was not unusual at ICE Ergonomics (even though the majority of her colleagues were physiologists and ergonomists). What set her apart seemingly, was something to do with her association with architecture. Sommer's work on personal space, and Hall's on "proxemics" had been seminal studies for her, inspiring an interest that, in 1977, led her to earn a Masters of Science degree from Strathcylde, Scotland, in architecture. She brought an unusual consciousness to ICE Ergonomics.

Home to the ICE campus is Loughborough University in the United Kingdom, which at that time was a technical university with a strong emphasis on applied psychology and biology. Fulton Suri was working on traffic safety and transit systems, "on people going through ticket barriers, buying tickets and interacting with machinery." The projects going on beside her addressed minimal space standards for public housing and new kinds of home appliances and machinery. But she had an odd sense at the time that if her team's design recommendations were to hit their mark more directly, she and her colleagues would need to think more about the meanings people assigned to their own behavior.

Consider the work we did on motorcycles. The question was why lads on bikes were having lots of accidents, and why drivers were failing to see them. We were tackling the problem at the level of putting on lights, and of wearing bright clothing. But then we realized that there had to be other forces at play in what boys were doing on motorbikes other than their getting from point A to point B. We wouldn't get far without tackling some of the issues to do with status, young manhood, and the meaning of clothing in the culture of motorcycles and adolescence.

To help solve these problems, she developed an empirical style and methodology that was to become her hallmark at ID TWO, and later still, at IDEO. But while at ICE, Fulton Suri met colleagues who would eventually introduce her to people in the American industrial design firms. One of them, Ian McClelland (of Philips in the Netherlands) was doing very interesting work with the San Francisco industrial design firm ID TWO. During a chance meeting with Fulton Suri at the University of California, Berkeley, in the late 1980s, he told her about the work. He also helped introduce her to a number of other people who were doing new kinds of work in design. They included Bill Verplank (formerly of Interval), a graduate of Stanford and of MIT and a human factors engineer, who had designed and tested human-computer interfaces at Xerox PARC in the late 1970s and early 1980s. Another was Bill Moggridge, president of ID TWO and an industrial designer who wanted to move ID TWO definitively toward software and computer interface design. Fulton Suri joined ID TWO in 1987. She remained there through 1991, the year the company merged with two other companies, David Kelley Design and Matrix Design, to form IDEO.

Fulton Suri's earliest intellectual relationships with colleagues in the American design world were with people who specialized in human-computer interactions. She mentions as an example the psychologist Joy Mountford (formerly of Interval), who, after beginning in military avionics at Honeywell, managed the Human Interface Group at Apple's Advanced Technology Group for nearly a decade. Fulton Suri felt a little unusual because she had little experience with computer software. And so when she joined ID TWO, her role initially was not always clear.

What exactly was her expertise? She recalls colleagues' confusion when she, having been asked a fairly straightforward human factors research question, responded by calling attention to the genuine complexity of matters.

I would be asked what kind of force would people be able to apply to the latch on the vacuum cleaner to get at the bag inside, in order to empty it. "Will users understand that that is what they are to do?" These are very clear questions. But I would tend to come back to that with more questions, such as: "Why would people have to do that?" And, "Under what circumstances?" And, "How frequently?" And, "Why have we assumed that that's the way the bag would be emptied?" . . . So my colleagues would be disappointed. But the re-learning was, "Well, maybe we need to start asking these questions earlier," and "Maybe we could go look at contexts of use and explore some of the opportunities." So gradually I became the person "who knows how to do that"—who knows how to pick up the phone and ask to come round and watch people doing things, and using products, as a way of inspiring design in strategic and tactical ways.

When IDEO was first formed, in 1991, she was the only person at IDEO consistently doing that. Since then, however, IDEO's human factors design and research staff has grown to seventeen people internationally, integrated into multiple "studios" within IDEO, each studio numbering fifteen to forty people.

SEARS

In 1979, Ron Sears (Design Consortium) was winding down a postdoc at Northwestern University. Rather than apply for another and abet his own anxiety about having to publish more articles than the guy down the hall, Sears gave up his rats. He gave away their temperature- and humidity-controlled cages and mazes, and looked for work. It was an unassuming beginning for the first psychologist to be hired by a design-consulting firm. Sears, however, was about to embark on a career trajectory whose corporate design strategies would spawn a new strategic design process and help reverse the ill fortunes of two American giants, the National Cash Register Corporation, and the Xerox Corporation.

At that point in Sears's history, though, the NCR Corporation in Dayton, Ohio, wasn't the first place one would have expected him to end up. He says he was "completely hooked on research, computers, and electronics," and wanted a way "to continue playing with behavior and technology." But he felt the work promised to be more challenging than safety studies or dog food taste preferences, which were some of the other options he'd considered at the time.

NCR had been building mechanical cash registers since the nineteenth century. By the time Sears joined, in 1979, it was making banking machines, automated tellers, and mainframes for financial systems. So his transition made a certain kind of sense, given the kind of experimental psychologist Sears had become. At DePaul University, and at Northwestern, where he had completed his postdoc, Sears was an avid builder of mechanical and electronic equipment. "I could order practically anything I wanted for the lab at DePaul from GSA (Government Surplus Authority) to support my research projects. And I did. I filled up the lab with everything under the sun, from electronic components, to recording equipment, to soundproof rooms. You name it." At NCR, this penchant for machinery led him toward the industrial designers in the company— people, he says, who belonged to "the profession of inventors."

NCR's own published material says of the 1970s that the times were "very difficult . . . partly due to a slow transition from mechanics to electronics in the cash register business." Sears is less sanguine about the company's fortunes at the time. "In 1978, the company had basically gone under," he says. "They had been using brass gears in their machines, and had produced millions of them. But now, anybody on the scene with TTL logic or microprocessors was killing them. I arrived in a company that had fired thousands, torn down most of their Dayton factories, and left blocks of empty parking lots." Sears's title was human factors specialist in corporate research and development.

At first, Sears worked on membrane switches: flat-panel keys that people tended to push too hard to activate. He developed several prototype keyboards for NCR, eventually developing and patenting a new design with better sensitivity. But actually inventing things tended to alienate him from his peers in the human factors department, who, according to Sears, were looking to dispense human factors wisdom from a chair. "We'd sit down at a few meetings with project engineers, with no time and no budget, and have to take a wild guess; and maybe they'd believe us." Sears kept inventing things anyway, submitting patents for some of his favorites and, as he remembers it, annoying people who wanted to keep a low profile, given the recent layoffs. "Nobody *told me* that human factors people are supposed to be passive advisers of the engineering process. That would have been an absurdity anyway, given my interests, background, and habits" (Sears, personal communication).

Events at NCR soon pulled Sears away from his switches and keyboards. As a primary person in the human factors department, who worked well with industrial designers, Sears was needed for a massive corporate plan aimed to help revive the company. The head of the design department at NCR had come up with the idea in 1979. The goal was to develop a corporate design strategy program that could define all the major design principles for the company's many products and product lines. The CAP or Corporate Appearance Program was meant to be far-reaching—too far-reaching, in fact, to be run by any single department at NCR. The project would have to be given to an outside design firm for implementation.

NCR took bids and handed the contract to the design firm of Richardson/Smith in Worthington, Ohio. The Richardson/Smith team, realizing that European ergonomic standards were increasingly important for business equipment design, requested that NCR expand the CAP plan to include human factors. Sears, along with two colleagues, was put in charge of the human factors part of the campaign.

My idea was to gather together the twenty-five people at NCR, worldwide, who were doing human factors and industrial design: the front-line product developers, who had hands-on experience that was recent and customer-informed. I suggested a grand conference, to be held at Richardson/Smith for a week, where we'd split up into cross-discipline teams to define all the major interaction problems and design principles.

That is what we did. And we redesigned the appearance and human factors of over 200 NCR products in the next two years, for everything from keyboards to cash registers, printers to ATMs. The idea worked. It quickly dawned on everybody that if we could create some basic standards, then huge numbers of

arguments, fights, and unproductive meetings—not to say crappy product designs—could be handled right up front, in terms of these basic design standards.

Sears found the Richardson/Smith approach congenial to his own. The
following year, he left NCR to accept a position at the consulting firm.
There, he would help administer a remedy, almost identical in some
ways to the CAP, to an ailing giant, the Xerox Corporation.

Arnold Wasserman, NCR's director of industrial design (now design
director at the Idea Factory), was directly responsible for carrying over
NCR's integrated human factors approach to product design at Xerox.
Wasserman had left NCR himself in 1980, to work at Xerox. So he was
there when Sears sent out a distress call from NCR, and helped Sears
get a job at Richardson/Smith.

Once ensconced at Richardson/Smith, Sears worked full time on the
Xerox Inter-Operability Study. To hear Sears tell the story, Xerox had it
even worse than NCR, more so for the frustration they suffered from
losing the low-end copier market to the Japanese.

Absolutely the only thing [Xerox] was interested in, apart from pushing expensive technical features into the low-end product lines, was improving copy quality. Get this: they hired a Ph.D. in psychophysics to help them design
experiments to allow human beings to *discriminate* between the copy quality coming out of their machines as opposed to the machines of their competitors. That's
called being way too far out on your Return-on-Investment curve.

The Xerox people knew the jam rates of the competitors, the number of
black specks, the amount of spilled toner. But they had no idea why
customers liked the Japanese competitors' machines better than their
own.

We took the question to be: "Why don't people like our equipment?" That was
a business strategy question. We would need to ask open-ended questions, not
questions about copy quality.

First, we asked people what they liked and disliked. "The damned thing is
broken all the time," they said. "Every time I walk by the equipment, it's down."
In fact, technically, Xerox's jam rate was better than that of competitors. The
problem was that servicing people were often required for relatively simple problems, which would tie up the machine. What customers tended to count as a
"jam" was any time they walked by and could not use the machine whereas on
the simpler Japanese copiers, the customers themselves could immediately fix
the jam. So it was not the machine, but the need for servicing people, that had
to be fixed.

As another example, one of the copiers used an air system to shuffle originals.
Some people hated that; the thing blasted their travel receipts all over the room.
We just kept finding this behavioral stuff over and over again.

Apart from its complement of industrial and graphic designers, the Xerox inter-operability team included a patent-lawyer-turned-designer, Chuck Leinbach, and eventually another psychologist, Liz Sanders. It was, by all accounts, strikingly interdisciplinary. The resulting intellectual synergy is precisely what its members most often credit with the far-reaching success of the project. The team not only identified the problems, but also was able to integrate those findings with specific design recommendations. The team produced mimic diagrams showing the paper cycling through the machine at various stages. They developed uniform color schemes. They designed keys, switches, inexpensive document handlers: a long list of innovations, which continued into the mid-1980s and well after Richardson/Smith was purchased by the British design firm of Fitch, Inc., in 1988. Sears occasionally finds articles discussing Xerox's "miracle" or "great turnaround" back in 1982. "Bull," he says. "That was us. Richardson/Smith woke those guys up."

Work on the Xerox study continued without Sears after 1985, when he left Richardson/Smith to form the Design Consortium. Sears's idea in forming the Design Consortium was to fashion a "virtual company," a consortium of companies that could cobble together instantly the talent and resources to complete almost any cross-disciplinary project. Key partners were Bally Design, in Pittsburgh, and GVO in Palo Alto. Under the urging of Alex Bally, Sears formulated a strategic model, called the Product Value Matrix^{SM}, based on his cumulative experiences. It was designed to help identify customer needs and expectations, as well as to develop concepts and design features. Sears's PVM^{SM} became the methodological cornerstone of the Design Consortium. One of the projects in which Sears applied this process was a competitive analysis of the original PowerBook for Apple Computer, Inc.

In the early 1980s, Sears and his compatriots at Richardson/Smith would inevitably get the chance to talk with researchers at Xerox PARC (Palo Alto Research Center). "Once Xerox saw what we were trying to do," says Chuck Leinbach, "Arnold [Wasserman] put us in touch with PARC." It is hard to know exactly how much each team influenced the other, but Sears and Leinbach have indicated that these meetings were very exciting, and that some of the ideas being floated at Palo Alto were circulating in Worthington as well. There is a good chance that there was some cross-fertilization of thinking, and maybe even some methodological sharing. Lots of people like to take credit for the first uses of video in design, for instance. But the credit should probably be shared among PARC, Richardson/Smith, and Bally Design. While Lucy Suchman and her compatriots at PARC were videotaping customers in California to describe workplace environments, Richardson/Smith was videotaping customers in Ohio to capture the errors of users plugging away at ATMs. Alex Bally, meanwhile, was using time-lapse film to study the use of anesthesiology equipment in surgery for Drägerwerk AG in Germany. Each team developed video ethnography from the needs of its research, and felt at the time that this was leading edge. It was a case of parallel evolution, also having much to do, one suspects, with video cameras first becoming relatively cheap and widely available in the early 1980s.

SUCHMAN

Lucy Suchman is one of the best-known anthropologists to be involved in applied design. Based at Xerox PARC since 1979, she is the founder of its Work Practice and Technology Area. She has written on participatory systems design, human-computer interaction, office work, ethnographic methodology, and artificial intelligence. She is best known for having led a massive multidisciplinary project on work practices that Steelcase undertook with Xerox (with consulting support from Jay Doblin and Associates). Principally through that project, known as The Workplace Project, Suchman pulled together people from a dozen, typically disparate humanities and science fields to form a critical mass of interest in workplace design.

The late 1970s was the heyday of artificial intelligence studies, and Xerox wanted to design intelligent, interactive interfaces. At the time, Suchman was a graduate student in cultural anthropology at the University of California, Berkeley, and she was interested in what humanlike intelligence might mean in the context of computers. She joined PARC in 1979, as an intern. "I wanted to raise awareness," she says, "among those in the design community about how hard a problem it really is to design an interactive machine in anything like the sense that humans are interactive." Her findings, published through the early 1980s as conference papers and articles, were to make a strong impact on the human-computer interface design and artificial intelligence disciplines. In 1987, these findings appeared in the form of a book, as *Plans and Situated Actions: The Problem of Human-Machine Communication*.

Suchman tended to see herself as a pure researcher. Traditionally, PARC has been a place that could accommodate such an orientation. Founded in 1970, PARC is unusual among industrial research centers in possessing an identity as an independent institution. It has a vigorous grant and internship program. Its staff maintains ties with people from universities and nonprofit centers. And in 1984, after Suchman finished her dissertation, PARC hired her as a full-time researcher. Suchman's mandate was to communicate with the product development teams at Xerox, to learn about the products they were developing, and to tailor her recommendations to their efforts. She was to provide an ongoing source of understanding about specific industries (e.g., law, transportation, engineering) and applications (e.g., marketing, customer relations, design) that her work might feed into. The deliverables consisted of presentations to product development teams in Rochester, New York, who from time to time would need to use the expertise her team had amassed. "Ideally, our research was running in parallel with the product program, but on a more ongoing basis, with longer time frames," she says.

In the early 1980s, another anthropologist, Jeanette Blomberg, joined PARC. She worked closely with Suchman. Blomberg was interested in how social interaction affects the ways we understand new technology (Blomberg 1987) and on how, conversely, technology affects the organization of our work, especially in offices (Blomberg 1988). In comparison to the Richardson/Smith team's findings on a similar topic—the user's perceptions of the performance of photocopiers—Blomberg's own findings drove home the social construction of meaning in these environments. A particularly interesting finding, for instance, was that users defined a machine's breakdown in terms of its severity, and hence, to the times when the breakdown occurred and the availability of someone who could fix it. By the mid-1980s, Suchman and Blomberg, along with anthropologist Julian Orr, had helped to establish firmly the formidable reputation of workplace studies at PARC that the institution has been able to enjoy in recent years.

But the watershed moment occurred in 1989, when the Chicago design firm of Jay Doblin and Associates needed to outsource a job on workstyles and work spaces. Steelcase (an office furniture manufacturer) asked Doblin to help it develop products for a variety of work environments. According to the then-director of research at Doblin, Rick Robinson (who went on to form E-Lab), the Steelcase managers understood that the effort would require a portfolio of multidisciplinary ethnographic field research efforts. The research team would not constrain itself to consider any single product specifically. Instead, its mandate was to explore multiactivity workplaces and work styles *as a whole*. The group at PARC, given its expertise on the workplace, was a natural place to look for help with the project. All that was needed was for Doblin's strategic planner, Larry Keeley, to broker a portion of the work to Xerox, as a project to be run by Lucy Suchman from PARC.

They created the Workplace Project. The Doblin and PARC teams decided to locate the study in an airport. According to Robinson,

the idea was motivated, in part, by an idea about the future of work. Airports are places where a lot of information is exchanged, where much communication is electronic, and where work behaviors extend through multiple kinds of space. The hypothesis was that work was tending toward high fluidity, high concentrations of information, incorporating various kinds of expertise. That made it an unusually interesting project, I think, for everybody who worked on it.

Since Xerox stood to gain from the research, it would help fund the project jointly, forming a temporary partnership with Steelcase. When the grant money arrived at PARC, Suchman found she had enough to form a research group, or area, with its own administrative identity. That entity became known as the Work Practice and Technology Area. It survived under Suchman's directorship for ten years. With the area's new resources, Suchman hired some unusually capable helpers—with extraordinary backgrounds.

Perhaps her most far-reaching achievement, beyond coordinating the mining efforts on this rich lode of new, multidisciplinary work, was to have helped forge new relationships between designers and social scientists. One of these relationships, of course, was with Rick Robinson, who was to develop a design research methodology that was more explicitly anthropological than anything yet seen (see the chapter by Wasson, this volume). But Suchman hired plenty of folks who hadn't before been a part of the world of industrial design: the anthropologists Brigitte Jordan, Susan Irwin Anderson, and Francoise Brun-Cottan; the sociolinguists Charles and Marjorie Goodwin of UCLA; and as consultants to the project, the anthropologist Jean Lave and sociologist Emanuel Schegloff.

SANDERS

Opportunities for social scientists in design began to widen perceptibly in the 1980s. By then, the earliest entrants to the field had not only created new job positions, but had also shaped new design philosophies and subtly altered client expectations, so that other social scientists could now more readily claim space in the field. Liz Sanders joined Richardson/Smith in 1982 at the start of the Xerox Inter-Operability study, about a year after Ron Sears had arrived. Sanders, too, remembers the Xerox study as having been just as intellectually exciting for its participants as it was productive of concrete applications for the client. "It was an opportunity to apply insights and implications from psychology and anthropology to the predesign portion of the product development process. We were breaking new ground." Sanders remained at Richardson/Smith, later Fitch, Inc., for seventeen years, where she continued to explore new applications of social science knowledge and methods to the design of products, information, interiors, and user interfaces.

Through the 1990s, Sanders became particularly well known as a leader in participatory design. At a general level, participatory design reminds us that there are other values in product development besides technical quality, efficiency, and high productivity. Helping customers and consumers shape the process and express their needs is also a necessary part of the whole business (Suchman 1993: viii). In line with this philosophy, Liz Sanders, along with three of her former teammates in the Research and Planning Group at Fitch, Inc., broke away in 1999 to form a new company they called SonicRim. "Our company provides predesign research services to clients who are willing to participate in the process," says Sanders.

Sanders likes to describe the company's eclectic approach to design by drawing a triangular diagram, consisting of "what people say" (learned from marketing research), "what people do" (learned from participant observation and applied anthropology), and "what people make" (learned from participatory design). The SonicRim practitioners have found that the most relevant insights occur at the interstices of the triangle. Yet it is "what people make" to which Sanders feels she and her colleagues have the most to contribute. "We believe that if you give people appropriate tools, they can express their tacit needs. They can tell you how they feel, and can communicate their aspirations."

Many of SonicRim's participatory tools rely on "projective" methods. I believe the term derives from the psychoanalytic concept relating to the externalization of unconscious wishes. Advertising and marketing have been the principal business fields to embrace it, to date, primarily in the context of focus groups. One of these tools is a three-dimensional collection of components called Velcro modeling. Potential users of the product, after participating in exercises designed to elicit their unspoken feelings, are seated at a table, in front of a vast array of Velcro-covered shapes, where they begin to make things out of the shapes. The Velcro-covered shapes come with a large assortment of smaller control elements (round, square, flat, protruding, angular, etc.), which the participants can employ to suggest buttons, dials, screens, or any other mechanical, decorative, or ergonomic component of a product. Sanders mentions a little black square, which participants in her studies have put to use as a screen, a button, and a fingerprint identification device. "People can very quickly, in minutes, actually, make things that express their unmet needs in experiences. It's amazing how creative people will become, even though they have no training in design, when they are in an open mindset and they have tools at their disposal that actually elicit ideas."

Core elements of the earliest participatory tools came from our watching designers "talk" to each other. Designers often make forms that show the innards of the thing—say, the fan, the hard drive, etc.—and then move these forms around, talking to each other all the while about where to put what. They call it "component volumetrics." We observed their visual way of communicating, and then turned those ideas into consumer tools: tools that consumers could use to express their unmet needs in products, and in spaces.

Sanders began using these tools and methods early in her career at Richardson/Smith. The earliest application was with preschoolers, involving an electronic learning product for Texas Instruments. The team's challenge was to design a single product that would appeal to both boys and girls (contrary to the current trend, which is to differentiate them, especially by color). No information was available to inform the design process. To make headway, Sanders took a participatory approach (Sanders 2000).

We had to get data. So we asked the children to draw things for us. We prepared large color selection boards so that they could select and show us their favorite colors. We asked them to color in pictures that we had made for them. We took pictures of the kids and analyzed what colors they were wearing. And in the end, we learned enough not only to solve the color challenge, but to help drive the overall design process as well.

The product that emerged from this particular study was the Texas Instruments Voyager, which received a Gold award in the annual *I.D. Magazine* awards in the 1980s in two categories: Consumer Product and Design Research.

At the generative end of a project, that is to say, when new concept ideas are critical, Sanders favors a method she calls image collaging. Here, participants make their own collages from a preselected set of images and words, and then they present them verbally. The idea is to help the team involved on a project, including members of the client organization, to communicate more effectively with one other about abstract, and often emotionally charged concepts, such as the brand of a particular product, or the company's corporate identity.

A great example of this is a big branding campaign we were doing with a major bank, while at Fitch. A man from the client side, someone who you would never have expected to share his feelings in a group situation, put the image of a clean, bright-white T-shirt on the group image-collaging wall. He then became amazingly expressive about what this white T-shirt meant to him and to his company, and how it made him feel. He went on and on about it. Everybody was flabbergasted. And from then on, all the other participants ever needed to evoke the feelings that he had expressed so eloquently was, "You know what I mean, it's like the white T-shirt," and it conveyed at once everything that this man had said before.

The participatory design approach, as Sanders construes it, requires more than just tools. It requires a new mind-set. Indeed, it can be taken to imply a critique of the premises of design consulting as a whole. On the one hand, Sanders advocates ceding to the user more creative authority than design has traditionally allowed. "Our goal," says Sanders, "is for the clients to learn to truly respect their customers as these customers become a crucial part of the process." On the other hand, Sanders advocates ceding to the client more authority than design consulting has allowed. "We also want our clients to learn to do this research themselves. We want to be an open-source company. We don't want to keep these methods proprietary." This, of course, flies in the face of the traditional consulting model, which holds that the specialized expertise of consultants is for rent, but never for sale.

But Sanders says she is convinced that in the long run, her sharing a fuller range of her knowledge with clients will be viable, financially, and that this strategy will turn out to be consistent with her philosophy and ethics. "I have been teaching for ten years, and have learned how valuable it is to share the knowledge. Many of our clients now are my former students. Sharing these methods can be hugely beneficial, because the more people are using them, the stronger the community of practitioners and the more demand there is for this way of working. User-centered design is much in demand these days. We are simply taking it to a new extreme."

WILCOX

Stephen Wilcox (Design Science) is one of the most outspoken proponents of human factors research in the business of design consulting. He was also an early advocate of bibliographic research in design consulting. In the mid 1980s, Wilcox left a college teaching job to join the design firm of Herbst, LaZar, Bell and Rogers (now Herbst LaZar Bell). There he helped formulate a tripartite model of design research (discovery research, human factors recommendations, and usability testing) that has since become adopted generally by the industrial design community. The distinctive features of the model were twofold. It insisted plainly that human factors analysis be prerequisite to any leading-edge design effort. And it argued in favor of prototype testing as early as possible in the design research process. Such testing would enable evaluation and usability testing prior to committing to production more resources than necessary to production.

A psychology Ph.D. out of Penn State who had been teaching for several years, Wilcox joined Herbst, LaZar, Bell and Rogers in 1984. "I felt like the academic world was self-indulgent. I really did; I felt that we were all writing articles for each other and it wasn't having any impact on anything. And as I began to study the underlying premises of psychology, its epistemology—my publishing area—I understood that the field would never tackle the real issues." By "real," Wilcox means both important and, more literally, perceivable. As he argues in a 1985 article for a symposium on human factors in consumer products, you can't turn to psychology "to find out whether or not to trust a witness who says a car was speeding." Although there are plenty of articles with the words "memory" and "problem solving," the number of these that are devoted to obscure, rare, and practically irrelevant perceptual phenomena outstrips those on the perception of actual physical motion by a factor of nearly 100 to 1 (Wilcox 1985: 194).

Because he had been saying the same kind of thing at Franklin and Marshall College (in Lancaster, Pennsylvania), his colleagues there told him in 1983, " 'If you really took yourself seriously, you would leave.' So finally I agreed with that," says Wilcox. "I accepted the logic of their critique, you could say." He sought an alternative field. Through networking and reading, he discovered industrial design and human factors.

In 1983, most of the human factors practitioners were either working for the government, or doing ergonomics in factory plants to try to eliminate workplace injuries. Though he knew of no one else who was doing empirical design research, it seemed logical to Wilcox that people developing products would have a need for somebody who knew something about the users of products. He lunched with Myrick Rogers from Herbst, LaZar, Bell and Rogers in Lancaster, and eventually sold him on the idea that such a need might exist.

That Wilcox was more or less at the same frontier as Fulton Suri, Sears, and Sanders is apparent from the way he speaks of his hiring. None of these early entrants really knew what they were supposed to be doing when they accepted the positions they were offered. They were "experiments" in interdisciplinary work. As Dave Smith told Liz Sanders in her interview at Richardson/Smith, "We don't exactly understand your role yet. But we hope that within a year or so, you'll know why you're here." Wilcox's story is similar, revealing the relative infancy of design research at the time:

In the beginning, the benefits of hiring me were theoretical, I'd be the first to admit. HLB was doing a lot of commodity-type items back then. I recall looking through their portfolio and seeing bowling bags, tackle boxes, the Pocket Fisherman, the Kitchen Magician, storm doors, kitchen goods, and hardware items. The big annual show for them at the time was the hardware show.

The thinking was that having a Ph.D. on staff would really give them a competitive edge. They must have figured that they could learn how to use me eventually. Having somebody like me around would help position them as a more sophisticated company, to get more medical and technological products. That's exactly what happened, as it turned out. Don't get me wrong, I didn't accomplish this myself. But it was part of HLB's strategic plan that we would start doing more medical, scientific, and complicated industrial projects; and we did.

The concrete usefulness of having somebody like Wilcox around emerged pretty quickly. Although the designers were adept and imaginative, they weren't much used to visiting libraries to solve their design problems.

Listening to them, learning from them, Wilcox started noticing that they often made design decisions in the dark, without hard information to answer their quite legitimate questions. "They were just guessing, or using intuition, where I knew there was real information that could influence the design decision." As a former academic, Wilcox found library work second nature. Much of what he did at first was to track down information. "On a job for a health care device for Clairol, I found a report containing the actual dimensions of the relevant anatomy. Depending on how the thing was going to be used, I'd determine strength requirements and limits; maybe I would even determine the size of the consumer market for the device. I had a sense that the data were out there, somewhere, based on what I had taught myself of human factors."

The whole process got a boost in the late 1980s from the rise of electronic database searching. As Wilcox remembers it, he and Dan Formosa (of Smart Design in New York) were two of the first design consultants to advocate it. Using PsychInfo (behavioral science), CompIndex (engineering), NTIS, and so forth, Wilcox and his peers could bring more information to the table, faster, than had been possible using print archives.

A project that helped shape methodology at Herbst LaZar Bell was undertaken in the late 1980s for Electrolux, a company that makes vacuum cleaners. Its evolution nicely illustrates the emerging difference between traditional marketing methods and a social scientific approach to design. Relying on data from focus groups, Electrolux had decided to pursue a product that would enable consumers to clean staircases more easily. The company had developed a product and was prepared to commit to tooling when it hired Herbst LaZar Bell to verify the design. Wilcox explains,

[W]e went into people's homes and hung out with them while they vacuumed, which I suppose was an early example of ethnographic design research. (I was an anthropology major as an undergraduate.) We also paid close attention to the physical behavior of people using vacuum cleaners. And it became apparent that Electrolux had solved a problem nobody cared about. People had grown accustomed to lifting their vacuum cleaners to access the stairways, and they had developed a lot of good strategies to access these spaces. More critical problems were the ones people seemed unaware of: repeated bending, too much noise, not wanting to pull on the hose to lug the machine around. Users never complained about these problems directly, or even realized they were problems. But when we noticed the behaviors and asked about them on site, people became more articulate, and we learned a great deal about these inconveniences and discomforts.

Design innovations included ergonomic changes, as well as a simplified electronic control that wouldn't intimidate technophobes, and a vacuum tube opening with a rounded edge to enable people to more efficiently and safely clean corners as they already did—by removing attachments. It was a good example of how to blend ethnographic research with human factors analysis.

Wilcox left Herbst LaZar Bell in 1991 to form Design Science in Philadelphia. His idea for the new firm was to specialize in helping to solve design problems by scientific methods. Design Science's clients would be design firms, or companies with in-house design and engineering capabilities, who had a need for research support in projects with behavioral, marketing, or human factors research components. In recent years, Wilcox has continued to proselytize for design research, serving as the chairman of the Human Factors Professional Interest Section of the Industrial Designers Society of America in 1999. He has distinguished himself particularly in the medical industry. In 1996, Wilcox helped define award criteria for the design research category of the IDSA awards. The same year, he guest edited an issue of the IDSA journal *Innovation* devoted to the role of anthropology in design, an issue representing the first articulation by the product development community itself of the value of ethnographic methods to industrial design.

ROBINSON

Rick Robinson is a principal and co-founder of E-Lab (now the experience modeling discipline of the Sapient Corporation), the first *design* consulting firm devoted purely to the use of ethnographic methodologies. Since the story of E-Lab is told in some detail by another contributor to this volume, I shall take the task here to be simply preparing the ground for that chapter with a quick sketch of Robinson's intellectual antecedents.

Robinson will be the first to tell you that he is not an anthropologist. Not, at least, by formal degree. His Ph.D. is from the University of Chicago's Committee on Human Development, whose overall emphasis is developmental theory of the human life span. But the program is so deeply interdisciplinary that it is pointless to label it according to any single traditional scholarly field. Some of the best known social scientists over the years have affiliated themselves with the human development program. Talking with me, Robinson framed the issue as a matter of ethos: "The University of Chicago's approach to *anything* is never that it's all in your head."

As a doctoral student, he was interested in the development of esthetic theories and of esthetic perception throughout adulthood—in whether people are born with an artistic awareness or must instead have it cultivated in them. His dissertation adviser, Mihaly Csikszentmihalyi, had authored a well-received book, titled *Flow*, on the kind of "peak experiences" that result in moments, sometimes very protracted moments, of intense creativity. An artist himself, and a painter and printmaker in his youth, Csikszentmihalyi had friends in the design community and was aware of New Bauhaus design. Through such interests, Robinson's mentor developed an acquaintance with Jay Doblin, of the design firm of Jay Doblin and Associates.

As Robinson neared the end of his Ph.D. research, Jay phoned Mike (Mihaly), wanting to know if he had students who could use a little extra work on the side—and who were good methodologists, too. "So, you work on people looking at art, huh?" Robinson remembers Doblin saying. "Do you think you could do research on architects designing spaces for work?" Robinson agreed to do a three-month summer internship at Doblin, which in the late 1980s numbered fewer than ten people.

The fit was ideal. Not only did Robinson end up doing real methodology development from almost the very beginning of his tenure at Doblin—a responsibility and opportunity that was unprecedented for a newcomer—but he also was producing work faster than ever before, thanks to the literal creativity of his colleagues at Doblin. "Having gone through a year and a half of editing a book, I was just really tired of endless wrangling over minor intellectual details. Here I was giving these people an idea and they were doing something with it right away. I would say, 'Well, this is how I think these people feel about furniture . . . and I would see these guys turn it into something almost immediately. It was a very different experience." Robinson became head of research at Doblin within the year, and in 1990 he helped conduct the Workplace Project, which brought him in touch with Suchman and her team. By 1994, he had launched E-Lab with fellow Doblin ex-patriots John Cain and Mary Beth McCarthy.

What's most interesting about E-Lab, from a historical perspective, is the way its clients and potential clients tended to understand its nature and purpose. The distinctive contribution of ethnography is, of course, self-evident to fellow social scientists (and to enlightened designers such as Jay Doblin), but this has never been true in the business world. No market could sustain so many feature stories and puff pieces about anthropology in design unless its real importance were not still badly misunderstood.

Robinson is the best person to tell us about that. When I spoke with him in the fall of 1999, before the merger with Sapient, Robinson told me that clients tended to misunderstand E-Lab as being a market research company. " 'Gee, you understand what people want, you understand needs, you understand motivations,' a client may say. 'You understand patterns of behavior, you understand how people do things.'

The questions sound a lot like traditional marketing questions. All of them, when framed slightly differently, are what people are likely to claim that market research has always done." The real problem, according to Robinson, came when someone from marketing research tried to compare the methodologies and techniques of data gathering of anthropology with those of marketing directly, without considering the different assumptions about the things to be explained. Without a proper brief, the anthropological tool kit can come out looking weak and ineffective or worse. It could seem "wrong."

You see, everybody that does this has to deal with the charges of anecdotalism, subjectivism, and small sample size. And the argument that what a good ethnography can describe is an underlying structure or dynamic is often hard to make when someone is asking about normal distributions, sample sizes, and all of the other elements of the empirical and statistical-positivist science traditions. The assumptions are different, and the nature of proof is different. But for many of the folks in market research, sometimes their measure is the only yardstick. Unless one recognizes this—realizes that it's likely to happen, and prepares for it—one is liable to end up with competing and incommensurate explanations. You will get into finger-pointing and name-calling. "Damned scientists." "Damned subjectivists." Solipsists in search of a common universe.

So we have spent a lot of time and effort working with people from those parts of the organizations, saying, "Listen, help us figure out how to make the *different* value of this approach clear." Accordingly, the stance we take is to demonstrate how our approach is to be added in, to be made complementary or parallel to the existing approach, and how in some places, our research is more valuable.

One of our major clients has designated us as one chunk of their overall development-planning chart. For every single product in this gigantic company, there is a phase in the beginning that says, "Do this kind of work." That's what we've been working toward. Our approach is not a panacea, not a cure-all, not the next greatest thing that will supplant everything the company already has in place. But to have this information, this different, useful information, will make the client more competitive. Now they know that. (Robinson, personal communication)

CONCLUSION

The behavioral scientists whose work I have discussed here have been taking on increasingly broad roles in the development process. Questions that business put to them about making better products became supplanted by questions about making products per se, which in turn, became supplanted by broader strategic questions. This process is somewhat apparent in the specific intellectual biographies of some of the individuals. Look at the career trajectories of Mauro, Sears, and Sanders, and you will see that design naturally draws participants into corporate strategy. Furthermore, this same process is a natural outgrowth of a developmental tendency toward the deepening and broadening of an individual's knowledge and expertise over the life course.

But at a higher level of abstraction the inclusion of behavioral scientists into design reflects a more fundamental historical development. Business decision makers are becoming increasingly aware that the experiences consumers undergo with their products are multiple. These experiences concern not only physical products, but also retail spaces, brands, company histories, and identities. The experiences arise constantly, not just when the product is purchased or used. And, those experiences require interpretation from these multiple points of view. It follows that behavioral scientists in design-related fields, posed as holists and integrators to begin with, may soon be perceived by business as a distinct breed of professional responsible for describing and acting on the complex experiences of consumers with products. They will map the multiplicity of experience that constitutes the customer interface in its broadest sense. An even greater receptivity to them from a more sophisticated understanding of their business leadership is in the forecast.

NOTE

Quotations from the seven individuals highlighted in this chapter appear with the permission of the subject. Product Value Matrix[SM], PVM[SM], Product Value Analysis[SM], and PVA[SM] are service marks of the Design Consortium, Worthington, Ohio.

REFERENCES

Baba, M. 1986. *Business and Industrial Anthropology: An Overview*. Washington, DC: National Association for the Practice of Applied Anthropology.

Blomberg, J. 1987. Social Interaction and Office Communication: Effects on User Evaluation of New Technologies. In *Technology and the Transformation of White Collar Work*, edited by R. Kraut. Hillsdale, NJ: Lawrence Erlbaum Associates.

———. 1988. The Variable Impact of Computer Technologies on the Organization of Work Activities. In *Computer-Supported Cooperative Work: A Book of Readings*, edited by I. Grief. San Mateo, CA: Morgan Kaufmann.

Hall, E.T. 1969. *The Hidden Dimension*. New York: Doubleday.

Hallowell, A.I. 1955. *Culture and Experience*. Philadelphia: University of Pennsylvania.

Helander, M.G. 1997. The Human Factors Profession. In *Handbook of Human Factors and Ergonomics*, edited by G. Salvendy. New York: John Wiley & Sons.

Kroemer, K., and K. Kroemer-Elbert. 1994. *Ergonomics*. Englewoood Cliffs, NJ: Prentice Hall.

Moroney, W.F. 1995. The Evolution of Human Engineering: A Selected Review.

In *Research Techniques in Human Engineering*, edited by J. Weimer. Englewood Cliffs, NJ: Prentice Hall.

Sanders, L. B.-N. 2000. Generative Tools for CoDesigning. In *Collaborative Design*, edited by S.A.R. Scrivener, L.J. Ball, and A. Woodcock. London: Springer-Verlag London Limited.

Sears, R., and M. Barry. 1993. Product Value Analysis[SM] Product Interactions Predict Profits. *Innovation* (Winter): 13–18.

Segal, L., and J.F. Suri. forthcoming. *Psychology Applied to Product Design*.

Suchman, L. 1987. *Plans and Situated Actions*. Cambridge: Cambridge University Press.

————. 1993. Foreword to *Participatory Design*, edited by D. Schuler and A. Namioka. Hillsdale, NJ: Lawrence Erlbaum Associates.

Whorf, B.L. 1941. The Relation of Habitual Thought and Behavior to Language. In *Language, Culture, and Personality*, edited by L. Spier, A.I. Hallowell, and S.S. Newman. Salt Lake City: University of Utah Press.

Wilcox, S.B. 1985. *Can the Human Factors Engineer Rely Upon Cognitive Psychology?* Paper presented at the Fourth Symposium on Human Factors and Industrial Design in Consumer Products, St. Paul, MN.

PART II

CREATING COLLABORATIVE CULTURES

Part II explores some of the issues that arise when attempting to create organizations that promote multidisciplinary collaboration.

Byrne and Sands argue that corporate management deserves the same kind of multidisciplinary collaboration that is often dedicated to products. Organizations can be designed using many of the same principles that guide product development. Both benefit from a sound understanding of the cultures of the relevant groups. After examining the apprenticeship system that forms the basis of the design culture, they look at some of the reasons that designers must change the firm's organization if they are to become multidisciplinary firms. They close by outlining eight tactics that industrial design firms have used to assimilate nondesigners.

Wasson follows with a detailed case study of E-Lab (now Sapient's User Experience Modeling Group). She explains how social researchers and designers together organize and create successful working processes.

Applin follows with a chapter that forcefully reminds us to avoid utopian hopes. Collaboration and interorganizational project management are very difficult and often inhibited by conflicting agendas, incompatible organizations, professional misconceptions, and the failure to communicate.

3

Designing Collaborative Corporate Cultures

Bryan Byrne and Ed Sands

Design managers must expend just as much effort in creating collaborative, multidisciplinary organizations as designers expend in creating breakthrough products (see Kelley, 2001). Indeed, managers can apply many of the ethnographic principles and methods described in this book to guide their own projects.

In this chapter, we will explain some of the cultural challenges and responsive strategies that are involved in transforming industrial design studios into full-service multidisciplinary innovation firms. We begin by examining how the apprenticeship system that guides professional development among designers also organizes design studios. Afterward, we discuss how the computer revolution and consequent call for multidisciplinary strategic design affect both the apprenticeship system and the studios. In particular, we outline some of the more difficult challenges managers face as they try to assimilate nondesigners into their firms. We have identified eight alternative strategies that design managers use to foster multidisciplinary collaboration with researchers and business strategists. Each strategy imposes significant consequences for corporate organization, project management, communication styles, human resource management, and professional development.

IMPETUS

Our work began in late 1997. GVO, a product design company in Palo Alto, California, was in the midst of making the transition from a design firm to a strategic innovation consultancy. By that time, GVO's research and innovation department was generating about as much business as its established industrial design and engineering departments. Surprised by the quick shift in its business, GVO's principals wanted to understand just how ethnographic research led to product innovation. Meanwhile, department directors wanted to document their generative working processes so they could codify their best practices. Everybody wanted a clearer, rational, and visual description of the processes to facilitate sales and training.

GVO assigned the project to Bryan as part of his internship. Previously, Bryan had conducted cross-cultural research about crafts professions (see Byrne 1994, 1999). Meanwhile Ed was consulting with GVO on a separate project. An entrepreneur with an MBA, Ed had seen many design firms risk the course that GVO had embarked upon. Throughout the project, we discussed the organization, operation, and developmental tendencies that design firms exhibit before, during, and after attempts to broaden their services and to assimilate nondesigners.

The research project revealed three small employee cliques and at least nine working processes within GVO's research department; each clique used its own theoretical and methodological approach to discovery, design, and evaluative analyses. Like most design firms that began the transformation process, GVO's directors and principals spent a great deal of effort negotiating the corporate mission, personal responsibilities, corporate and project processes, and sales messages. In a sense, clique leaders were searching for common ground; they were trying to create and present a unified, coherent company that provided a variety of related services. In light of the conversations we were having about design firms in general, the internal findings just raised even more salient questions about the nature of design firms and the options open to those that dare navigate the rocky shoals of strategic design.

APPRENTICESHIP

Designers are members of a profession that configures esthetically pleasing, meaningful, and functional artifacts. Good designers are—by their own definition—creative, insightful, and prolific artisans. Historians explain that people become designers by passing through an apprenticeship system that evolved from European medieval guilds (Lucie-Smith 1983; Sparke 1987; Epstein 1991).

Broadly speaking, apprenticeship is an institutionalized, hands-on educational process (Coy 1989; Goody 1989). Apprenticeship systems have been found in nearly every society. They are particularly common among groups who must become proficient in standardized techniques that involve motor-physical coordination. Potters, smiths, textile makers, clergy, physicians, and even some scientific research specialists (e.g., forensic anthropologists and, occasionally, archaeologists) rely on apprenticeship systems. In contrast, business professionals and most social scientists (e.g., psychologists, sociocultural anthropologists, sociologists, literary critics, market analysts, business strategists, etc.) tend to rely on formal or informal mentoring programs in which seniors may advise but seldom take responsibility for their junior colleagues' employment and performance.

All apprenticeship systems have three important socioeconomic consequences (Goody 1989). First, they regulate the labor supply. Second, they create predictable professional relationships. And third, they set performance standards. Apprenticeship systems regulate the labor supply by limiting the number of recruits to roughly approximate the demand for them in the regional markets; senior practitioners instruct as many apprentices and journeymen as they can financially support and train. Although apprenticeship systems create competitors, senior artisans are protected by law and benefit from the relatively cheaper labor of younger artisans.

Apprenticeship systems are inevitably shaped within and adapted to the dominant infrastructural conditions and the prevailing political and economic institutions of their day. The contemporary apprenticeship system familiar to designers barely resembles the apprenticeship system of the European medieval guilds. Even so, there are cases that demonstrate their direct evolutionary connection. For example, twentieth-century schools such as the Bauhaus tried to synthesize the apprenticeship tradition with the practices of modern industry. The Bauhaus distinguished among apprentices (students), journeymen (tested students and staff), and the masters (teachers). Guild masters from nearby towns gave students and staff annual tests to determine their status.

Masters were experienced practitioners. They had demonstrated to other masters a thorough knowledge of the guild arts, techniques, rules and regulations, and mysteries. The master was permitted to open and manage his own business, to hire journeymen, and to teach apprentices. Furthermore, they were expected to be active in their local guild and to represent it in local commercial and political affairs.

Masters taught apprentices and journeymen physical skills, conceptual distinctions, and organizational principles. Their instructive styles varied—and vary—among masters. Some took an active part in guiding and instructing subordinates. They showed subordinates how to execute specific tasks and how to plan the creative process. Others took more passive approaches, encouraging apprentices to understand and adapt trade secrets through observation and practice. Whatever the style, masters did not expect to learn much from their apprentices.

Apprentices during the medieval era were novices (Renard 1918). Relatives of the apprentice frequently paid the master a fee as a token of the fact that they were buying instruction—and knowledge—from the master for the apprentice. In one sense, the fee was a form of tuition. In turn, the master paid for the room, board, and materials, sometimes even providing a small stipend. Since apprentices had no right to the fruits of their own labor, a skilled master could gain more from the labor of his apprentices than he spent—even though the apprentice system itself presumed that the master was giving more than he got. As the landless European populations grew, the value of crafts professions grew, and masters frequently turned to sons and nephews as successors of the workshop.

Journeymen were competent professionals who had passed tests of workmanship and proved they could work independently. They could instruct novices under the supervision of the master but were not permitted to open their own businesses or take on their own apprentices. Instead, the journeymen were legally free to travel and find work—thus, their name. The laws of supply and demand combined with strict guild regulations forced many journeymen to travel for years or until they attained the status of master.

CONTEMPORARY APPRENTICESHIP

The contemporary apprenticeship system among designers barely resembles its historical antecedents. Contemporary academic institutions, design firms, and industry associations all share the responsibility for cultivating young designers. There are now several thousand design schools around the world. Some offer bachelor's and master's degrees in design. Fine arts programs offer degrees in design studies. A few now offer doctoral degrees for basic and applied research.

The degrees and curriculum required to receive them are closely linked to the needs and abilities of trade associations and the companies that employ designers. During the twentieth century, trade associations made concerted efforts to unite art schools and technical schools. The British Design and Industries Association and the British Council of Industrial Design made recommendations about training, certification, and business practices requirements for British designers and firms. Contemporary associations and schools continue to set explicit goals. For example, the Industrial Designers Society of America (IDSA) is a national nonprofit association that publishes guidelines, provides grant monies, establishes competitions, publishes journals, newsletters, and industry reports, and creates a natural communication forum. It is itself a member of the International Congress of Societies of Industrial Design (ICSID) and the American Design Council. The councils are coalitions of organizations that represent graphics arts, fine arts, architecture, fashion, packaging, interiors, and newspapers. IDSA is also associated with a strong network of museums and major universities that house information on arts, crafts, and manufacturing processes.

Although it does not advocate certification tests or enforce standards, IDSA has published guidelines for entry-level professionals (IDSA 1996a: 19). Ideally, graduating students should be familiar with human and social factors, esthetics, technology, business practices, design history, and contemporary design issues. They should demonstrate problem-solving skills to meet the needs of marketing, sales, engineering, manufacturing, servicing, and consumer/user needs and expectations. That means they should define problems, relate variables, conduct secondary and primary research, manage and analyze data, and conceptualize and evaluate alternative theories. They should be able to act on the implications of the research to perform their own tasks in industrial or graphic design, user-interaction architecture, or engineering. Whatever their specialty, they should be able to work in teams that transform the research findings into viable two- and three-dimensional renderings, engineering plans, and scale models. Finally, they should be able to make oral and written presentations.

Since it is impossible to master all of these skills and bodies of knowledge without prolonged multidisciplinary experience, IDSA encourages students to focus on a fairly narrow range of technical skills in school and to master other skills after graduation. Design education is therefore becoming more specialized.

The general and specialized knowledge bases are developing so quickly that formal classroom education must be supplemented with practice as interns and entry-level employees. IDSA supports short-term engagements at this level, explaining that "Through mentoring and internships, students can learn more about the profession while still in school. This knowledge of professional practice will complement their education and help students prepare for an entry-level position in the field" (IDSA 1996a: 19). Although the experience of "mentoring" is more akin to apprenticeships as we defined them earlier, the IDSA recommendation is not completely off base. As we will discuss later, computerization and the emergence of global labor systems are challenging the apprenticeship system and compelling designers to adopt multidisciplinary mentoring relationships.

Major manufacturers and design consultancies help novices make the transition from academic study to professional practice by providing teachers, financial resources, and job opportunities. For example, General

Motors helped to establish the Art Center College of Design. This school has been supplying the auto manufacturer with highly skilled designers since the 1950s. In Chicago, the late Jay Doblin left Loewy Associates to establish his own firm. He helped to establish the School of Design at the Illinois Institute of Technology (IIT) in the 1980s. Today, The Doblin Group's (formerly Jay Doblin and Associates) employees teach IIT students. The firm draws on the school for interns and entry-level designers. Similarly, the founders of IDEO and other well-established firms in the Silicon Valley teach and recruit from "The Loft," Stanford University's graduate program in design and engineering.

Young designers prefer to work at consultancies even though they earn lower wages and work longer hours, because consultancies are tremendous training grounds. They provide young designers opportunities to learn many skills and rapid working processes, and to learn about business and many industries.

Consultancies choose recruits carefully because the apprenticeship system demands that employees be talented, well trained, and personally compatible with their colleagues. Interpersonal compatibility among designers is critical, because the firm relies on nonadversarial and competitive forms of teamwork. Designers rely on internships, subcontracts, and probationary employment to test the suitability of candidates because these methods do not require a long-term commitment or benefits and compensation packages.

DESIGN STUDIOS

The contemporary apprenticeship system facilitates the transition from apprentice-student to master designer and businessperson. The principles that organize design firms stem both from the prevailing economic conditions and business practices, and the apprenticeship system.

According to a recent survey by the Industrial Design Society of America (1996b), more than 70 percent of the two thousand U.S. industrial design firms are proprietorships that employ fewer than ten people and earn less than a million dollars a year. They are normally owned by the founders and, to a lesser extent, their families and friends. Most are composed of a small group of designers and engineers. The majority of the revenues in consultancies come from project contracts based on time and material costs or fixed-fees terms. As many as 25 percent of design firms employ up to fifteen people and earn $1–2 million a year. Larger design consultancies are almost always privately held corporations that enjoy revenues of more than $5 million. A few firms are either wholly or partly owned by manufacturing firms or holding companies that seek to guarantee consistent design while reducing the cost of business. Major manufacturing and service companies such as Qwest, Intel, AT&T,

Whirlpool, Samsung, Hitachi, and Laerdal Medical Corp. often create internal semiautonomous design consultancies.

Design firms are organized and operated as studios. The very name of the studio attests to designers' primary allegiance to art and craftsmanship rather than to business. One creates in studios and conducts business in offices. Therefore, designers tend to divide their studios according to function. The largest firms normally have several conference rooms, testing labs, modeling shops, video and photography rooms, cubicles, offices, reception areas, libraries, and kitchens. Company principals tend to have offices set apart from cubicles where the designers can work individually and common project areas where everybody works together.

The architecture and interior decor of the studio reflects the design proclivities of the senior designers. Since esthetic styles pass in and out of vogue, contemporary industrial designers tend to work in postmodernist buildings and interiors that leave piping and ventilation systems exposed. The entire studio setting is an exercise in versatility and a constant reminder that designers must create interior and functional components, not just beautiful and meaningful surfaces.

The pace of work is fast and chaotic when times are good. You can hear a muffled cough from the other side of a large studio when times are bad. Secretaries and bookkeepers occasionally arrive at 7 A.M. to work undisturbed for an hour or two before the principals and directors arrive. Everybody checks their e-mail, gets coffee, and talks with colleagues about personal activities and business before they concentrate on projects. By 9:30 A.M., the studio is filled. Everybody spends the rest of the day shifting between work at their own desks, workshops, project areas, and meetings. Designers leave the studios to conduct research, work with vendors and clients, have lunch, or do personal errands. Normally, the studios begin emptying out between 5:30 and 6:30 P.M. Employees habitually meet after work to go cycling, climbing, or hit the clubs at night. Meanwhile, employees facing tight deadlines work late into the night, if not the entire night. Many return to the studio during the weekends.

The long hours and stressful deadlines tend to be offset by the sheer playful thrill of discovery and creation. Designers recognize that creativity is a process that involves both conscious and subconscious thought. They are willing to work the long hours because, apart from the purely financial and professional reasons, they are driven by all the questions and possibilities that each project raises. Designers are really never off the clock; they think about their challenges whether or not they are in the studio. For many, the studio is not an onerous workplace. It is a playground for artists, engineers, and scientists who dare to challenge the status quo of industry, consumer culture, their professions, and ultimately, themselves.

STATUS

Design studios are hierarchical institutions. They are not egalitarian cooperatives—no matter what designers might claim. One's position within the hierarchy is explicitly marked by a job title. Every job has an attendant set of responsibilities, limits of authority, accountability measures, and access to resources. That means every individual has specific roles within the organization. The managerial design of the firm itself seeks to optimize the interlocking roles. In the process, it recognizes status and creates incentives and disincentives.

Principals are executive officers who usually hold property interests in the company. They are typically designers who have had more than ten years' experience. Occupying prominent offices or centrally located areas, they are responsible for sales, negotiating contracts, administration, business strategy, human resources and facilities management, financing, legal issues, and public relations. They provide internal direction, make policies, and referee disputes. Although they may occasionally work with junior designers on projects, they are not extensively involved in any single project. Instead, they usually attend key meetings or provide occasional artistic direction and business advice.

Department directors and project managers occupy the second tier in the hierarchy. Differences in their status are more pronounced in larger studios. Directors are more likely than project managers to have ownership interests in the company. They usually occupy cubicles or offices near their junior colleagues. They are responsible for some elements of business development, sales, project design, team organization, scheduling, work performance, and billing. Principals and directors may double as project managers in small studios.

Project managers are usually treated like journeymen since they engage in business-related tasks but are not primarily responsible for the business itself. Project managers are responsible for the execution of multiple projects (occasionally up to twenty at a time). They write proposals, assemble teams, calculate budgets, set schedules, handle expenses, manage clients, and advise team members.

The next tier in the corporate hierarchy is composed of apprentice and journeymen designers, engineers, modelers, and researchers. They tend to be between twenty and thirty-five years old with less than seven years of experience. They spend most of their time working on one to five projects. Although they are assigned cubicles and computers as a base of operations, they spend a great deal of time working in common project areas. Most are full-time employees, but design studios are shifting to part-time employees and consultants to trim fixed overhead costs.

The bottom rung consists of interns. Students attending B.A. and M.A. design programs are given three-month internships. They are given in-house tasks and roles in projects as additional designers; their presence is usually not needed. Their entire reason for being there is to learn, not to contribute or to assume business responsibilities.

A parallel hierarchy composed of salespeople, administrative staff, and facilities-support workers operates in larger firms. These are essentially the people who make the company function as a legal and solvent entity. The marketing staff is responsible for acquiring projects. Typically working on a combination of sales commissions (2–5 percent) and a flat rate salary, the salespeople search for and contact potential clients, explain the working processes of the company, and work with the project managers to write proposals. The administrative staff handles the bookkeeping, facilities, travel, human resources, publicity, and anything else that comes their way during their hectic days. From the perspective of the apprenticeship system, they are all nondesigners who make it possible to work but who cannot do the work itself.

FOSTERING CREATIVITY

The entire purpose of strategic design is to break through current circumstances and to create elements of tomorrow's experience. The mission has tremendous implications for corporate organization and operations (Kelley, 2001). Design firms thrive on projects that set seemingly impossible objectives. The rapid, dynamic, and varied working conditions actually help them propose and then—just as quickly—abandon their own ideas. The apprenticeship system facilitates design by training designers in technical and conceptual and social skills that are consistent with incessant ideation and experimentation.

The world's most successful design firm, IDEO, presents us with an excellent example of a negative case in which the apprenticeship system is challenged. When David Kelley founded his first studio, he envisioned an egalitarian artistic cooperative where peers could create without suffering heavy-handed managers. Although he did avoid instituting an oppressive corporate bureaucracy like those among large manufacturers, he was unable to create an egalitarian cooperative. Senior employees enjoyed the relative creative freedom of Kelley's system, but junior employees complained that they were not being trained adequately. By seeking formal guidance, the junior colleagues compelled Kelley to re-institutionalize the apprenticeship system although he may never have thought of it that way. They made more formal distinctions among titles and encouraged greater, more formal lines of authority and oversight (Detwiler 1999).

STATUS AUCTIONING

The fact that designers have expectations for their own professional growth suggests that there must also be some mechanism to change status. Taking their cue from anthropological research on initiations to closed societies, Andrew Hargadon and Robert Sutton found it in the status auctioning that they observed at work in IDEO's Palo Alto studios (Sutton and Hargadon 1996; Hargadon and Sutton 1997). Although Hargadon and Sutton focused on the individual consequences of status auctioning, we would like to suggest that it also has implications for groups and studio dynamics.

Status auctioning is simultaneously a way to validate and change an individual's position, and a way to establish, reinforce, and challenge internal competitive groups. The most pronounced instances of status auctioning occur during weekly meetings and brainstorming events. Typically, designers gather on Monday mornings to review previous events, communicate ongoing projects, and discuss upcoming issues or projects. The meetings are led by principals. Directors and project managers make announcements and give kudos to individuals who have performed well.

Status auctioning is also evident in brainstorming sessions. These create-athons are usually fun efforts to clarify and propose viable alternatives for design and engineering challenges (see Kelley 2001). Brainstorming participants draw on their diverse experiences, skills, and interests as they banter and build a tremendous variety of ways to get the job done. The sessions also function as status auctioning events because the entire process forces designers to provoke and receive the valuation of their peers. Their status rises and falls as their colleagues agree, disagree, defer to, or dismiss them. They are typically evaluated according to their technical and creative abilities as well as their interpersonal skills. Those who don't contribute are dismissed. Those who dominate and alienate their colleagues are also dismissed. Those who are prolific, entertaining, and helpful see their reputations improve, their networks deepen, and their professional status rise.

The auctioning process is part of a more general process of validating and modifying everybody's responsibilities and financial rewards (Sutton and Hargadon 1996). Firms tend to evaluate the value of an employee by a simple, informal process. Executives assume that employees who consistently report a high percentage of billable hours are in high demand. Thus, the reasoning goes, they are creative, effective, and well respected. Conversely, those who report few billable hours are inactive because nobody wants to work with them; they lack technical, business, or personal skills.

Status auctioning among individuals often translates into status auctioning among cliques. Aspiring designers augment their value by bringing in and satisfying clients. Both increase company revenues. Since designers tend to work in small cliques of senior and junior colleagues, the billable hours can also be seen as an indirect measure of the success of the entire clique. The relative power of the clique grows from its ability to bring in a higher portion of total revenue than competitive cliques. A relatively small percentage of clique leaders eventually acquire property interests in the firms themselves.

STUDIO DYNAMICS

Studios grow and contract in relatively predictable ways. The apprenticeship system is one factor in the creation of a developmental cycle for the entire firm. As we will explain later, the developmental dynamics must be considered when making attempts to change the corporate culture to assimilate nondesigners.

Design managers often say that the optimal size of any studio is twenty to twenty-five people. This includes one or two directors, two or three project managers, up to twelve junior staff, two secretaries, a business manager, and an assistant. Each director can typically support a maximum of ten people without drastically reducing the effectiveness of the teams. By limiting the size of the studio, senior designers retain control over the studio's creative and business activities.

Studios dynamics change when they support more than twenty-five employees. To be effective, they must change their managerial structure from one based on the cooperation among small cliques to more formal corporate organizations with internal departments that distinguish among professions and functions. The organizational change creates more opportunities for maturing designers to assume greater responsibilities. It also means that competition increases. Either way, the transition period requires that the designers and administrators learn new skills and adapt to new working relationships.

Design firms try to reduce the fiscal and internal political volatility by planning ahead. They try to predict workloads and finances six months to a year in advance. Executives rely on a wide variety of normal accounting indicators to assess corporate health. Design directors and managers often focus on two ratios to get quick insights into the productivity of cliques and individuals. The first is the ratio between projected revenue from *committed* projects to income from *potential* projects. That measure tells directors and clique leaders what their sales success has been and what it must be to maintain the budget. It also helps determine how many designers the firm might have to hire or fire. The second measure is the ratio of billable to unbillable hours. To be profitable, design firms have to make sure their designers are billing approximately 80 percent of their hours. The ratio helps directors get a fix on which employees are making or losing money for the company.

These measures can be particularly useful to make decisions about employment. When the ratio of employees who bill clients and those who do not falls to 2:1, the principals frequently cut support staff (such as secretaries), eliminate the weakest cliques, and occasionally change business strategies. In good times, when employees bill 90 to 110 percent of their time, managers are in a better position to expand the firm. They typically either purchase struggling firms or help their senior designers open new studios. Growing firms have commonly established branch studios in booming metropolitan areas. These include Austin, New York, Boston, Detroit, Chicago, San Francisco, Los Angeles, London, Milan, Barcelona, Tokyo, Buenos Aires, Mexico City, Tel Aviv, Singapore, and Shanghai. The studios quickly take on the personal characteristics and design orientation of the senior designers. Once a parent company starts opening satellite studios, it must maintain its growth rate until all satellites stabilize at an optimum configuration.

One might argue that the rapid growth of design firms such as IDEO suggests that all design firms should retain the apprenticeship system and make no effort to modernize it. But that is not an option, even for IDEO (see Kelley 2001). Two forces compel design managers to tinker with their corporate cultures. The first is the rapid rise of a young, technologically sophisticated, internationally mobile cohort of designers. The second is the rise of multidisciplinary work teams that include professionals who know little if anything about design.

A GENERATION GAP

The generation gap has been growing for more than twenty years (Essex and Gluskin 1999; Neumier 1999; Gold and Bernard, 1999). As Rob Curedale, a seasoned industrial designer (personal communication, 2001), explains, "The tools of the trade are constantly changing. In the last 20 years designers have evolved from using ink to polymer pencils on a drawing board to a variety of computer programs. This has tended to dilute the value of the apprenticeship system." Senior designers lost a great deal of control over maturing designers when they installed computers. Senior designers may control their studios, but they rely more than ever on junior designers to stay competitive. Not only are junior designers more familiar with state-of-the-art technologies, they often match the cultural profiles of young consumers, are more receptive to strategic design work, and are in higher demand in the marketplace.

When combined, the young designers have gained a relatively great degree of influence over corporate working processes and artistic direction. In addition, young designers often complain that senior colleagues cannot teach them about either the craft of design or how to conduct business in today's global multicultural economy.

Because younger designers are questioning the authority and direction of their senior practitioners, it follows that the iconic image of the design master is also under assault. Corporate dynamics are becoming much more fluid. Young designers are freer to express themselves. Brainstorming sessions are far more playful and experimental than ever. On the other hand, there is less artistic direction and a greater emphasis on technical skills. As Curedale (personal communication 2000) explains,

There are two types of design studios. The first is led by the design hero. Examples would be Philip Starck, Marc Newson, Ron Arad, and Ettore Sottsass. In these studios, the novices feel that they are learning to become more creative. Traditionally novices from these types of studio do not do well when they try to set up their own studio because they have learnt to work only under the direction of the strong master. Ziba Design may be an example of this type of studio in the U.S. context.

American clients prefer a design solution adapted in style and detail to their needs. They prefer not to go to a design hero type of studio that has only one style because it dilutes their own brand identity. Most U.K. and U.S. studios are of the second type. The novices at places like Fitch and Hauser learn technical skills rather than raw creativity. There is not one creative director influencing all designs. In fact their creativity would possibly be reduced working in these environments but their ability to actualize the ideas would increase. They also learn to work in a real life actualization group that is a necessary part of complex design solution such as a vehicle.

The demand for designs that reflect corporate needs rather than designer inspirations forces more designers to more carefully consider criteria and perceptions of their clients and the ultimate consumers.

Meanwhile, the digitization of design technologies and designers' heightened mobility are reducing the chances that designers will learn at the feet of any master. These days journeymen and apprentice designers are constantly on the hunt for jobs where they can learn marketable skills. Design masters lose apprentices if they cannot teach them how to apply design concepts to new technologies. Many young designers consider the first few firms they work for as little more than personal training grounds. And the burgeoning transoceanic demand for experienced designers is so intense that skilled designers spend at least a few years abroad. On the other hand, corporate managers who neither offer star-quality creative supervision nor control the latest tools of the trade are more likely to treat junior designers like interchangeable parts of a greater machine. The result of these conflicting sets of interests is that design studios, even the best of them, can hold on to junior staff only for an average of five to eight months. If and when conditions permit, senior designers entice junior designers to remain by granting them more autonomy and authority. In a few cases, principals help maturing designers open new studios. Otherwise, they might help promising designers enroll in graduate school or find employment with clients.

The Internet is part of the digital equipment that challenges the apprenticeship system. Designers from around the world use Internet discussion lists such as IDFORUM and the DRS list of the Design Research Society to examine and lend support on a variety of issues. The discussions seem equally peppered with requests for information about specific techniques, tools, contacts, jobs, and ethics as with more philosophical discussions about those qualities and activities that mark design as a profession, art form, business, and approach to life. By participating in these discussion lists, designers not only declare their status internationally, but also help guide the professional development of other participants and influence the profession itself.

The effect of the Internet on internal corporate dynamics is ultimately subversive, because junior designers can readily receive advice from senior designers other than their direct supervisors. Furthermore, they can and do provide and receive job tips. Thus, although the Internet may help designers solve immediate problems, it also constitutes a tool to change the relationships among designers and to modify the nature of apprenticeship and design itself.

ASSIMILATION IS DIFFICULT

The technological pressures compelling designers to modify their apprenticeship system are aggravated by calls for strategic design or one-stop service packages. The apprenticeship system facilitates professional growth and innovative work among designers. However, since apprenticeships are ultimately skill based, design firms encounter tough, frustrating problems whenever they try to assimilate marketers, administrators, salespeople, or researchers. Thus, the challenge facing design managers is to figure out how to modify the corporate culture enough to assimilate nondesigners without destroying the apprenticeship system.

The difference between design and strategic design is a matter of perspectives and starting points. Industrial design typically starts with a description of the product or system, including its functions, features, and forms. Managers or clients often tell the designers what they want configured. The designers lend their artistic and engineering skills to make it. Strategic design does not confine designers to any detailed brief.

The design team members must first figure out what consumers need and offer managers alternative ways to achieve those ends. Strategic design projects may compel managers and project members to assess corporate objectives, review product portfolios, and consider external trends in law and society to lay the conceptual foundation for design ideation.

The move toward strategic design has even more profound and troubling implications for design studios than digital technologies. They are being *compelled* to work with nondesigners. Collaborative modes of interdisciplinary work represent another threat to the apprenticeship system and the image of the "design hero" (Ellis 1984; Detwiler 1999; Morris et al. 1998).

However heartfelt their mutual respect and admiration might be in the best of circumstances, designers and nondesigners have a long way to go before they can work collaboratively with any ease. It is clear that designers and nondesigners cannot rely on their traditional modes of training, interaction, and evaluation. Designers cannot assess nondesign colleagues the way they might each other. Nor can nondesigners be appointed and evaluated according to the criteria with which they are familiar.

Designers, social scientists, and managers don't have to master each other's professions, but they must know them well enough to form reasonable expectations about what they must provide in the entire creative process. For example, designers are making efforts to become more familiar with the sociocultural concepts, research designs, and methods for data collection and analysis presented elsewhere in this volume. They are also developing stronger design management programs to teach the financial, organizational, and market concepts that drive their executive clients. Similarly, social scientists must do more to train students to prepare for product development.

Strategic design work puts designers in a terribly uncomfortable position, one to which nondesigners are not necessarily sensitive. Social scientists and business managers often unknowingly create conflicts by doing exactly what they were trained to do; their perspectives, preferred roles, and methods violate the tenets of the apprenticeship system. Researchers challenge design masters by attempting to define project goals, by designing research, and by setting schedules. They presume the primary responsibilities of the project managers and senior designers by setting creative directions. Throughout the project process they question the cultural and business assumptions of all of their coworkers and too frequently impose their own impressionistic explanations of abstract sociocultural and financial processes. The coup de grace comes when they evaluate concepts that designers develop according to the criteria they establish through their own research.

From the point of view of many designers, researchers and business strategists habitually overstep their bounds. Rather than collaborating with designers, they seem to try to dominate them—even though they lack any basic training in design. Thus, researchers and business strategists can seem arrogant, uncooperative, disrespectful, and incompetent.

The basis of the interactions among designers, businesspersons, and researchers are seldom explicitly understood or resolved. Managers tend to handle conflicts as exercises in crisis management among strong personalities. Designers tend to view the conflicts as interpersonal clashes among people who are more creative (designers) and less creative invaders (nondesigners). Researchers tend to view the conflicts as irritating cultural phenomena that beg for explanation from the safe distance of academic institutions. Business analysts tend to view the conflicts in terms of organizational culture and personality types—shortly before sending their resumes to more traditional and stable companies.

Managerial efforts to assimilate consumer researchers and to transform studio cultures might be easier if the designers could treat nondesigners as a homogeneous group, but they cannot. Researchers, for example, are a terribly fragmented and contentious lot. They tend to have in-depth training in one or more of the following disciplines: anthropology, sociology, psychology, economics, business, history, literature, religious studies, arts, and drama. There are few consistent conceptual or methodological trends among these fields.

As one might expect, a professional's intellectual background does influence the likelihood that he or she can be assimilated. Judging from Reese's history (see chapter 2, this volume), cognitive psychologists with backgrounds in human factors or human-computer interface have had the easiest time assimilating into the design industry. The reason, we suspect, is that cognitive psychologists are brought into projects after the consumer needs and project briefs have been established. They are free to concentrate on the interaction of individuals and external artifacts within a given environmental context.

Conversely, the cognitive psychologists miss many of the more abstract sociocultural processes that catch the eye of sociologists and anthropologists. By focusing on interaction, human factors analysts trained in cognitive psychology reduce the temptation of examining how gender, race, class, age, nationality, religion, family membership, and so forth affect the human-artifact interaction. They are less likely to examine the changing nature of the American household on nutrition or communications equipment (e.g., computer, phones, refrigerator notes, walkietalkies, Post-it notes, calendars, and so on). They are also less likely to figure out why educational programs and educational products fail in schools or what can be done to improve their utility. Of course, as any designer and human factors analyst will tell you, social scientists must guard against the temptation of focusing almost exclusively on these more abstract issues while ignoring more concrete interactive processes. But the trick is incorporating those critical cultural and business factors, too.

In addition to variations among disciplines, there are profound intellectual and technical disputes within each of the disciplines. Anthropologists and business administrators are also divided by intellectual backgrounds that affect how they approach design—if at all. Anthropologists, for example, are in the midst of a protracted decade-long dispute between postmodernists, poststructuralists, structuralists, cultural materialists, historical determinists, neo-institutionalists, symbolists, and sociobiologists (see Borofsky 1994; Harris 1999). The principal theoretical conflicts include topics that define anthropology as a discipline. These include the definition of culture; the interaction between biophysical, psychological, institutional, and ideational aspects of human life; appropriate time and geographic frames of reference; one's point of view; modes of explanation (theory versus interpretation); research design; quantitative versus qualitative methods; communication processes; and ethics.

Fortunately, change is on the horizon, at least among anthropologists interested in innovation and change management. Design provides anthropologists with more concrete opportunities to address and, perhaps, resolve some of the disciplines' most intractable puzzles. By addressing design in terms of science, art, politics, and commerce, every anthropologist is forced to address disciplinary conflicts about epistemology and subdisciplinary interaction. For example, sociocultural anthropologists, archaeologists, and ethnoarchaeologists are just beginning to dovetail scientific concepts and techniques that could be very useful in creating operation data languages and theories about human-artifact-environment interactions (see Schiffer 1999).

OPTIONS

There are strong financial and intellectual advantages to multidisciplinary collaboration. It is not going away. Design managers have to create ways to offer multidisciplinary services without destroying the benefits of the designer's evolving apprenticeship system. The managerial effort takes creativity, persistence, and, as we have argued here, a knowledge of the sociocultural and business principles shaping design.

Design firms have tried at least eight strategies to assimilate researchers as they move toward more multidisciplinary corporate cultures. Each carries a mixture of advantages and disadvantages.

Self-Sufficiency

We call the most common strategy *self-sufficiency*. This is a default strategy in which designers offer strategic services without working with nondesigners. In a sense, it's the natural inclination that designers might follow first—and often last. The apprenticeship system teaches maturing designers lessons about consumer culture, marketing, and finance. The advantage is that there is no challenge to the authority structure. The drawback is equally obvious. Designers risk alienating clients by providing substandard analysis.

Design Support

The second strategy is *design support*. Researchers are supposed to "feed" the designers' creativity by providing them with raw information. Researchers are likely to earn good marks by providing designers with ethnographic information and hip-shot interpretations; one of the constant challenges is to do enough structured work to use theory and evidence to arrive at those interpretations and recommendations. To be effective, researchers must grasp the fundamental skills of their own discipline and operate in accordance with the manager's assimilation strategy. In this case, they have to ally with senior designers and create working processes that the designers approve of. The senior designers must legitimize and support work done by nondesigners.

Of course, there are broader corporate advantages and disadvantages. The principal advantage is that designers can maintain control over creative and corporate apparatus, make relatively small capital commitments, and still benefit from interdisciplinary teams. The principal danger is that the senior designers and nondesigners will alienate each other by arguing over sales messages, client management, project definition, project design, and performance measures. Mounting conflicts create interpersonal rifts that make it difficult to collaborate. Given the feast or famine model of design consultancy funding, the nondesigners search for more favorable working environments.

Internal Unit Development

In the *internal unit* strategy, design firms create departments according to profession or project focus. If the departments are managed well, clients benefit from projects built on the interaction of professionals who can combine consumer insights, technical prowess, artistic sensibilities, and financial planning. Employees may benefit by forming enduring relationships based on mutual respect and experience. The challenge is to make each unit an integral part of the company.

Some companies form departments along disciplinary lines that roughly correspond to their roles as "analyzers" or "researchers" and "creators" or "designers." E-Lab took this approach. Its principal advantage is that researchers and designers can rely on each other to organize, solve problems, learn skills, and communicate. The chief disadvantage is that it tends to create insular disciplinary cliques if the firm's executives cling to the apprenticeship system and resist efforts to cross-train.

Other advantages and disadvantages arise if the design firm chooses to create units based on the projects they work on. The project types might include, for example, consumer research, corporate innovation management, interaction design, industrial design, or engineering and modeling. GVO, for example, formed multidisciplinary teams based on project types and the cliques created by the existing apprenticeship system. Each group operates in a semiautonomous fashion that still leads back to the firm's principals. This approach draws on the strengths of each clique but offers little opportunity for cross-training or individual professional growth.

Strategic Innovation

There are a few remarkable instances in which design firms have gone so far as to virtually abandon design. For example, The Doblin Group started as an industrial design firm, headed by a charismatic and talented designer, Jay Doblin. After Doblin's death, his successors moved with the times by shifting the firm's weight from designing things toward conceiving alternative products, services, and working processes based on their own extensive consumer and market research. Doblin Group is one of the few firms to build a dynamic multidisciplinary set of consumer researchers, business analysts, and designers that is *not* controlled by industrial designers or engineers.

Partnership

Partnership is common but rarely successful. Design firms may ally themselves with consultancies that specialize in consumer research, marketing, and business strategy. These partnerships are fragile and tend to be unprofitable. They demand extraordinary flexibility and a willingness to collaborate but offer limited financial gains because the firms cannot commit enough resources to generate sales that leverage their mutual interests. The fiscal ebb and flow within the partnering corporations make it even more difficult to coordinate sales and project schedules. Profit margins on the projects tend to be fairly low because each firm must cover unanticipated administrative and transaction costs. Any personal or professional conflicts that arise from the first few experimental engagements spell the end of the partnership.

Entrepreneurial Alliances

Entrepreneurial alliances occur when design firms make use of independent consultants. Corporate downsizing and the growth of the Internet in an expanding knowledge economy are creating more opportunities for entrepreneurial alliances. Unfortunately, they tend to fail for the same reasons that partnerships fail. It is difficult to identify mutually beneficial income streams or to create stable expectations regarding responsibilities, authority, accountability measures, and access to resources. Given these conditions, the chances that allies can sustain enough work to create those expectations is slim.

Mergers

Design firms may enlarge their offerings by merging with manufacturing companies or consortia. The acquiring company enjoys the resources, location, and contacts of the studio. The studio gains access to other professionals and larger clients, and enjoys larger economies of scale and, sometimes, more stable revenues.

The chief danger is that the parent and subsidiary companies may not balance the fundamental conflicts between stable operations, profits, and creative experimentation. Parent companies expect consistent and growing profits. Employees lose status (relative to the senior executives of the parent corporation). They may react to profit-oriented policies and any threats to their creative control by reducing expenditures on unpaid overtime work. In an industry founded on the principles of artistic and scientific experimentation, failure and overtime are essential to train maturing professionals. By trimming budgets to save pennies for investor dividends, managers destroy any chance for creativity or profits. Thus, it should be no surprise that large, profit-driven consultancies typically do not produce the most creative and innovative design work. That is why small, independent firms are still viable.

Conversely, parent companies are much more likely to create a viable internal design unit if they treat it as a semiautonomous cost rather than a profit center. The parent companies can profit by manufacturing or licensing commodities rather than by billing hours to clients. The success of the internal units can be measured by subtracting revenue their products generate from the cost of enabling the unit to work. Inasmuch as parent companies demand continually growing profit margins and minimize failure and experimentation, they are frequently forced to sell the unit or spin it off as an independent, privately held company.

Foundation

Some designers have gone as far as to establish their own multidisciplinary companies. The *foundation* strategy is by far the riskiest and probably the most rewarding. Rather than trying to assimilate nondesigners into a design firm, entrepreneurs implement new corporate models that promote collaboration among design and nondesign units. E-lab and SonicRim are wonderful examples of companies that used the foundation tactic successfully.

As Wasson will describe in the next chapter, *foundation* permits greater opportunities for experimentation because the founders start fresh. Although they bring their own professional biases, they avoid established institutional obstacles. They define corporate missions, make investments, find employees willing to experiment with the tentative rules they establish, and find companies willing to risk large sums of money on their services. However, even here, there is a temptation for designers and nondesigners to maintain distinct professional views of the working process and for the principals to maintain an apprenticeship system in which they claim authority over both design and nondesign.

In practice, design firms are far more likely to shift among the eight strategies in a frenzied effort to find an appropriate corporate structure and working process. For example, they may start with either the entrepreneurial alliance or partnerships before trying to create internal units only to be acquired by a consortium that stresses design and uses other internal professionals to provide consumer research and business planning. Occasionally, design firms may start by building an internal unit, shift back to a self-sufficiency tactic, and inspire several entrepreneurs to break free and found their own multidisciplinary firms. Whatever the approach, the firms must adapt to highly dynamic markets and lead slower academic institutions.

CONCLUSION

Organizations are cultural creations; they are designs that change with the external circumstances. In some respects the process of designing and changing corporate culture is similar to the process of creating breakthrough products. Teams must understand the culture of the groups involved, figure out their own objectives, generate alternative structures and processes, and then implement them. And, like product design, organizational innovation is best done in an environment that favors experimentation, dedication, and iterative modifications.

REFERENCES

Borofsky, R. 1994. *Assessing Cultural Anthropology*. New York: McGraw-Hill.

Byrne, B. 1994. Access to Subsistence Resources and the Sexual Division of Labor Among Potters. *Journal of Cross-Cultural Research* 28 (3): 225–250.

———. 1999. Subsistence Strategies and the Division of Labor by Gender among Clothes Makers in Non-Industrial Societies. *Journal of Cross-Cultural Research* 30 (3): 307–317.

Coy, M. 1989. Introduction to *Apprenticeship: From Theory to Method and Back Again*, edited by Michael W. Coy. Albany: State University of New York Press.

Detwiler, M. 1999. Management by Design: IDEO Thwarts Traditional Models to Increase Creativity among Product Designers. *The Edge*. http://www.edgeonline.com/archives.

Ellis, S. 1994. Toward the Design Era: The Evolution of the Designer as Functional Interface with Marketing and Engineering. *Design Management Journal* (Summer) 31–34.

Epstein, S. 1991. *Wage Labor and Guilds in Medieval Europe*. Chapel Hill: University of North Carolina.

Essex, J.M., and L. Gluskin. 1999. Certification Is Here. *Critique* 10 (Winter): 10–17.

Gold, E., and N.E. Bernard. 1999. Educating Design. *Critique* 10 (Winter): 18–25.

Goody, E. 1989. Learning, Apprenticeship, and the Division of Labor. In *Apprenticeship: From Theory to Method and Back Again*, edited by Michael W. Coy. Albany: State University of New York Press.

Hargadon, A., and R. Sutton. 1997. Technology Brokering and Innovation in a Product Development Firm. *Administrative Science Quarterly* 42 (1997): 716–749.

Harris, M. 1999. *Theories of Culture in Postmodern Times*. Walnut Creek, CA: Altamira Press.

IDSA. 1996a. *Directory of Industrial Designers*. Great Falls, VA: IDSA.

———. 1996b. *Consultant Office Operating Study*. Great Falls, VA: IDSA.

Kelley, T. 2001. *The Art of Innovation*. New York: Random Books.

Lucie-Smith, E. 1983. *A History of Industrial Design*. New York: Van Norstrand Reinhold.

Morris, L., J. Rabinowitz, and J. Myerson. 1998. No More Heroes: From Controllers to Collaborators. *Design Management Journal* (Spring): 22–25.

Neumeir, M. 1999. Secrets of Design: Mentoring. *Critique* 10 (Winter): 26–37.

Renard, G. 1918. *Guilds in the Middle Ages*. London: G. Bell and Sons.

Rothstein, P. 2000. "Re-emergence" of Ethnography in Industrial Design Today. Paper given at the Chicago IDSA Design Education Conference. http://www.idsa.org.

Schiffer, M. 1999. *The Material Life of Human Beings*. London: Routledge Press.

Sparke, P. 1987. *Design in Context*. New York: Chartwell.

Sutton, R., and A. Hargadon. 1996. Brainstorming Groups in Context: Effectiveness in a Product Design Firm. *Administrative Science Quarterly* 41 (1996): 685–718.

4

Collaborative Work: Integrating the Roles of Ethnographers and Designers

Christina Wasson

In this chapter, I describe some of the issues that arise when designers and ethnographers work on projects together. Who takes on which tasks? How do they communicate their insights to each other? How do they build on each other's contributions? How do they have to modify their work process to collaborate effectively?[1]

In the world of design, innate creativity and intuition tend to be glorified. Although becoming a designer involves the acquisition of certain technical skills, true excellence in this field tends to be measured more by the creative brilliance of the objects or services a designer has developed, the way these items blend esthetic beauty with an elegant functionality and ease of use. Although designers recognize that their inspirations are shaped by their engagement with various external sources, ranging from market surveys to observations of consumers, they nonetheless highlight their internal processes as being the essential locus of new ideas. This emphasis has a long history. Practitioners have traditionally represented design "as an autonomous, inward-looking relationship between designer and product . . . One of the most outstanding post-war British designers, Misha Black, affirmed the designers' own view of their role: 'That creativity is the foundation of their work, is the faith that motivates all designers' " (Heskett 1980: 7–8). Such a bias also resonates with the American ideology of highlighting personal autonomy and control in most spheres of life (Bellah et al. 1985; Varenne 1987; Wasson 1999).

In the political landscape of design firms, research has traditionally played a secondary role. Researchers were primarily thought of as support personnel who produced fodder for the designers' internal creative processes. Their work process was seen as just the gathering of facts, not as a creative endeavor in its own right. They made up a small minority of a firm's members, and tended to have less of a voice in important areas than designers did. For instance, they might have little control over the content of proposals, and their contact with clients might be limited. This approach, or aspects of it, is still current in many design firms, and has resulted in frustrations for the ethnographers who have started to join these enterprises.

Good design can no doubt come from many sources of inspiration and many kinds of work processes, involving a wide range of specialists. I certainly would not want to claim that good design always requires ethnography. However, I do want to argue that for those occasions when ethnography can be useful, there are more and less effective ways for ethnographers and designers to collaborate with each other. The concerns of the former seem to revolve around a sense that their expertise is not fully appreciated and that they are underutilized. Designers, on the other hand, encounter frustration when they are given research results that do not point to practical applications in any obvious way. The key questions, therefore, are how to integrate the work processes of both groups, and how to establish a balance between them that enables each to contribute their full value.

Solutions to these questions are explored in this chapter by using the consulting firm E-Lab, LLC as a case study. E-Lab, located in Chicago, was founded on the principle of an equal partnership between research and design; all design recommendations are based on ethnographic research. I should note that because E-Lab is a novel kind of enterprise, the firm's structure and practices are continuously under development. It is intended as an example of creative innovation, to point out some of the organizational possibilities and inspire further ideas. It is not meant as a template for other firms to follow exactly. I also wish to note that E-Lab was acquired by Sapient Corporation in late 1999, and no longer uses its original name. Since I am describing the firm prior to this merger, however, I will refer to it as "E-Lab."

Three overall guidelines for effective collaboration between researchers and designers can be gleaned from E-Lab's experience. These themes suffuse the story I tell below; they can be summarized as follows:

• Ethnography needs to be recognized as a creative process. It is much more than a way of collecting data. More importantly, it is about discovering cultural patterns and developing models to explain those patterns. This is a high-level analytical process grounded in extensive training, prototypically a Ph.D. in anthropology. The creativity involved in doing this well is parallel to the effort of generating a good design. Adopting such an understanding of ethnographic research has implications for how design firms organize their research work processes. For instance, they might want to budget time for ethnographic analysis in between the data collection and design phases of a project.

- Ethnographers need to be given a voice in project development and execution. It is unlikely that a manager trained in design would, on her own, be able to develop a research plan that fully utilized the value of ethnography. To do their best work, researchers should be included in the process of developing new projects, including client meetings and proposal writing. In particular, they should have a strong voice in designing and carrying out research methodologies.

- The work activities of researchers and designers should be integrated. The results of an ethnographic study should not simply be handed off to designers. Members of both disciplines need be involved in a project from beginning to end. Although their involvement is naturally greater in some phases than in others, they should nonetheless invade each other's territory to a certain extent. Some individuals find that participating in the activities of the other discipline is uncomfortable at first, but they often end up enjoying the creative stretch. This kind of collaboration helps immeasurably in ensuring that the research process generates insights that are useful to designers.

In portraying E-Lab's collaborative work processes, I will describe not only "objective structures" but also the ways that members of the company conceptualized them (Bourdieu 1990). E-Lab created a visual representation of its research-design collaboration, which was referred to as the "bow tie model." This model formed a tool that employees used to think about their work practices. It can also function that way for readers of the chapter who seek ideas about how to structure their own cross-disciplinary collaborations. Multiple versions of the image accompany the text, below.

For anthropologists casting an ethnographic eye over E-Lab, the bow tie model offers several further points of interest. First of all, it was a native visual representation of local practices, connected to extensive discursive representations (Keane 1997). Members of the company were highly self-reflexive about the challenges of integrating research and design. Both visual and discursive representations were dynamic and integrated with action; work processes were frequently subjected to scrutiny and reconfigured (Chaiklin and Lave 1993; Engeström and Middleton 1996; Lave and Wenger 1991).

Second, the graphic nature of the bow tie model is richly indexical of the visually oriented culture of the design profession. In conversation, for instance, designers frequently get up and make sketches illustrating whatever topics they are talking about, using the whiteboards that plaster the walls of their work spaces. This practice and others indicate that members of the profession make an unusually close link between *thought* and its *visual representation*—these two aspects form a single system of distributed cognition (Cole and Engeström 1993).

A final point of interest is the question of how this reliance on graphics shapes the reasoning of designers. The bow tie model did, indeed, seem to influence the way members of E-Lab thought about research-design collaboration. As company members' understandings of their work interactions changed, they drew new versions of the model to express their altered perceptions. These images in turn functioned as tools for further reasoning about work processes.

E-LAB

E-Lab was founded in 1994 by three individuals who left The Doblin Group to pursue their own vision for a consulting firm. Rick E. Robinson had been the head of research at Doblin, John Cain had been the head of design, and Maribeth McCarthy had been in finance. The three of them sought to create a novel kind of firm that would embody an equal partnership between research and design. All design recommendations were to be based completely on ethnographically oriented user research.

E-Lab did not quite fit into any preexisting categories; it was neither a traditional design firm nor a typical research group. Although E-Lab's principals no doubt built on their experiences at Doblin Group in general ways, they had to invent much of their new company's work process, staffing approach, and organizational structure from scratch. By creating a kind of enterprise that had not existed before, they took on the challenges that attend such efforts: the need to learn through a process of experimentation what worked and what did not.

Much of the inspiration for E-Lab's collaborative philosophy came from Robinson and Cain's work together at The Doblin Group. They had formed a cross-disciplinary partnership in which the activities of generating research insights and developing creative solutions became closely integrated. This co-work formed their mental model for the kind of work process they wanted to institute at E-Lab. For instance, they understood the importance of having researchers and designers work side by side on projects, rather than letting the former simply hand off their results to the latter.

Robinson had first become aware of the potentialities of ethnographic research in the early 1990s, when Doblin was asked by a mutual client, Steelcase, to collaborate with Xerox PARC on part of their Workplace Project (C. Goodwin 1996; Goodwin and Goodwin 1996; M.H. Goodwin 1995; Suchman 1992, 1996). At the time, Xerox PARC employed a number of anthropologists who were pioneering the use of ethnographic methods as an aid to developing more user-friendly software. Their approach was shaped by a mixture of Vygotskian activity theory (Engeström and Middleton 1996; Lave and Wenger 1991) and ethnomethodology/conversation analysis (Drew and Heritage 1992; Garfinkel 1967; Goodwin and Heritage 1990).[2] For instance, they drew on the conversation analysis technique of making video recordings of naturally occurring behavior— in this case, capturing interactions between users and the new products being developed (Blomberg et al. 1993; Brun-Cottan and Wall 1995; Suchman and Trigg 1991). One of the primary figures in the development of this approach was Lucy Suchman (1987, 1995). The Xerox group, in turn, was part of a larger network of researchers in the field of computer-supported cooperative work engaged in similar activities (Button 1992; Hughes et al. 1994; Luff et al. 1992; Shapiro 1994).[3]

Suchman was the leader of the project, which brought The Doblin Group and PARC together. It was through her and the other Xerox participants that Robinson was exposed to the advantages of using ethnographic research. He quickly realized its usefulness for a wide range of design projects, and started to experiment with an increasingly ethnographic approach to data collection in his own work. Over time, these efforts led to E-Lab's suite of research methodologies. To the best of my understanding, Robinson acted as the initial bridge through whom ethnography entered and become adopted in the world of design consulting firms.

I was hired by E-Lab as a project manager in mid-1996, following the completion of my dissertation in anthropology. I remained there until mid-1997. The picture of the company that I present below is therefore a snapshot of a single year; as time passes, the firm will undoubtedly continue to evolve. Prior to working for E-Lab, I had been negotiating the boundary zone between anthropology and the business world for some time. I had spent two years working as a project manager at an investor relations consulting firm. I had conducted my dissertation fieldwork at a large high-technology company, gaining access by consulting on the topic of "empowerment." In addition, I had cofounded and acted as president of a Chicago-area association for anthropologists involved with the private sector.

At E-Lab, I occupied a matrixed set of roles that encompassed a number of responsibilities. As project manager, I led client projects, from developing the plan and budget, to coordinating the efforts of the project team, to maintaining good relationships with the client. I also participated in new client development activities such as meetings and proposal writing. In addition, I joined the other managers in ongoing efforts to coordinate the company's activities and plan future directions. As a "research lead" on projects managed by designers, I guided the fieldwork process. Finally, as one of the senior ethnographers, I participated in efforts to develop new methodologies and train other researchers in our areas of expertise.

During the time period I focus on, 1996–1997, the company had about twenty-five employees. It was in the River North neighborhood of Chicago, an area of craft and interior design galleries. Although the firm was quite young, it had already attracted a range of clients, from office furniture companies to high-technology industries. It was also receiving quite a bit of media attention; for instance, it was featured in the October 1996 issue of *Fast Company* (Posner 1996; also Coleman 1996; Heath 1997; Nussbaum 1997; Smith 1997).

ORGANIZATIONAL STRUCTURE AND STAFFING

The principle of an equal partnership between research and design was embodied in E-Lab's organizational structure and staffing practices. The most stable internal structure was a discipline-based division. All employees (except a few administrative personnel) were categorized as either "researchers" or "designers." These groupings played an important role in staffing, both with regard to the makeup of the company as a whole and on individual projects. For the company as a whole, E-Lab strove to maintain an equal ratio between researchers and designers. On particular projects, employee assignments were also based on the principle of balance. The project manager was chosen for the kind of expertise that seemed to be most important; some projects had more of a research focus, whereas others were more design oriented. But, ideally at least, a second project manager from the opposite discipline was assigned to the project in a subsidiary role. For instance, a manager who was a designer would have another manager as "research lead" on each of her projects. The rest of the team was usually composed of about half researchers and half designers, although the ratio could shift somewhat depending on the nature of the project.

E-Lab's hierarchical structure was fairly fluid; it continued to evolve as the number of employees grew and other pressures for efficiency emerged. While I was there, the firm essentially had a three-level hierarchy: at the top were the principals; in the middle were the project managers; and at the bottom were the rest of the employees, the "staff" or "team members." An unusual feature of this hierarchy was that the team members had multiple reporting relationships. Since they regularly worked on two or more projects at a time, they reported to several project managers. At the same time, they also reported directly to the principals. Lines of authority were thus not always clearly drawn. E-Lab maintained a strongly egalitarian ideology that further de-emphasized the existence of power differences and relations of inequality.

THE WORK PROCESS

To facilitate collaboration between ethnographers and designers, E-Lab developed a team-based work process that integrated the two disciplines in a balanced way. To adapt to this process, members of each group had to undergo significant shifts in their ethos and practices: designers had to surrender their creative autonomy, and ethnographers had to target their activities to the needs of designers and clients. I will highlight five phases in the work process: data collection, data analysis, the development of frameworks, general design implications, and specific design recommendations. Of course, these phases all "bled" into each other—describing each one separately is to some extent a heuristic device.

Also, before a project could begin, E-Lab representatives had to work with clients to identify their problem, negotiate a proposal, and structure the project. These initial efforts were most often conducted by a two-person team, designer and researcher, at the level of project manager or principal. From a practical point of view, this was useful because members of each discipline could respond to some questions better than others. At the same time, such pairings sent a symbolic message about the importance of collaboration at E-Lab.

On each project, the trajectory of the work process started with an emphasis on research, and gradually shifted to an emphasis on design. However, there was no clear moment of a "handoff" from research to design. On the contrary, the company's philosophy encouraged all team members to participate in all phases of the project, although the intensity of their efforts shifted over time. When a project's research and design activities did disengage from each other, employees recognized this as a problem. Projects could be as short as a few weeks, or as long as a year or more. They were typically staffed by three to seven team members.

Data Collection

A number of different research methods were included in E-Lab's repertoire during my time there, and they continue to evolve. There is a certain amount of secrecy in the design world concerning research techniques, since new ones may temporarily constitute a competitive advantage—until other design firms learn about and copy them. I therefore discuss only E-Lab's most basic and widely known activities (Wasson 2000).

The firm's research approach centered on the observation of *naturally occurring* consumer behaviors. In other words, project members watched, and talked to, users of the relevant products in the settings where they ordinarily engaged with those products, be it at home, work, school, or play. Their shopping activities were often monitored as well. This emphasis on learning about the activities of social actors "in the wild" through participant observation and unstructured interviews is, of course, one of the central tenets of anthropology. It became one of the ways that E-Lab differentiated itself from traditional design and marketing firms early on. As one article about E-Lab put it, for instance, "don't just ask people what they want, go out and watch how they live" (Posner 1996: 105).

Observations of naturally occurring consumer behaviors were captured in various ways, but the most significant technique was videotaping, using either mounted cameras or Handicams carried by roving project members. As Robinson put it,

Once we decide where the best place to watch people using things is, we take a bunch of cameras, a bunch of computer controlled video decks, miles of cables, microphones, and small gray computers with little colored logos out into the real world. For hours at a time, for days and days, we videotape people doing the things they do, without interference, where and when they usually do them. (1994: 7)

Considerable expertise was required to plan and coordinate the data collection efforts. A Ph.D.-level researcher almost always played a major role, either as project manager or as "research lead" when the project manager was a designer. Problems arose in those rare cases when a project did not have adequate involvement from such an individual.

This was not surprising, since anthropologists have long found that effectively carrying out fieldwork requires a complex of skills that are developed through long education and experience (Agar 1980; Van Maanen 1988). Ethnography is an inductive process, not a deductive one. Rather than going out to the field to test predetermined hypotheses, practitioners try to keep an open mind and discover what "the natives" regard as the key issues. Such an approach requires creativity, intuition, self-reflexivity, and the ability to gain rapport with the people being observed. Fieldworkers need to learn how to become an unobtrusive part of ongoing events, a "fly on the wall." They need to understand the interpersonal and ethical dilemmas of the observer role. They need to become good at noticing the details of scenes they watch. They need to learn how to elicit deep issues from their subjects in conversation, without leading them. This constellation of skills is hard to explain and can be fully learned only through experience. For these reasons, anthropologists have long talked about the "mystique" of fieldwork.

There are also a number of practical planning issues that ethnographers need to attend to creatively and with skill. What activities and settings should be observed for a given project? How should the topics under investigation be defined? Since the ultimate goal is to find out what meanings a particular product has in the lives of its consumers, a wide range of cultural domains and spheres of activity may need to be examined. Appropriate field sites need to be found, and the data collection efforts must be managed. This can involve challenges such as coordinating the efforts of eight people who are mounting eight video cameras in the high ceiling of a grocery store in the small hours of the morning.

At E-Lab, it was generally believed that someone with a research background needed to be involved in planning the fieldwork process, to ensure that maximally useful data would be gathered. This was important because the quality of data had a direct bearing on subsequent design recommendations, and thus on client satisfaction. However, the firm found that Ph.D.-level training was not a requirement for team members to master the basics of fieldwork. Many individuals became highly adept fieldworkers as they acquired experience. And this activity was not limited to researchers. As much as possible, E-Lab tried to make sure that designers engaged in participant observation and interviewing as well. They usually spent less time on these activities than the project members who were researchers. Nonetheless, the company found that placing designers in the field was invaluable for their ability to understand the context for which they were designing a product. It also gave the whole project team a common basis for group discussions concerning data analysis.

Data Analysis

The process of analyzing and interpreting ethnographic data was crucial to the success of any project, yet ironically, its importance was often not intuitively obvious to clients. Demonstrating its significance was one reason for the extensive client contact E-Lab maintained. In a nutshell, what E-Lab needed to communicate was that ethnographic data do not speak on their own. Simply watching a videotape of consumer behavior does not transparently reveal design recommendations that are both far-reaching and accurately targeted to user needs (although some members of some design firms appear to think it does).

For one thing, it is easy to be overly influenced by a single, dramatic example of consumer behavior. Although isolated examples can occasionally lead to useful insights, the crucial behaviors are those that are repeated over and over. These are the ones that reveal the underlying cultural beliefs and practices that influence large numbers of consumers. Second, an analytic process is needed to reveal the cultural meanings that lie beneath the surface of particular activities, tying together different kinds of user behaviors that may seem unrelated at first glance. This again is a creative process. It involves the ability to see patterns in a kaleidoscope of individual actions. Furthermore, the ability to contextualize these behavioral patterns broadly requires training in social theory and knowledge of a wide range of existing cultural beliefs and practices. Such a contextualization of consumer behaviors enables more far-reaching design recommendations and creates bigger client opportunities. "[I]f you do this well . . . you begin to control the rules of the game and leave your competitors in the dust, not because you've got more features than they do, but because you have redefined what is valuable about the thing and they are still playing by the old rules" (Robinson 1994: 10).

At E-Lab, all team members participated in data analysis. Researchers spent more time on it, but designers participated as well. Team members started by examining the ethnographic materials, such as videotape, and collecting "instances" of consumer behaviors that they thought might be relevant. E-Lab had created a sophisticated software program to capture and annotate video clips. As "instances" accumulated, project participants began to identify clusters of similar examples, which they eventually grouped into "patterns." This work process was both individual and collective; team members alternated between watching video on their own and in groups. One of the big advantages of video ethnography, in fact, was that it made ethnographic materials easy to share. Team members who had not participated in a particular fieldwork encounter could see it through the eyes of the original observer's Handicam. Likewise, multiple project participants could all watch an episode together and contribute their individual perspectives on it. Group meetings were particularly productive occasions for brainstorming interpretations of data. The collaborative process of teams was further enhanced by having project-specific work spaces, with whiteboards, bulletin boards, and shelves. Such areas made it possible for a team to distribute its emergent insights across various participants and objects (Cole and Engeström 1993). Individuals and groups could leave insights and artifacts for other team members to find and play with.

Development of Frameworks

The goal of data analysis was to develop a *framework* that both interpreted the ethnographic materials that had been collected and envisioned a solution for the client. The framework told a story. It offered a coherent narrative about the world of user-product interactions—how the product was incorporated into consumers' daily routines and what symbolic meanings it held for them. These insights, in turn, were framed to have clear implications for the client's product development and marketing efforts.

Developing a comprehensive, coherent, and catchy framework was an iterative process that team members turned to again and again during data analysis. Generating such a model was the activity in which researchers and designers played the most equal roles. It thus revealed most clearly the extent to which members of both disciplines needed to modify their work practices to collaborate successfully. Designers were limited by having to base their suggestions for frameworks strictly on research insights; they had to sacrifice the autonomy of their intuition. Researchers were often intrigued by discoveries that were tangential to the client problem; their analytic efforts had to be kept focused on topics that could lead to design opportunities. In collaborative meetings, designers pushed researchers to think more about the practical implications of their work, whereas researchers pushed designers to base their ideas on the insights that had emerged concerning user-product interactions and their cultural contexts.

The frameworks E-Lab offered clients always comprised both a verbal narrative and a graphic representation. Because visual models are endemic to design culture, they also shaped the ongoing collaborative efforts of researchers and designers as they developed frameworks. When team members met, they usually sketched images on whiteboards as they talked. These visual accompaniments influenced the course of their discussions; an idea that could be given a catchy visual representation was more persuasive and memorable than one that could not. Meeting participants also used each other's pictures as aids in reasoning about ideas: they drew additions onto sketches and reformulated them, accompanying their efforts with explanatory verbal narratives. For most researchers, reasoning this way was a new skill that they had to develop.

General Design Implications

Once a project team had developed a satisfactory framework, it turned to developing recommendations for the client. Here, the role of the researchers diminished while designers took on an increasing prominence. However, the collaboration between them continued. Designers might brainstorm solutions together with researchers. Or they might work out ideas on their own and then ask researchers for critiques. The design solutions developed by a project team began with general implications, broad formulations of new product and marketing directions based on the discoveries encapsulated in the framework.

Specific Design Recommendations

Subsequently, the team—especially its designers—might develop specific suggestions for how these overall directions could be given shape in particular new designs. They usually represented their ideas through

Figure 4.1
Early Bow Tie Model

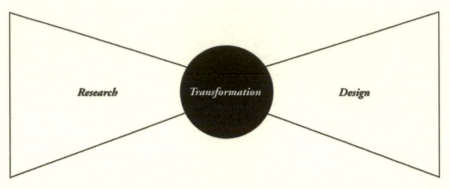
Research   Transformation   Design

Image courtesy of E-Lab LLC.

sketches or computer simulations; in some cases, they might even build three-dimensional prototypes. The more concrete the representations of these product ideas became, the more they required basic design skills, such as training in technical drawing, computer graphics programs, or the ability to work with foam core. Since most researchers did not have these skills, their participation in such activities was small, limited primarily to evaluating product and marketing ideas for their fit with research findings.

THE BOW TIE MODEL

E-Lab's principals and employees were highly self-reflexive about the way researchers and designers worked together. This was a topic of frequent discussion and concern. Organization members created and modified several visual representations of the process. Most images were variations on a pattern informally termed the "bow tie model." This image was used in publicity materials and for client presentations. But it was also used internally, as a tool that organization members used to reason with.

In the model's earliest formulation, the left side of the bow tie represented research, the right side represented design, and the knot in the middle showed the transformative alchemy that occurred when these two fields came together (Figure 4.1). A second version, used concurrently, focused more on the chronology of the work process (Figure 4.2). The left side represented activities with a research emphasis: "Instances" and "Patterns" stood for the data analysis process as it moved toward the development of frameworks. The knot of the bow tie represented the achievement of satisfactory frameworks, a task collaboratively accom-

Figure 4.2
Second Bow Tie Model

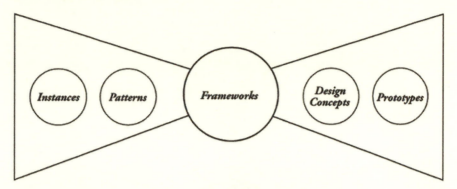

Image courtesy of E-Lab LLC.

plished by researchers and designers in equal measure. The right wing of the tie depicted activities with a design emphasis, moving from the creation of general "Design Concepts" based on the frameworks, to the formulation of particular "Prototypes" that encapsulated these concepts and gave them form. The data collection phase that I described earlier is not represented in this diagram. As Figure 4.3 shows, the two versions of the bow tie could also be combined. This image was included in E-Lab's 1996–1997 publicity materials.

These representations of the company's work process were widely used by organization members for a year or two. Subsequently, however, they came under criticism from two directions, leading to a reformulation of the bow tie image.

Integration Concerns

The first kind of criticism arose in the winter of 1996–1997, and it came mainly from the designers at E-Lab. They were concerned about the degree of separation between research and design activities that the bow tie seemed to imply. The fact that they started to "see" the model this way after it had already been in use for some time reflected other changes that were happening in E-Lab's work process.

Research and design work had been solidly integrated at E-Lab until shortly before that time. However, the number of employees approximately doubled between the summer of 1996 and the following winter, and as the company grew larger, research and design had drifted apart. The informal kind of collaboration that had occurred without any effort when there was only a handful of employees diminished as their num-

Figure 4.3
Combined Bow Tie Model

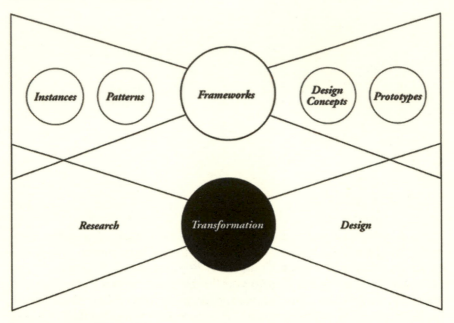

Image courtesy of E-Lab LLC.

bers grew. The development of a more structured approach to collaboration, and training for newcomers, lagged behind the hiring process.

Interestingly, it was designers who pointed out the problem. They reminded everyone that E-Lab's strength lay in the integration of research and design efforts, and that the work process should not become a "handoff" from research to design. Designers should be actively involved from the first day of the project, and researchers should participate until the end. The complexity and depth of ethnographic data meant that the designers needed to be exposed to them over time in order to utilize them most fully.

The concerns voiced by the design community helped alert the rest of the firm to what was happening, and various steps were taken to reintegrate research and design. A greater effort was made to assign designers to each project from the beginning. Meetings that brought all team members together were made more frequent. Designers were given more time to watch ethnographic videotape. The company acquired more space so that teams could again be given project rooms where they could display new ideas and develop frameworks in a way that was accessible to everyone. One project manager experimented with a team work proc-

Figure 4.4
Double Bow Tie Model

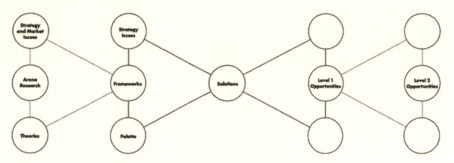

Image courtesy of E-Lab LLC.

ess in which research and design looped back and forth in innumerable small cycles.

In voicing their concerns about the danger of separating research and design, designers offered a variety of visual representations of a more integrated work process. None of these took hold, however.

Client Focus

The second critique of the bow tie model occurred in the spring of 1997. In discussions among project managers and principals, there was an emergent sense that the work process had become too internally focused, and that more emphasis needed to be placed on the client. One afternoon, planning a presentation for a prospective customer, a project manager envisioned a new kind of bow tie that would show a balance between E-Lab's internal activities and the deliverables it could provide to clients. She drew a double bow tie, shown in Figure 4.4. The two wings on the left showed the company's research and design collaboration, and the two wings on the right represented the two kinds of opportunities E-Lab could uncover for the client: modifications of existing products, and entirely new ideas.

Figure 4.5 was an expansion of the left side of the bow tie. This half of the new model described E-Lab's work process, and in this sense was similar to earlier versions of the whole bow tie. Yet even this piece was much more focused on client needs. The image clearly pointed to the goal of "Solutions" for the customers. Furthermore, E-Lab's work process was situated in external contextual factors. The diagram illustrated the importance of three kinds of information in shaping the initial stages of a project: the client's "Strategy and Market Issues," preexisting "Arena Research" on the client's industry and consumers, and the "Theories"

Figure 4.5
Expanded Half of Double Bow Tie

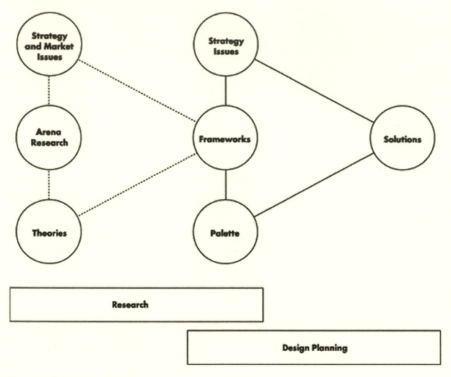

Image courtesy of E-Lab LLC.

that informed E-Lab researchers' understandings of social phenomena. The diagram also highlighted two external factors that shaped the later stages of a project. Again, the client's "Strategy Issues" played a role in what kinds of solutions E-Lab offered. The client also usually had preferences regarding the "Palette" to use in design recommendations. For instance, with regard to marketing suggestions, the client might prefer to focus on packaging, or advertising, or store displays.

This new version of the bow tie resonated with the concerns of principals and project managers, and quickly became popular. At the same time, a variety of concrete efforts to improve customer focus were under way. In E-Lab's earlier days, there had been an idealistic tendency to regard the quality of ideas delivered, and the attractiveness of written reports, as the most important factors in determining customer satisfaction. This perspective became more nuanced in the course of discussions in the spring of 1997. Project managers and principals started to focus more on matching the form of the deliverables to the client's work culture. They also started to think more about the role played by the deliverables in making their contacts look good to the rest of the client organization. The presentations that E-Lab was often asked to make to client groups were accorded greater importance.

This new perspective on deliverables complemented E-Lab's preexisting focus on working closely with clients over the course of a project. Project managers always made sure that clients bought into research findings and design directions as the team was developing them. Also, the depth and complexity of the firm's work meant that clients usually needed repeated exposure to a project; they needed to be brought into the story as it developed. To this end, E-Lab developed a type of interactive work session that incorporated a number of techniques to help draw in clients. A series of such sessions took place over the course of each project.

THE PALE SHADOW OF ETHNOGRAPHY

What does "ethnography" mean in the design world? What does it mean to clients? A conceptual model of "ethnography" circulates in these groups that is quite divergent from anthropological understandings of the term (Wasson 1999). E-Lab's use of the concept lay midway between them, resulting in a particular set of challenges for the company.

For anthropologists, "ethnography" is a complex process that encompasses fieldwork (usually entailing immersion in some culture for a year or more), interpretations of the phenomena observed, and the articulation of these insights in textual form (Agar 1980; Van Maanen 1988). From the anthropological point of view, designers have greatly thinned out and reduced the notion of "ethnography." The concept has become a pale shadow of itself. In its most emaciated form, the term is simply used to refer to a designer with a video camera. Even in somewhat richer versions, the term has become closely identified with the act of *observing* naturally occurring consumer behaviors. The need to *analyze* those behaviors and situate them in their cultural context is poorly understood, even though these activities are essential parts of developing a model of user experience that leads to targeted and far-reaching design solutions. One might speculate that the visual orientation of design culture makes the value of observation more immediately obvious than that of analysis.

I believe that the potential effect of "ethnography" is reduced to the extent that it loses its grounding in the kind of training anthropologists (and members of related disciplines) receive. Such training involves gaining a background in social theory, mastering a variety of fieldwork methods, and learning how to interpret the observations, conversations, and artifacts collected. Observation on its own is a less powerful tool for design. A videotape alone cannot answer questions about how, for instance, particular user-product interactions are situated in the consumers' family dynamics, work pressures, and cultural beliefs.

Although E-Lab's research process was much shorter than traditional anthropological endeavors, it was still longer and more in-depth than that of many competitors. This placed a particular burden on the company, of justifying the need for the greater time and expense. Communicating the power of its approach to clients was an ongoing challenge.

NOTES

1. This chapter developed out of a presentation I made at the 1997 meeting of the American Anthropological Association, in a session on "Assisting in the Solution of Corporate Problems: A Self-Assessment by and for Anthropologists." I wish to thank Elizabeth Briody for organizing the panel, and the discussants, Frederick Gamst and Marietta Baba, for their useful comments. Some of the ideas in the paper were shaped by presentations made to the Anthropology Department Colloquia at Northwestern University and Northern Illinois University. In addition, I would like to extend my appreciation to Susan Squires, Charline Poirier, and Rick E. Robinson for helpful conversations. Finally, I extend a special thanks to all E-Lab employees for teaching me about their occupational community.

2. For further reviews of the approach to ethnography developed at Xerox PARC, see Blomberg et al. 1997, Shapiro 1994, Wasson 2000.

3. Integrating the work of ethnographers and designers was an ongoing challenge in CSCW (computer-supported cooperative work), just as it has been in industrial design. For thoughtful discussion of the challenges, see Blomberg et al. 1993, Blomberg et al. 1997, Hughes et al. 1994, Shapiro 1994.

REFERENCES

Agar, M.H. 1980. *The Professional Stranger: An Informal Introduction to Ethnography*. New York: Academic Press.

Bellah, R.N., R. Madsen, W.M. Sulllivan, A. Swidler, and S.M. Tipton. 1985. *Habits of the Heart: Individualism and Commitment in American Life*. New York: Harper and Row.

Blomberg, J., J. Giacomi, A. Mosher, and P. Swenton-Wall. 1993. Ethnographic Field Methods and Their Relation to Design. In *Participatory Design: Principles and Practices*, edited by D. Schuler and A. Namioka. Hillsdale, NJ: Lawrence Erlbaum Associates.

Blomberg, J., L. Suchman, and R. Trigg. 1997. Back to Work: Renewing Old Agendas for Cooperative Design. In *Computers and Design in Context*, edited by M. Kyng and L. Mathiassen. Cambridge: MIT Press.

Bourdieu, P. 1990. *The Logic of Practice*. Translated by R. Nice. Stanford: Stanford University Press.

Brun-Cottan, F., and P. Wall. 1995. Using Video to Re-present the User. *Communications of the ACM* 38 (5): 61–71.

Button, G., ed. 1992. *Technology in Working Order: Studies of Work, Interaction, and Technology*. London: Routledge.

Chaiklin, S., and J. Lave, eds. 1993. *Understanding Practice: Perspectives on Activity and Context*. Cambridge: Cambridge University Press.

Cole, M., and Y. Engeström. 1993. A Cultural-Historical Approach to Distributed Cognition. In *Distributed Cognitions: Psychological and Educational Considerations*, edited by G. Salomon. Cambridge: Cambridge University Press.

Coleman, C. 1996. Perverse Fascination. *Perspective* (Fall): 1–46.

Drew, P., and J. Heritage, eds. 1992. *Talk at Work: Interaction in Institutional Settings*. Cambridge: Cambridge University Press.

Engeström, Y., and D. Middleton, eds. 1996. *Cognition and Communication at Work*. Cambridge: Cambridge University Press.

Garfinkel, H. 1967. *Studies in Ethnomethodology*. Englewood Cliffs, NJ: Prentice-Hall.

Goodwin, C. 1996. Transparent Vision. In *Interaction and Grammar*, edited by E. Ochs, E.A. Schegloff, and S.A. Thompson. Cambridge: Cambridge University Press.

Goodwin, C., and M. Harness Goodwin. 1996. Seeing as Situated Activity: Formulating Planes. In *Cognition and Communication at Work*, edited by Y. Engeström and D. Middleton. Cambridge: Cambridge University Press.

Goodwin, C., and J. Heritage. 1990. Conversation Analysis. *Annual Review of Anthropology* 19:283–307.

Goodwin, M.H. 1995. Assembling a Response: Setting and Collaboratively Constructed Work Talk. In *Situated Order: Studies in the Social Organization of Talk and Embodied Activities*, edited by P. ten Have and G. Psathas. Washington, DC: International Institute for Ethnomethodology and Conversation Analysis & University Press of America.

Heath, R.P. 1997. Seeing Is Believing: Ethnography Gets Consumers Where They Live—and Work, and Play, and Shop. *Marketing Tools* (March): 4–9.

Heskett, J. 1980. *Industrial Design*. New York: Oxford University Press.

Hughes, J., V. King, T. Rodden, and H. Andersen. 1994. Moving Out from the Control Room: Ethnography in System Design. In *Proceedings of the Conference on Computer Supported Cooperative Work*. New York: ACM Press.

Keane, W. 1997. *Signs of Recognition: Powers and Hazards of Representation in an Indonesian Society*. Berkeley: University of California Press.

Lave, J., and E. Wenger. 1991. *Situated Learning: Legitimate Peripheral Participation*. Cambridge: Cambridge University Press.

Luff, P., C. Heath, and D. Greatbatch. 1992. Tasks-in-interaction: Paper and Screen Based Documentation in Collaborative Activity. In *Proceedings of the Conference on Computer Supported Cooperative work*. New York: ACM Press.

Nussbaum, B. 1997. Annual Design Awards: Winners—the Best Product Designs of the Year. *Business Week*, June 2, 92–95.

Posner, B.G. 1996. The Future of Marketing Is Looking at You. *Fast Company* (October/November): 105.

Robinson, R.E. 1994. The Origin of Cool Things. Paper read at the conference, "Design that Packs a Wallop: Understanding the Power of Strategic Design," March 8–9, at New York.

Shapiro, D. 1994. The Limits of Ethnography: Combining Social Sciences for CSCW. In *Proceedings of the Conference on Computer Supported Cooperative Work*. New York: ACM Press.

Smith, A. 1997. Shoppers under the Microscope: Watching How Different Types of People Use Goods and Services Can Supply Useful Information. *Financial Times*, December 5, A1.

Suchman, L. 1987. *Plans and Situated Actions: The Problem of Human-machine Communication*. Cambridge: Cambridge University Press.

———. 1992. Technologies of Accountability: Of Lizards and Aeroplanes. In *Technology in Working Order: Studies of Work, Interaction, and Technology*, edited by G. Button. London: Routledge.

———. 1995. Representations of Work. *Communications of the ACM* 38(9): 9.

———. 1996. Constituting Shared Workspaces. In *Cognition and Communication at Work*, edited by Y. Engeström and D. Middleton. Cambridge: Cambridge University Press.

Suchman, L.A., and R.H. Trigg. 1991. Understanding Practice: Video as a Medium for Reflection and Design. In *Design at Work: Cooperative Design of Computer Systems*, edited by J. Greenbaum and M. Kyng. Hillsdale, NJ: Lawrence Erlbaum Associates.

Van Maanen, J. 1988. *Tales of the Field: On Writing Ethnography*. Chicago: University of Chicago Press.

Varenne, H. 1987. Talk and Real Talk: the Voices of Silence and the Voices of Power in American Family Life. *Cultural Anthropology* 2 (3): 369–394.

Wasson, C. 1999. The Paradoxical Discourse of "Ownership." Paper read at the 1999 International Conference on Language in Organizational Change and Transformation: What Makes a Difference?, May 14–16, at Columbus, Ohio.

———. 2000. Ethnography in the Field of Design. *Human Organization* 59 (4): 377–388.

5

Team Roles in the Design Process: Living with and Creating Legacies that Benefit Design

Sally Ann Applin

What makes a usable and well-designed product? Which members of a product team are responsible for a product's design? If you answered that good design is derived from all the members of a product team and is the sum of their combined experience, then you got it right. Although this book is written primarily for designers and anthropologists, many others collaborate on projects including engineers, marketing representatives, and product and project managers. These professionals are critical to success in good design.

In my opinion, good design process is the result of the combination of (1) successful education and collaboration of group members, (2) the combined experience of the team and (3) an eye for the intended product, and most importantly (4) an understanding of the product's intended audience. From the beginning, a well-rounded design team should include at least one engineer, one marketing representative, and one project manager. Although they aren't always included in the entire product development process these "other" professionals must be included for a successful product design to emerge. Once a team is formed, it is up to every member to create a dialogue with, and develop an understanding between, these different professions. My intention in this chapter is to share with you what I have learned and observed from collaborating within these groups as we moved toward the goal of designing usable products.

WHO AM I?

I have worked on designing the interfaces between people, products, and information for the past twelve years, and there are four words on my business card: "conceptual, design, interface, architecture." These seem to capture what I do and what interests me.

Although my profession began with the name "human-computer-interface design," it has gone through several naming cycles over the years. It has been called "interface design," "interaction design," and "user-interface architecture." The alternative names reflect the preferences of the professionals who design people's experiences with objects and software. The cognitive scientists, designers, and human factors engineers all have different interpretations of what their profession means and how to label it.

I say that I "design how people use things over time." To me, "things" can be software, remote controls, telephones, information, services, or any other temporal activity that may require some thought and process applied to its use.

I started my career designing science museums and working on how to display information to people who might be viewing and learning about it for only a short period of time. I later worked on understanding computer software, and how people are able, or not able, to complete their tasks. I'm currently interested in what I call "service design." How does one design specialized or preferential access to services that deliver products or information? Over the years, I have worked in many multidisciplinary design and engineering groups. When I write about collaborating with design groups, it is usually through my role as a designer, though there have been instances when I've worked as a researcher. I use the term "researcher" to connote an anthropologist, sociologist, or other "person-focused" professional on a design team.

BUILDING THE IDEAL TEAM

Each member of a design team brings something important to the design process. I like to believe that every competently trained professional has informative, accurate, and significant expertise to bring to the process. In an ideal product design scenario, team members work together to share their expertise as they move through the design process. Let's examine a scenario where there is research, marketing, engineering, and design. In this first stage, research is expected to have, or have the ability to gain, an understanding of the product's intended audience. Next, marketing will have clear goals and objectives of how to reach and educate that audience. The engineers will have a clear idea of how to build for these goals within the limits of the technology. Finally, the designers interpret the marketing goals, user needs, and engineering limitations into a viable, usable design. And of course, in this ideal scenario, each team member comes together with the desire to work with one another. But what happens when there isn't an ideal scenario?

Many issues can get in the way of building the ideal team. They may include differing opinions about the goal of the product, interoffice politics, prejudices against the professional disciplines of certain team members, and communication styles between members of the same group. To further complicate matters, outside the "design profession" itself are scores of clients, companies, or groups who hire the designers, researchers, and other team members, because they like the idea of the process, but have a reality of wanting to save money and/or see quick results. Thus, sometimes a design budget can be translated into "no design at all." Multidisciplinary design teams have to do a lot of work to sell and justify themselves. In short, the idea of an "ideal team" is a good one, but there may be obstacles to creating one.

Some research or design professionals may have the impression that multidisciplinary, collaborative design teams are the usual mode of operation for innovative design groups, and that clients are willing to fund and utilize members of those professions on a regular basis. Unfortunately, even having a "researcher" on a design team still seems to be the exception rather than the rule. For some reason, clients need to "see" something visible as a first result of a nonengineering team's efforts. Researchers often provide reports that are not directly interpreted as "screens" or "things" and therefore, sometimes have a more difficult time justifying their work to their clients. This latter phenomenon seems to be especially true in the software industry. In other industries, design is hired to appease a managerial request, but not utilized because of a lack of understanding of the process or changes in scope or budget.

Though the design profession is learning to work with anthropologists and other researchers, it rarely includes engineers in the early development of a product. Occasionally an engineer is included in initial meetings. More often, engineers are left as end-of-cycle "implementers," a position that can create stress on a team. This stress can be significant when a product is doomed to failure because an engineer wasn't consulted on the feasibility of actually building the product in the first place. The best thought out ergonomic and "usable" design needs feedback, and needs it early on to determine whether it can actually be built. Conversely, the software engineering profession often does not include designers, anthropologists, and/or other researchers in the early development of its products. Instead, it uses them as end-of-cycle "quick-fix" repair people. This often leads to a product being doomed to failure because it was never determined whether or not it had a useful application for the end user.

Figure 5.1. Some individuals prefer to be the front line "point of contact" with the client and may tend to keep other members of the team less informed.

DESIGN TEAM DYNAMICS

It is obvious then, that when working with multidisciplinary teams, each discipline is important and valuable. However, determining when and how to include each member's input is a tricky balancing act that requires sensitivity and knowledge of a holistic design process. Is this a knowledge that all professions on a design team have? Do different professions have their own unique philosophies and ideals for varying types of products? How do teams learn to work together? How do teams learn about each other to forge a healthy, productive working relationship?

In my experience, the importance of various team members depends upon the product that is being designed. If the product is a "thing," then the initial meetings will involve all team members, but very quickly the designers will become the initial first points of contact—often not even working with researchers, marketing representatives, or engineers until later in the cycle. If the product is software, the engineers are often the primary contact, shunning the designers and anthropologists because the engineers themselves are the designers and builders. If the product is a service, often the researchers take the lead, and sometimes neglect to include the designer or engineer in the beginning (see Figure 5.1).

The ideal case, of course, is when all possible members of a team are present to kick off a client meeting, know each other's strengths and weaknesses, know when to include each other in their individual processes, and are respectful of each other. In addition, each team member carries the client's goal in mind when developing his or her portion of the project. Unfortunately, sometimes even with the best intentions and training, team members are still shaped by the environment in which they work, and have worked. Hence, there can be legacy issues that preclude thoughtful design and that need to be addressed.

CASE STUDY—ACME CORPORATION: LEGACY DRIVING THE DESIGN PROCESS

This story is about a project in which engineering and upper management drove the design process. Acme Corporation was a manufacturer of computer widgets. As a research experiment, Acme Corporation decided to partner with Big Network, a communications company. At the executive level, it was decided that the two corporations would partner on a project to make a communications widget that they would jointly test in the market. Acme Corporation assembled a team, consisting of a product manager, a low-level programmer, a user-interface designer, a high-level programmer, and a hardware engineer. There were a few others, separate from the core team, who were involved at different stages of the product, including a contract employee, who assembled the prototype units; the industrial design division of Acme Corporation, which worked on the physical design of the unit; and a project manager, who came on board as the units were being assembled and distributed. Big Network's team included a marketing representative, a programming technician, and a customer service representative.

Acme Corporation's core team began on the design of the project. There was a "kickoff" meeting with Big Network regarding expectations of the product, and then the software and hardware engineers began the design process. The pecking order internally had been established early within Acme Corporation as a legacy from other projects: software and hardware engineers ran the projects and pretty much dictated what resources they needed to support their vision. Although some attention was paid to human factors, in the form of a single user-interface designer, there was no real budget for research outside of the core team. Once the engineers decided on a software and hardware platform, they consulted with Acme Corporation's in-house industrial design division to come up with a hardware design that would reflect the features they thought should be in the widget. (Note: In software design, "features" are the parts of a program that support various tasks the users might want to accomplish.) At this stage of the project there was a key feature mistake. To save money, the engineers decided to add a few hard buttons (buttons actually on the widget's hardware) to the widget, and have the remaining buttons displayed on a soft keypad on the widget's touch screen. Unfortunately, the remaining buttons on the soft keypad were for features that were needed for communications. All potential users of this device had a standard legacy model for these features, but to save money, the engineers decided with no supporting research to move standard mapped hard key features to soft keys. This decision was made without any user study evidence or research. Furthermore, the engineers together with the industrial designers decided on a form factor for the widget that had no supporting input from either potential users or their environments. The legacy of Acme Corporation was in full force.

In this particular project, Big Network had features that they wanted to include in the design, because they were interested in testing and marketing them, and not because anyone had determined that the user group needed those services as a feature. This proved to be an enormous problem because Big Network added these features at the last minute. The features were part of Big Network's agenda for expanding their outreach to customers, and had little to do with the widget they were building with Acme Corporation. However, it gave the team from Big Network an opportunity to appease their management and economize by conducting one trial for what essentially amounted to two separate products. Acme Corporation really wanted the partnership with Big Network and was willing to accommodate these requests, even though they further diluted the integrity and usefulness of the widget. Although both Acme Corporation and Big Network wanted to test residential users, Big Network's new requests soon changed the charter to include small-business users. The marketing representatives from Big Network began to assemble "users" with whom they wanted to first test the widget—users who were actually friends and colleagues of the team from Big Network.

While the design for the widget was already being determined, the engineers asked the user-interface designer to conduct a small study of the end users. The study interviewed end users at their homes and businesses, trying to catalog and understand their communications usage habits with regards to the widget. The results of this study showed that some of the features that existed in the software and hardware of the prototype were useful to end users, and that some were missing. The study was able to influence the software somewhat, but the hardware features had already been determined and could not be changed because of schedule and budget constraints.

After the units were assembled, the user-interface designer, along with representatives from Big Network, went to the small-business and residential end users to watch them install and try to use the prototype widget. The hardware buttons were useless to the end users, and the modified, engineering-driven soft key features confused end users who had legacy issues with their current communications devices. In addition, the features added by Big Network further confused end users as to the overall purpose of the widget. Subsequent visits to the end users' homes and small businesses were recorded and analyzed. Although some of the results were incorporated into patch releases of the software, none were incorporated into final software. The widget trial lasted three months.

The widget project was not a success for either Acme Corporation or Big Network because of the following factors:

• politics of both Acme Corporation and Big Network (there were reorganizations in both companies during the project)
• lack of a clear vision amongst the teams in the two companies
• lack of clear marketing goals between the companies
• budget
• time

A big flaw of the project was the lack of a defined feature set that suited the hardware platform, the software architecture, and the needs of the users. More effort was put into appeasing the partnerships between Acme Corporation and Big Network than determining end-user needs and goals. In short, internal company problems took precedence over designing a product for the end user.

So what happened? In Acme Corporation, there was a legacy that projects were engineering driven and thus, precluded any early work on user research. In spite of that, some research did manage to get done and incorporated, though it was, unfortunately, conducted in parallel with the engineering effort, and conducted by an interface designer, not a researcher. Mostly, within Acme Corporation and within Big Network, individual team members were harmonious and enjoyed working together. But the lack of management for the project, unclear goals, and the acceptance of Acme Corporation's legacy process created a widget that was lopsided in its development. The widget trial became an engineering-driven project with little room for a design or research process, which subsequently compromised a lot of its potential. At the time, none of the team members questioned the legacy of Acme Corporation, and in fact, felt that they were actually doing a bit "better" by including any research at all.

Because decisions for the widget's feature set and design were determined early in the process without any research included, the project was already subject to those early decisions, and thus negatively biased. Both corporations deemed the widget unsuccessful, and further plans for any relationship between Acme Corporation and Big Network were cancelled.

In summary, although team members liked each other and enjoyed working together, there was no formal agreement between these com-

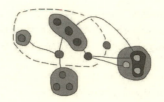

Figure 5.2. Communication between
groups and between clients/partners
is not always clear or direct for team
members (Acme Corporation shown
in light, Big Network in dark).

panies to create a single unified team (see Figure 5.2). The prior project
cultures of both Acme Corporation and Big Network were stronger than
the individuals' yen to make a better team. If individuals on the design
team had worked to understand each other earlier, it may have had more
positive results:

• The designs proposed to cut costs might have been discussed before they could
  be implemented badly, and a better solution might have been proposed, and

• It may have been possible to present to Big Network and Acme Corporation
  the consequences of their disparate company politics and how they affected
  the product design.

   It can be a lengthy process to educate companies about the value of
collaborative, multidisciplinary design teams. Often, companies have political or legacy issues that existed long before teams are assembled to
work on a project together. Some teams spend hours helping their clients
communicate with other members of their teams or companies. Sometimes good design is listening and translating, and sometimes it is actually providing an insight.

CASE STUDY—MEGA COMMUNICATIONS CORP.

   This is a story about a research team and how their assumptions created internal problems between them and their organization.
   Mega Communications Corp. hired Design It Now to help them understand and design products for a certain market demographic. Mega
Communications Corp. had a hunch that this demographic was going to
be the next big thing, but they didn't know how to market, sell, or design
products for it. Design It Now had a successful track record of helping
clients define and design their products and was a fine choice for the
job. Mega Communications Corp. had teams consisting of marketing rep-

resentatives. Design It Now's teams consisted of an anthropologist, an interaction designer who was learning Design It Now's research methodology, and a research manager who periodically acted as a program manager. In addition, a Design It Now salesperson was involved at various stages of the project to ensure that there would be a potential for follow-up business from Mega Communications Corp.

The first task for Design It Now was to try to understand the demographic for which Mega Communications Corp. was interested in developing a product. Design It Now conducted various research activities consisting of field studies in different segments of the market demographic requested by Mega Communications Corp., as well as literature searches and examinations of other case studies for the particular desired end-user group. Design It Now analyzed the data and then had an odd occurrence: the product that needed to be designed wasn't a product at all; it was a service. These research findings were not standard to the experience and approach of Design It Now. They were used to designing things, and a service didn't fall into this category. All of their legacy products had been things. In fact, Design It Now had only recently been designing software, mostly as companion pieces to the hardware products they were designing. The Design It Now research manager was not particularly comfortable with this idea, or convinced that a client would accept a research report recommending various service designs instead of "things." The anthropologist had previously designed social and business services, and the interaction designer had designed software, indeed itself not a "thing." Both were familiar and comfortable with the idea of a product being a "service" and felt that their research findings were complete enough evidence to present a final report to Mega Communications Corp. In the report they could allude to service design directions that would help Mega Communications Corp target their chosen demographic end-user group.

Externally, the project was successful. Mega Communications Corp. was so pleased with the final report and research findings that they used them to educate their outreach staff. Internally, because of legacy issues, other team members from Design It Now felt that the team had failed because they hadn't produced a tangible "thing" as a deliverable. There was an oversight at Design It Now: instead of stopping to educate other team members about the potential and previous experience with a product being a "service," the anthropologist and interaction designer assumed that the other team members understood this phenomenon and proceeded with preparing their report. Had the anthropologist and the interaction designer realized this earlier, the report might have been stronger with the buy-in and feedback from the other team members. When this experience was finally analyzed with others, the long-term

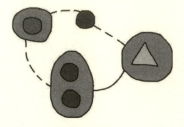

Figure 5.3. The Design It Now creative
team communicated directly with the
client, but did not include the sales or
research director in their work (Design
It Now shown in light, Mega Communications Corp. shown in dark).

result for Design It Now was that they incorporated "service" design
into their client offerings, thus removing the legacy issues.

Although this story had a happier ending than the previous one, the
problems could have been avoided if the research team had shared their
prior knowledge and experience with their management and worked on
including them into the team at an early stage (Figure 5.3).

THERE ARE NO PERFECT TEAMS!

These case studies show that even in the best circumstances, where
"best" is defined as team members working well together, each team
member needs to be aware of issues beyond the expected scope of personality and profession in order to create successful products. Companies are constructed of individual team members, and it's easy, as we
learned in Case Study—Mega Communications, to think that our colleagues know and understand what we are working on. An enormous
amount of understanding of the design profession lies in educating our
colleagues, our companies, and ourselves, whether they are consultancies
or corporations, about each other's working styles and professions. Although good planning and management is essential, awareness and education of all team members seems to be the key to successful
collaboration and design.

Our professions are subjective, and because we aren't hard scientists
or engineers, it may take longer to educate companies founded by those
types about the value of our professions. Sometimes, opposites attract,
and they embrace us.

As you begin to work together with designers and other professions
on a design team, remember the uniqueness that each member brings to
the design process, and try to teach and learn from each other.

PART III

EMERGING COLLABORATIVE PROCESSES

Part III focuses on some of the collaborative processes the authors have developed in partnership with their design colleagues.

Anthropologist Susan Squires outlines three ethnographic research platforms (discovery, definition, and evaluation) and associated rapid quantitative and qualitative methods. She discusses rapid ethnographic research and suggests that social scientists working for product development firms today can benefit from the rapid assessment methods that social scientists developed while working in international development.

George Walls, an executive who specializes in new product development, explains how and why corporations value ethnographically driven breakthrough product development. After distinguishing between the kinds of risk associated with breakthrough and derivative product development, he outlines an effective eight-step process that he and GVO created over the course of five projects.

Rita Denny, an anthropological linguist who works at B/S/R, follows with an essay on how researchers can effectively interact with businesspersons during the course of a project. She examines some of the assumptions and investigative steps that help reframe the fundamental concepts that define how businesspersons understand their relationships with customers and guide the development of their products, services, and brand images.

Mark Dawson then explains some of the techniques he developed to communicate with designers during his tenure at Hauser Design and Design Continuum. His techniques are based on the principle that researchers should function as cultural guides, translating abstract notions into sensible, graphic, and self-explanatory forms.

Heiko Sacher's chapter shows how semiotic and cognitive domain analyses can provide a common framework in which social researchers and designers can partner. He provides several case examples where understanding the principles that guide communication has led to the development of breakthrough media products.

6

Doing the Work: Customer Research in the Product Development and Design Industry

Susan Squires

The role of research in the creative process is to discover and draw out design implications of real cultural phenomena. Researchers must command a sound working knowledge of the concepts and methods that make culturally driven design possible. Since sociocultural concepts such as culture, ethnography, and research design are not typically well understood, researchers guide colleagues through these working processes. Every project demands that we carefully—and quickly—determine appropriate outcomes, project constraints, and research methods. We must demonstrate that our conclusions are logical and founded in the data created during the project itself so that the design team can create new ideas and then, be able to explain the reasoning for the design, execution, and application to our clients.

However, the dynamic nature of contemporary research and design continues to fuel debate about what constitutes appropriate research for design. Despite the differing opinions, many research designs and methods are either applicable or can be modified for design. The sheer number of options makes it even more important to clarify research concepts now and to identify the most effective combinations of concepts, research designs, information sources, and methods.

In this chapter I will concentrate on one critical issue that would be integral to any larger effort. Most researchers and designers are unfamiliar with the concept of research platforms when they enter the industry. But they are fundamental to customer research. After I define my terms, I'll outline the relationship between the research platforms and some of the methods I've used to collect and analyze information.

THREE RESEARCH PLATFORMS

Design researchers have independently distinguished three research platforms that correspond roughly with principal stages of product development. They are discovery, definition, and evaluation.

- Discovery research is an open-ended exploratory effort to learn about consumer culture. It is useful for developing original product and service ideas or finding new applications for existing and emerging technologies.
- Definition research is a more focused effort. It assumes that there is already a product concept. It helps define the products by identifying the implications of consumer culture for design and market strategy. It is particularly useful for gaining knowledge that can guide business decisions, and for matching products with appropriate customer groups.
- Evaluation research assumes that there is already a working product or prototype. It helps refine and validate product prototypes, design usability, market segments, and consumer preferences. Any project may start with any one research platform and lead to others. Teams might start with discovery research and proceed to definitional research once a concept has been selected. Or they might start with evaluative research and find opportunities that lead directly to definitional or exploratory research.

Although businesses frequently tout their proprietary methods, there are few methodological secrets among researchers. The vast majority of the methods can be found in books that should be at least known to graduate students who have taken classes in research design, advanced statistics, ethnoarchaeology, ethnographic interviewing, and content analysis.

The immediate challenge is not so much in creating new research methods, although there are plenty of opportunities to do so. The greater challenge is to figure out exactly when, how, and why to use them to draw out the implications of their findings for design. The research platforms make it possible to select the appropriate qualitative and quantitative methods for data collection and analysis (see Trotter and Schensul 1999; Bernard 1998).

Qualitative and quantitative data and analysis techniques help us discern among processes that may be more or less prevalent among the customer groups we study. Data collection methods are just that: standardized techniques that enable researchers to gather valid and relevant information. Qualitative data such as descriptions of perceptions about

Table 6.1
A Sample of Data Collection Instruments in the Customer Research Toolbox

DISCOVERY	DEFINITION	EVALUATION
• Contextual observation (tours, maps, inventories)	• Contextual observation (tours)	• Product simulations
• Focus groups	• Directed and semi-structured interviews	• Product modeling
• Open-ended interviews	• Free-lists, ratings, rankings, definitions, explanations	• User-experience scenarios
• Drawing	• Role-playing	• Usability tests
• Participant observation (active or passive)	• Concept mapping	• Surveys
• Videography	• Scenarios	• Focus groups
• Tracking	• Displacement research	

how people use or classify objects, the nature of their personal interactions, and opinions about the world around them provide tremendous clues about people on a group level; it yields us clues about culture. Quantitative data such as the amount of time spent at displays in museums or the number of phones a family might have are great for the same reason. When combined, we can create and distinguish among the most important human processes within and across groups of people.

Researchers are just beginning to understand how to match research platforms and methods. We know that some methods are better than others to discern patterns and others to test specific ideas. Some methods are better to describe behavioral phenomena, others opinions. Some methods are terrific ways to document the way people interact with things. Others are better to figure out how they interact amongst themselves. Some methods are better for figuring out just how similar things or people are. Others are better at teasing out causes from consequences.

I have found that open-ended qualitative observational and interview methods are most useful for discovery research because we may not know the appropriate questions or issues to address, let alone have a coherent theory (Table 6.1). Once we know more about the product con-

Table 6.2
A Sample of Data Analysis Instruments in the Customer Research Toolbox

DISCOVERY	DEFINITION	EVALUATION
• Categorical matrices	• Categorical matrices	• Product simulations
• Time series analysis	• Concept mapping	(usability tests)
• Scaling (Guttman, multidimensional scaling, property fitting)	(multidimensional scaling and property fitting)	• Standard inferential statistics
	• Similarity/dissimilarity	• Scaling (Guttman, multidimensional scaling)
	• Correspondence	
• Network mapping	• Activity flow diagramming	
• Content analysis (text, audio, and video)	• Decision modeling	
	• Displacement activities	
• Cultural history	(customers use, experiment	
• Semiotic analysis	with, or redefine prototypes)	

cept, more focused techniques can be used precisely because we know more about the cultural domains. Definition and evaluative research grant us far greater opportunities to conduct naturalistic and field experiments than open-ended exploratory research. We know something about the culture group, the relevant products, and the context in which they are to be used.

The data analysis techniques are also widely known. Data analysis methods are methods that enable us to identify patterns and make inferences from that information about the relationships among cultural phenomena (Table 6.2). Again, the challenge is in selecting the appropriate techniques for the research platforms.

This is only a sample of the qualitative and quantitative data collection and analysis methods that researchers use in customer research. Researchers tend to favor other techniques, partly in response to their own intellectual predilections as well as to the projects they undertake and the preferences of their colleagues.

Rather than try to summarize the breadth of techniques that might be used, I will provide some examples from my own research of ways I've used these research platforms and methods.

DISCOVERY RESEARCH

The goal of discovery research is to uncover and understand the cultural system that frames human action to provide a direction for creating new products and services. Researchers collect and analyze a combination of verbal, observational, and contextual information to identify what people say and do in their natural environment. The consistencies and, more frequently, the inconsistencies help identify unarticulated or unrecognized needs, gaps, and adaptations called "work-arounds" and "disconnects." By reframing disconnects in terms of sociocultural systems, teams essentially change the assumptions that guide their own attempts to create products or services. Clients and consumers almost always perceive the new products and services as innovative or novel because existing products usually ignore many of the cultural attributes of a product or treat them in stereotypic ways.

Discovery research is the most open-ended research of the three research platforms described in this chapter and the most time consuming. Researchers assume they must explore the culture of a group of people, learning about the questions to ask just as much as their answers.

The key to a successful discovery research project is the use of rapid ethnographic assessment methods. Most of the data collection analysis methods that I mentioned above are frequently used by the social scientists who developed rapid ethnographic assessment during the course of their international development projects. Since at least the mid-1970s, rural development projects requiring quick results have been called rapid appraisal, rapid assessment, and rapid rural appraisal (Chambers 1983; Hildebrand 1982; Rhoades 1982; Honadle 1979; Shaner, Philipp, and Schmehl 1982; Collinson 1981). More recently they have been used to describe new research directions in health (Beebe 1995; Bennett 1995; Higginbothom 1994; Manderson and Aaby 1992; Manderson et al. 1996; Trotter and Schensul 1999) and product innovation (Squires 1999; Sunderland 1999).

The objective of rapid ethnographic assessment in discovery research is typically to construct a sociocultural model of the local living system that is both consistent with the way local people understand it and uses local (emic) categories to describe and categorize their reality (Galt 1985: 14). All rapid ethnographic approaches share three important characteristics "(1) a system perspective, (2) triangulated data collection, and (3) iterative data collection and analysis (Beebe 1995: 42)."

Rapid ethnography, as applied in product innovation, differs from other rapid ethnographic approaches in three important ways. First, whereas rapid rural appraisal requires the participation of sizable multidisciplinary teams, small teams usually do rapid ethnographic research for product development. Thus the teams have to be quick, almost self-supporting, and well coordinated. Second, the outcome of the work is most likely a product rather than complex state-subsidized programs and public policies. Third, the teams use video whenever possible to document interviews, behavioral activities, and the relationship among things so that individuals who could not be present might review and exchange information.

I use rapid ethnographic approaches that stress open-ended interviews, site tours (contextual observation), participant observation, literature reviews, cultural history, and semiotic (content) analysis. I occasionally use time series analysis, multidimensional scaling (cognitive mapping), focus groups, and telephone surveys. Let me give you an example of how discovery research can be used to generate cultural insights that lead to successful products.

My colleagues and I were asked to learn about family morning routines and breakfast time behavior. Our client, a large breakfast food company, was particularly interested in learning whether or not "participant observation," the hallmark of anthropological ethnographies, was useful in generating insights that might facilitate its own product development. We formed two teams. Each was composed of one social scientist and one designer. I teamed up with Sally.

We went to have breakfast with the Kellys, a family residing in a northern California suburb. They were one of several families we visited. We arrived at 6:30 A.M. with bags stuffed with video cameras, film, batteries, tape recorders, and paper and pens. I knocked on the door and waited. The door opened into a dark, empty hall, and a woman's voice echoed from the kitchen, "Come on in. We've been expecting you." And then she added, "Close the door, Jack." Sally and I looked down to see the silent upturned face of a smiling four year old. Jack pushed the door shut and ran ahead of us down the hall and into the kitchen. We followed.

The first minutes are always awkward, but soon Sally and I were sipping coffee at the kitchen table and engaging in small talk with Mom and Jack's older brother Kevin, age six (see Photo 6.1). Jack had left us in favor of the family TV that was booming away in the living room.

Mom led the conversation. We let her talk. "Well, I'm not sure I have anything more to tell anyone. If you want, I'll tell you what I told the people at the focus group."

We had recruited Mrs. Kelly because she had participated in a traditional focus group sponsored by the client. As we normally do, we had already familiarized ourselves with the latest understanding of breakfast food consumption. The material included industry reports and market research. Market research is often a good source of information about what is currently the "right" or "acceptable" thinking on a topic. The focus group in which the Kelly mom participated provided us with in-

Photo 6.1. A breakfast interview conducted by Tom Williams. Photo by Steve Portigal.

formation on what people say about breakfast and breakfast food. The focus group data indicated that the American breakfast of the 1990s was occurring very early in the morning. The data also revealed that American moms are very concerned about the quality of the breakfast food they buy. They want to give their kids a good start to the day, and a good breakfast, they told the market researchers, was key to providing that start. We were visiting the Kellys to learn whether their breakfast time activities matched what moms had told the market researchers in the focus group.

Jack's mother began our visit by telling us what she had told the market researchers at the focus group. "As I already said," Mom continued, "I only feed my kids whole grain, nutritious food. Gives 'em a good start to the day. I know Kevin does better on his tests when I make sure he's had a good breakfast."

Mom took out a package of whole grain waffles and put a couple in the toaster to back up what she had just told us. "Want some waffles?" she smiled. Sally and I shook our heads. I didn't feel like having a waffle at 6:45 A.M. It was tough enough to concentrate on the long list of questions we wanted to ask:

- What were the morning routines at the Kelly house?
- Who was there and who was not?
- What other foods might be available?
- What was it like to coax a four year old to eat at 6:30 in the morning?
- What else had to get done before the family left the house?
- Where did the family go after leaving the house?
- Did anyone pick up food after leaving the house?

Sally and I were looking for the answer to these and a multitude of other questions. We began by watching what Mom was doing as she spoke to us. As Mom talked, she moved rapidly around the kitchen, adding a banana from a bowl and yogurt from the fridge, packing lunch for the boys. The toaster popped up, and Mom put the waffles on plates and buttered them while she told us about her day.

"My husband left just before you got here. He never eats breakfast. I think he grabs something at a 7–11 later on. But I make sure the kids eat. Jack, get in here and eat your waffle," she interrupted to call the four year old. Jack paid absolutely no attention to her and continued to watch cartoons on TV.

Mom smiled at us and put a plate of waffles in front of Kevin. "Jack's in day care. I drop him off first. Then I take Kevin to school. He's in the first grade. I'm usually out of here by seven or seven-fifteen. It's so early for them, but what can I do? My husband has to be at work pretty early, so it's up to me to take the kids to school before I go to work."

While Mom was telling us about the nutritious lunch she had just made for her two sons, we made our first "discovery": a disconnection between Mom's verbal reports and the family's breakfast behavior. Kevin left the table. He returned with a bowl of red, white, and blue Trix cereal and milk. Meanwhile, Mom was showing us how she got her kids to eat fresh fruit by mixing it into their yogurt. She paid no attention to Kevin as he ate his cereal.

"Where did you get that?" I asked Kevin, pointing to the cereal.

"From the cabinet, of course," he told me with a puzzled look. He knew I had seen him get the cereal.

"How is it?"

"It makes the milk turn blue." Kevin stirred the cereal in his bowl to demonstrate. The milk turned blue.

"Pretty cool," I noted. "Did your mom buy this for you?"

Kevin looked at me. "Not her. My dad—he likes it, too."

Mom came over to the table and began taking things to the sink. "Oh, that." She pointed to the cereal. "His father buys that," she explained as she picked up Kevin's waffle and ate it, licking the syrup off her fingers. She headed to the dishwasher with Kevin's empty dish and Jack's uneaten waffle.

"Jack, are you ready to go?" she shouted at the living room as she shoved Jack's waffle down the garbage disposal. During the time we were with the Kelly family, we never saw Jack eat anything.

Jack appeared with a blanket wrapped around him. Mom handed him his lunch container and said, "Here, take this and get in the car. You too, Kevin." Mom picked up her car keys. "Well, that's about it," she told us.

Sally and I slowly began to pack up our equipment when the phone rang. Mom ran to the counter and picked it up.

"I'm late," she informed the caller. "Yeah, whole grain waffles, juice, milk. Hey, I've got to go. Talk to you this afternoon."

She hung up and turned to Sally and me. "My mother-in-law," she explained. "Calls almost every morning to see if the kids have had a good breakfast. She thinks I should stay home with the kids. Doesn't think I have time to feed them good food when we're always on the run. What does she know? In her day, she fed her kids (my husband being one of them) bacon and eggs in the morning—cholesterol. Just goes to show you. Hey, I'm watching out for my kids. I'm a good mom."

As Sally and I left the Kelly home, we talked about what we would need to do next. We recognized that spending breakfast at the Kelly home was only a first step in the discovery process. Back at our office we spent hours examining the videotapes and transcripts from this and other breakfast visits, looking for a pattern in what people had told us and what they did. If this were a typical research project, we knew we would probably identify more questions than insights during the first analysis phase. That would mean we would be out "in the field" again at 6:30 in the morning.

From the analysis of our visit to the Kelly home and other breakfast visits, we learned that morning food consumption is not just about the individual decisions that moms make. A network of family and friends is involved in defining what is acceptable and made available for breakfast.

The existence of this network of family and friends was not a surprise. Underlying the rapid ethnographic approach is the understanding that all people belong to one or more networks of interlocking social relationships in which all members share a common or core set of beliefs, values, and behaviors. Anthropologists and other trained ethnographers use various methods to uncover the core sets by

- gathering individual (emic) perspectives from members of these sociocultural groups;
- examining the collected information to identify patterns of shared beliefs, behaviors, values, and rules;
- constructing group "mental models" from identified patterns to understand the meaning at the core of the system;
- interpreting how the members of a sociocultural network use their mental models to construct and express appropriate shared behaviors, beliefs, and values, to provide a contextual frame of meanings for products and services;
- identifying disconnects in the mental model where shared beliefs don't match behavior or where beliefs are not shared or break down, causing points of stress. For example, among the Kelly family adults there was a shared understanding that breakfast is an important meal. What constituted a "good" breakfast, however, was in disagreement and was causing tension in the family.

Because we were interested in placing breakfast in the context of the Kelly family's lives, we continued to follow various Kelly members in the following days. We called Dad at work and conducted a telephone interview. He told us about Saturday morning breakfast with Kevin and about shopping with his kids, buying cereal like the "stuff [he] ate when [he] was a kid." We also arranged to observe at Jack's day care. We were interested in learning whether he ever got anything to eat during the day, and if so, when and what.

We made our second discovery the day we visited Jack's day care. The kids were playing outside. While some of the kids were participating in a teacher-led activity, we found Jack sitting on the grass near the edge of the playground area.

"Hey, Jack, remember us?" I asked, walking over to where he sat.

"Sure, I have to go. Bye."

"Wait, Jack, what are you doing over here anyway?" Sally asked. She had noticed that Jack had his lunch container with him.

"Eating my lunch." Jack looked first at Sally, then me.

"Lunch at ten o'clock in the morning?"

"It's all right, you know—Miss Barbara said it's okay. I got hungry."

Now we knew that something was up. Jack may not have eaten in the early morning, but he could not wait until the school's proscribed lunchtime to eat. The fieldwork with the Kelly family and others confirmed much of the information collected in the focus group. Breakfast time for today's families is very different than the idealized breakfast of the 1950s. Other findings were more unexpected. We certainly didn't expect to see

Mom eat Kevin's breakfast. Nor did we expect to see blue cereal or Jack eating his lunch before lunchtime.

We began to see the whole picture of food consumption in the morning once we constructed shared mental models and a contextual frame for observed behaviors. By doing so, we identified the disconnects between beliefs and behaviors that provided insight about what happened at breakfast, what didn't happen at breakfast, and what happened outside of the home. Although we recognize that we will never be able to actually get inside the heads of the Kelly family, we can infer quite a bit from what moms, dads, and kids told us, and from what we observed.

We began to look at what was common to all the families in the study. We constructed a set of understandings of the food consumption habits of families that put the focus group data in the context of an evolving American family.

Because both moms and dads are working, breakfast in today's American homes is under stress. There really is no time for breakfast. Yet, there is a belief among parents that breakfast is the most important meal of the day, especially for the kids. Kids, we are told, will do better in school and by extension better in life if they eat a good breakfast every morning. Parents are under a lot of pressure to provide their children with a good start to the day and to their future. Although it appears that moms, dads, and their relatives all share the belief that breakfast is the most important meal of the day, they differ about what constitutes a "good" breakfast. For Mom, a good breakfast is whole grain or preservative-free foods. Dads value foods similar to those they had as children. They enjoy sharing these "comfort" foods with their kids although they may not be the nutritional food moms value.

Grandparents are typically more worried about the changing role of moms in the family and more likely to doubt the ability of moms to juggle work and child care. They are not convinced that today's mom can provide the breakfast their grandkids need to succeed in life. However, the foods of a generation ago that the "good mom" provided are not perceived as good by today's standards. As the mom in this story told us, she would never provide a breakfast of cholesterol-laden foods to her kids.

Finally, kids are not cooperating. They may not want to eat so early in the morning. Physiologically, they may not be ready to eat. If they do eat, they want something that has a value to them: blue milk. Getting kids to eat Mom's ideal breakfast is another point of stress.

The opportunities we found during this research were not just about trying to reconcile the differing beliefs about what constitutes a "good" breakfast for moms, dads, kids, and grandmothers. We also looked at the food consumption patterns of all the family members during the day, and it became clear that the "traditional" breakfast time at the beginning of the day might not be the best time to consume food. In fact, most of the family members in our study were not eating breakfast at home. Dad stopped at a convenience store. Mom picked up food where she worked. The kids were eating their lunch at school when they got hungry. Presented with this pattern of food consumption in the morning, it is easy to dismiss the eating at school and work as snacking. But it is not about snacking. It's breakfast; it's about a meal that has culturally proscribed beliefs about its appropriate time, activity, and location.

A deeper look at the food concerns of the family and the behavior using cultural and physical anthropological theory suggests a more pervasive nutritional problem in the American middle class. Selling people another snack food will not solve this problem, even if it is a healthful snack.

The combined information we gathered from the literature and our field studies suggest that Americans are facing a structural conflict. Time pressures are forcing American families to start their day earlier than ever before—so early that, for all intents and purposes, we are still "asleep." Recent studies of sleep cycles among children and teenagers suggest that they need more sleep time. The majority of us are ready to eat and begin our day between 8 and 10 in the morning. By looking for opportunities holistically, we found that the problem was not just about what to eat (breakfast food). It's about the inconsistency between when it is culturally appropriate to eat and when people are ready to eat.

We shared our insights with our client. It considered the evidence and created Go-Gurt. Despite limited distribution, Go-Gurt brought in $37 million in sales in its first year. Two years later, *Newsweek* featured Go-Gurt in a story. The magazine quoted one California mom who said that her child "thinks she's eating a Popsicle for breakfast, but it's better for her" (*Newsweek*, October 11, 1999). Go-Gurt succeeded because it resonates with the kid's need for fun and mobility and the mother's need to provide nutritious food.

DEFINITION RESEARCH

Definition research helps turn a product concept or idea into meaningful form. Rather than trying to figure out if something should be, definition research focuses on just what the thing should do, how it should be used, and how it should communicate its place in the world to consumers and others alike. Therefore, it focuses on finding the use, use features, and meaning to configure a fully featured conceptual prototype.

The methods used in definition research differ from discovery research because we know the parameters of the topic, the concept, and something about the consumers. Furthermore, since all of that is known, we usually start with a series of questions that the consumers and designers have about applications and the meaning that consumers might ascribe to alternative designs that have already been suggested.

Therefore, researchers can dispense with broad-based cultural assessments and focus on the immediate use context, user, and product. Researchers can compare existing products in context to make inferences about how the proposed changes in concept and design might fit into the routine daily lives of their users. This allows the researcher to better understand how the new product might be perceived.

Many of the data collection methods used in discovery research can be used in definition research, too. Rapid ethnographic assessment is also important for definition research. Fieldwork concentrates on observing and eliciting detailed descriptions of activities about specific product or service use. Combining interviewing with videotaping is particularly useful for product exploration. Because definition research is focused on a new concept or idea, interviews are often more structured than in discovery research. They follow a set of well-understood rules that builds rapport in the first segment and then looks for deeper information. Details are summarized at the end of the interview in order to confirm the data with the respondent. Verbal statements are validated through observed actions. Researchers listen for native language—words, terms, and descriptions—to fully understand the use context.

For example, several years ago my colleagues and I worked on a project for a personal care product manufacturer. The goal of the definition research was to understand personal care products in their traditional context—the home—as well as a potentially new context—the office. Personal care products, traditionally reserved for bathroom use, can be redesigned for use in public or office environments. A large manufacturer of personal care products wondered why their customers did not use more of their products during the workday. People need to wash their hands during the day, brush their teeth after lunch, or moisturize their skin in dry office environments, yet most individuals did not engage in these grooming activities. Why? Was there a need for new products for use outside the home?

Many different potential customers might have been included in the research. After a review of market research and extended conversations with our client, we decided to focus on young adults working in an office environment. After learning that the target customers tend to work in bounded social groups, we turned our attention to sampling. We found our participants following strict guidelines so that we would have valid data and not a random collection of anecdotes.

One of the advantages of discovery and definition research is that the relevant cultural patterns can be discerned by doing ethnographic interviews with a relatively small number of customers to learn about the shared understandings and behaviors in a group. Theoretical mathematicians and social scientists suggest that small samples are appropriate for studies of beliefs and behaviors in social networks. Theoretical mathematician Duncan Watts points out that "the world that we live in is not at all random. We are very much constrained by our socioeconomic status, our geographical location, our background, our education and our profession, our interests and hobbies. All these things make our circle of acquaintances highly nonrandom" (Shurman 1998). He and fellow mathematician Steven Strogatz have been examining highly structured social networks to understand and predict membership connectiveness using mathematical formulations. Their work is built on, and extends the work of, the theoretical mathematician Paul Erdise. Erdise has been indirectly responsible for popularizing the idea of six degrees of separation: the idea that only six other individuals link all humankind through their social networks to almost everybody else in the world.

Whereas Watts and Strogatz are most interested in the interconnectiveness of social networks, others such as Borgatti and Everett (1997) among many others (see also *Mathematical Social Sciences* and *Social Networks*) are focusing on the highly nonrandom nature of social networks and devising statistically reliable mathematical formulae to predict the number of individuals who need to be interviewed to capture the shared characteristics of social networks: shared beliefs, values, and behaviors. Using a set of mathematical calculations, Handwerker and Wozniak have suggested the surprisingly low number of seven. This number is reliable only if certain criteria are met.

1. The information gathered is about shared or core understandings within the social network. This is not about group variation.
2. The cognitive domain of the social network is internally consistent and ordered.
3. Information is gathered from key members of the social network: cultural experts.
4. Informants must be interviewed independently of others in their social network. Informants cannot be allowed to confound information by checking or comparing notes with other members of the network.
5. There are no known divisions within the social network: no subgroupings that might have their own set of core knowledge and behaviors (Handwerker and Wozniak 1997).

One way of determining whether one has bounded a social network is by analyzing the patterns that emerge from the data. Highly redundant information about the membership of a group and their perceptions of cultural norms is strong evidence that there is consensus about who is in the group and what they consider appropriate. However, if any of these criteria are not met, one should interview another individual. Once it has been determined that there is consensus, one can put it down as a discovery and move on.

In our case, the stories, activities, and observations we collected during the fieldwork were consistent and clear. Everyone told us that the personal care products on the market were fine and that they would like to use some personal care products during the day. However, everyone also agreed that they could not do so in public view. Most wanted to use personal care products such as toothbrushes but felt they had to do this covertly at work. They all shared a concern that coworkers might see engaging in personal care during the day as "obsessive" and that they would be seen as "weird."

We found that some products are appropriate for "front stage" public space, whereas others are appropriate for "backstage" private space (Goffman 1996). The cultural attitudes about what is appropriate for a backstage or a front stage determined where people could use products. We also discovered that some "backstage" products were finding their way onto the "front stage." The products were not changing. The packaging was.

Hand lotion or tissues, for example, have traditionally been backstage products. In the last few years they have been finding their way into the office in designer containers where they have become acceptable "front stage" products. One solution for personal care products was clear. Repackaging backstage products to fit into a front stage context might make them acceptable in the office environment. We told our client they didn't need a new product concept, just new, context-sensitive packaging for existing products.

EVALUATION RESEARCH

The goal of evaluation research is to learn whether something works. Typically companies perform some sort of evaluation research at the end of a product's development. They do it to (1) validate the product, (2) test customer usability, and (3) refine or "fix" feature details. These goals are fairly consistent with the two main forms of traditional evaluation research done for social programs.

Like rapid ethnographic research, evaluation research has its own history that can be traced back to the middle of the twentieth century. In 1967, Michael Scriven proposed that all evaluation could be broken down into two distinct types, formative and summative evaluation.

The main focus of formative evaluation is to determine how a program or product might be improved. He described it as "evaluation designed, done, and intended to support the process of improvement, and normally commissioned or done by, and delivered to someone who can make improvements" (Scriven 1991: 20). Here evaluation is used to test or validate products.

Summative evaluation answers the question "Assuming the program should be continued, then to what extent?" It is "done for, or by, any observers or decision-makers (by contrast with developers) who need valuative conclusions for any other reasons beside development" (Scriven 1991: 20). In other words, it helps people decide if something is worth continuing. He used this example to explain the difference between formative and summative evaluation. "When the cook tastes the soup, that's formative evaluation; when the guest tastes it, that's summative evaluation."

Although this seems pretty straightforward, a formative/summative evaluation debate is ongoing in American evaluation circles. It has been a central topic at several evaluation conferences, and a whole issue of *Evaluation Practice* (1996, 17: 2) has been devoted to a discussion of formative and summative debate (Patton 1996: 131; Wholey 1996: 145; Chen 1996: 121–130).

I think the distinctions that Scriven makes are valid and useful. For example, a client once asked how a product could be improved. We started by investigating how it might be improved, but our findings led us to change the nature of the question to make recommendations about whether the product was worth purchasing. Thus, formative evaluation can lead to summative evaluation.

Evaluation researchers use a toolbox of methods from many of the social sciences. They are all used to understand "what is" as a baseline, because one must be able to explain what is in order to determine whether or not it's worth continuing or just how it can be improved. Although it does not seem to be widely employed in the industry, evaluative research as conceived of by Scriven is useful for testing a product's usability or how well a service is functioning.

An example should make my point. In December 1994, an information system services division of a large international firm sponsored a study of desktop conferencing. It wanted to know if desktop video conferencing would "work" in their business setting. The four objectives for the study were to

- assess customer opinions of the desktop conferencing concept;
- explore the perceived need for desktop conferencing within the business setting;
- identify current and future uses and users of desktop conferencing; and
- determine those features of desktop conferencing most useful for the firm.

We compared two desktop conferencing products: desktop conferencing with video and desktop conferencing without video. We designed

Figure 6.1
Likelihood that Participants Would Use Desktop Conferencing

our research using three different methods of data collection: (1) direct observation, (2) focus group interviews, and (3) on-line surveys.

By triangulating our methods, we tend to get more robust answers to the many questions we ask.

1. We could see how people interacted with the conferencing product.
2. We learned what they said in directed group conversations.
3. And, we found out what they thought individually.

Ultimately, the multiple data points created by the different methods helped us understand the end user from a variety of perspectives.

We used a "hands-on" simulation to observe participants so we could help them form direct opinions about desktop conferencing and authentic business experience interacting with colleagues. It also provided us with the opportunity to observe participants actually operating the products. We designed the simulation so that twenty-seven pairs of participants interacted. Half used the desktop package with video, and the other half used a platform without video. Each pair explored the desktop conferencing package for about twenty minutes. After participants were comfortable with the software, we asked them to work jointly on a problem of their choice using the whiteboard, a shared work platform that is one of the major components of the software. We videotaped and took notes on their interaction and use of the technology itself.

We supplemented the experiment with a survey and focus group. Surveys make it relatively easy to systematically collect comparable data that we can use immediately to test for statistically valid differences within a sample (see Figure 6.1). The focus groups provide excellent information collection tools for quickly gathering perceptions and opinion shared by a group. Both are based on what people say rather than on direct observations of what they do.

Before beginning the experimental trial, we asked the participants to complete an on-line questionnaire. We designed the questionnaire to measure expectations regarding video conferencing products as well as background information on computer use. We conducted two focus groups each night after the experiment. One consisted of people who had used the product with video. The other included those who did not use video. The focus groups helped us collect additional qualitative data about the viability of desktop conferencing.

Once we finished collecting our data, we began analyzing it. We used qualitative procedures to analyze the direct experimental observations and the focus groups. We used quantitative procedures to analyze the survey data.

We found that regardless of the desktop conferencing package used, the majority of participants believed that desktop conferencing could (1) encourage colleagues to work together more often (72 percent), and (2) improve the quality of communication with both colleagues (84 percent) by "allow(ing) for greater sharing of information between offices," and by providing "quicker, more effective communication." The majority of participants said they preferred a desktop conferencing package that contained a video window. Seventy-five percent of those who used the video package and 65 percent of those who did not have a video option said they would prefer video. "It would make the communication more personal," noted a nonvideo user.

Although all participants responded positively to the concept of video-enhanced desktop conferencing, only 33 percent of those who used the desktop package with video reported that it actually enhanced communication. Video and nonvideo users disagreed about the benefits to collaboration. Nonvideo users were more likely to respond "yes" in statistically significant higher numbers ($p < .05$) when asked if desktop conferencing would encourage working with colleagues than video users (Figure 6.2). The video users were far more likely to answer "not sure."

Video and nonvideo users also disagreed about the value of communication. Nonvideo desktop conferencing users reported that their ability to communicate was enhanced more often than video users.

The focus groups and questionnaires told us what people said. We juxtaposed that information with our own observational data and found a strong discrepancy between what people told us and what they did. We observed that almost all the participants who used the video turned off their camera or eliminated the video window from their screen within the first ten minutes of the simulation. Those who actually had an opportunity to use video conferencing became somewhat disillusioned with it.

Figure 6.2
Response Rates for the Utility of Desktop Conferencing

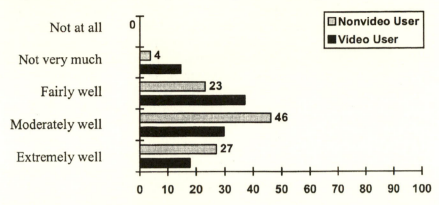

The discrepancy between the perceived value of desktop video conferencing and its observed functionality may be in part caused by the pervasive belief in new and cutting-edge technology that is a core value within the organizational culture of the study participants. Recent research in the culture of organizations suggests that "cultural meanings are not only in people's heads: rather they are ideas that are shared by social actors. They occur between, as well as in them. In this sense, cultural meanings have some public manifestations and therefore must be somewhat observable" (Trice and Beyer 1993: 43). In this case, that cultural process manifests itself in the participants' stated preference for the technological superiority of video conferencing.

Furthermore, the belief in new and cutting-edge technology is strong enough that participants continued to hold those beliefs even after they disabled the video feature. When this was later brought to their attention, they indicated that they had not been aware of their behavior and continued to believe that video contributed to the quality of their communication.

The desktop conferencing evaluation provides significant information about the uses of desktop conferencing technology in business organizations. Although there is a strong, positive perception for a video option in desktop conferencing, the majority of participants did not use the video option when given the opportunity. As a result of our formative evaluative research, the firm decided not to purchase desktop video conferencing for the organization.

We demonstrated a principle that is well known to any evaluation researcher and those doing international development work: One must consider the influence of the shared cultural values and beliefs of the organization to evaluate whether or not specific products or policies can and should be introduced (see also Keeney 1994).

CONCLUSION

Although the research platforms and methods discussed in this chapter have immense potential, they will succeed only if our cultural analyses are translated into meaningful products and services. Such a translation necessitates multidisciplinary teams of researchers (analyzers) and designers (creators) to take an idea from discovery to reality.

"The things humankind makes and uses at any particular time and place are probably the truest representation we have of values and meaning within a society. The study of things, material culture, is thus capable of piercing interdisciplinary boundaries and brings forward meaningful discussions and interactions among . . . many disparate fields. No one denies the importance of things, but learning from them requires rather more attention than reading texts" (Kingery 1996: ix).

REFERENCES

Beebe, J. 1995. Basic Concepts and Techniques of Rapid Appraisal. *Human Organization* 54 (1): 42–51.

Bennett, F.J. 1995. Qualitative and Quantitative Methods: In-depth or Rapid Assessment? *Social Science and Medicine* 40 (12): 1589–1590.

Bernard, H.R. 1998. Introduction: On Method and Methods in Cultural Anthropology. In *Handbook of Methods in Cultural Anthropology*, edited by H.R. Bernard. Walnut Creek, CA: Alta Mira Press.

Borgatti, S., and M.G. Everett. 1997. Network Analysis of 2-mode Data, *Social Networks* 19 (3): 243–269.

Chambers, R. 1983. Rapid Appraisal for Improving Existing Canal Irrigation Systems. *Discussion Paper Series* No. 8. New Delhi, India: Ford Foundation.

Chen, H. 1996. *Evaluation Practice* 17 (2): 121–130.

Collinson, M. 1981. A Low Cost Approach to Understanding Small Farmers. *Agricultural Administration* 8: 463–471.

Csordas, T. 1992. Anthropology's Integrity as a Research Discipline. *Medical Anthropology Quarterly* 6 (4): 394–400.

Galt, D. 1985. "How Rapid Rural Appraisal and Other Socio-Economic Diagnostic Techniques Fit into the Cyclic FSR/E Process." Paper presented at the International Conference on Rapid Rural Appraisal, Khon Kaen, Thailand.

Goffman, E. 1996. *The Presentation of Self in Everyday Life*. Garden City, NY: Doubleday.

Guyton, W. 1992. *Guidelines for Marketing Information Needs Assessments (MINAs): AMIS Project*. Quezon City, Philippines: Abt Associates.

Handwerker, W.P., and D. Wozniak. 1997. Sampling Strategies for the Collection of Anthropological Data: An Extension of Boaz's Answer to Galton's Problem. *Current Anthropology* 38(5): 869–875.

Heath, R.P. 1997. Seeing is Believing. *Marketing Tools* (March): 4–9.

Higginbothom, N. 1994. Capacity Building for Health in a Social Science: The International Clinical Epidemiology Network, Social Science Program and

International Forum for Social Science in Health. *Acta Tropica* 57 (2/3): 23–137.

Hildebrand, P. 1982. Summary of the Sondeo Methodology Used by ICTA. In *Farming Systems Research and Development: Guidelines for Developing Countries*, edited by W.W. Shaner, P.F. Philipp, and W.R. Schmehl. Boulder: Westview.

Honadle, G. 1979. Rapid Reconnaissance Approaches to Organizational Analysis for Development Administration. Paper presented at the RRA Conference, at the Institute of Development Studies, University of Sussex, Brighton.

Keeney, R. 1994. Creativity in Decision Making with Value-Focused Thinking. *Sloan Management Review* 35 (summer).

Kingery, W., ed. 1996. Editor's preface to *Learning from Things: Method and Theory of Material Culture Studies*, edited by W.D. Kingery. Washington, DC: Smithsonian Institution Press.

Leonard, D., and J. Rayport. 1997. Spark Innovation through Empathic Design. *Harvard Business Review* (November-December) 102–113.

Lieber, R. 1997. Storytelling: A New Way to Get Close to Your Customer. *Fortune*, February: 3.

Manderson, L., and B. Aaby. 1992. An Epidemic in the Field? Rapid Assessment Procedures and Health Research. *Social Science and Medicine* 35 (7): 839–850.

Manderson, L., A. Almedom, J. Gittelsohn, D. Helitzer-Allen, and P. Pelto. 1996. Transferring Anthropological Techniques in Applied Research. *Practicing Anthropology* 18: 33–35.

Newsweek, By Loosing the Spoon, General Mills Wins Big. October 11, 1999.

Patton, M. 1996. *Evaluation Practice* 17 (2): 131–144.

Rhoades, R.E. 1982. The Art of the Informal Agricultural Survey. (Training Document 1982–2.) Lima, Peru: Social Sciences Department, International Potato Center.

Scriven, M. 1991. Beyond Formative and Summative Evaluation. In *Evaluation and Education: At Quarter Century*, edited by G.W. McLaughlin and D.C. Phillips. Chicago: University of Chicago Press.

Shaner, W.W., P.F. Philipp, and W.R. Schmehl. 1982. *Farming Systems Research and Development: Guidelines for Developing Countries*. Boulder: Westview.

Shurman, Polly. 1998. From Muhammad Ali to Grandma Rose. In *Discover*, Dec.: 85–89.

Squires, S. 1999. Rapid Ethnographic Assessment, American Breakfast and the Mother-in-law. Paper presented at the American Anthropology Association meetings, Chicago.

Sunderland, P. 1999. Glancing Possibilities: Three Weeks to Understand the Nature of Family Life in the United States. Paper presented at the American Anthropology Association meetings, Chicago.

Trice, H., and J.M. Beyer. 1993. *The Cultures of Work Organizations*. Englewood Cliffs, NJ: Prentice Hall.

Trotter, R., and J. Schensul. 1999. Methods in Applied Anthropology. In *Handbook of Methods in Cultural Anthropology*, edited by H.R. Bernard. Walnut Creek, CA: Alta Mira Press.

Van Arsdale, P. 1996. Ethnography, the Life Course, and the Use of Event Calendars: A Research Note. *Cultural Anthropology Methods* 8 (3): 11–12.

Werner, O. 1995. Short Take 15: The Case for Verbatim Cases. *Cultural Anthropology Methods* 7 (1): 6–8.

Wholey, J. 1996. Formative and Summative Evaluation: Related Issues in Performance Measurement. *Evaluation Practice* 17 (2): 145–149.

7

A Client's Perspective on User-Centered Design

George Walls

Ethnography and social science had little meaning for me until mid-1997, when I began a journey from neophyte to advocate. This chapter draws on those experiences to address several issues. First, internal product developers and marketers face an impasse or chasm of misunderstanding between each other and between customers. Social science represents one possible bridge over the chasm. Second, as with any new activity, there is a learning curve. Chronicling my first experience with social scientists should provide some perspective on us novices. Third, I outline the process of successful projects. The case studies show how social scientists who interact with marketers and new product developers can uncover unarticulated needs, develop ideas to meet those needs, and define a product for development. Finally, once an organization identifies a core skill, most will try to internalize it. To illustrate this, I summarize another development project in which the management used some of the anthropological concepts and ethnographic lessons on their own.

My functional background is largely in sales and marketing with three assignments in product development. The most recent position was director of product innovation at Laerdal Medical Corporation. As one of five reporting to the CEO, I directed all aspects of new product development through four development teams. Product innovation included several teams: medical device development, multimedia software development, and product managers. My professional experience includes na-

Table 7.1
Primary Foci of Product Developers and Marketers

Concept	Product Development	Marketing
Planning Horizon	Quarters and years	Months and quarters
Proper Marketing Input	Customer problems	Perspectives and insights
Priority of Development	Top priority	Second or third (at best)
Reward System	Project performance	Product line performance

tional accounts and sales management, product management, marketing, and senior management. Aside from my own personal experience, I have kept up with relevant literature (see Reis 1999; Heiman and Sanchez 1998; Leonard and Rayport 1997) and attended executive training sessions such as those offered by the Management Roundtable (1999) and the Product Development Management Association (1999) whenever possible. This breadth is what led the CEO to ask me to create and lead a fully integrated, cradle-to-grave product management and development department. He wanted customer-driven product development and reasoned that no one knew the mind of the customer better than a former salesperson.

One of the fundamental problems I had to surmount was the fact that marketers and product developers are essentially two subcultures with very different viewpoints (see Table 7.1). If product developers are focused on product development within the time span of quarters, if not years, then marketers are interested in shorter time horizons and are far less interested in developing new products than they are in selling those that already exist. Furthermore, product developers want to know what problems consumers are trying to solve so they can design new products, whereas marketers are primarily interested in learning things about their current customers. These fundamental differences create a cultural schism that causes poor communication, misunderstanding, and the conflicts they engender.

We learned that ethnographic research can help the marketers and product developers resolve some of these conflicts. An experienced consultant can help bridge the internal subcultures (development and marketing) and thereby, boost the chances that all those involved will leverage their differences to learn about customers and markets.

THE BEGINNING

Early in a project to develop a new CPR manikin, a conflict between developers and marketers arose that revealed a need for a deeper, and perhaps new, understanding of our customers. Though complicated at the time, in retrospect, the conflict was simple. Marketing wanted a new manikin that met a general specification (size, weight, and cost). Development wanted to know what user problems the new model would solve.

In this particular case, the developers would not compromise their request for full and complete information, and for good reason. About five years earlier the same team had developed a manikin at the same general price point. Although it won a major design award, it failed in the marketplace. The designers' question to marketing was, "What has changed?" They wanted to know what new information we had uncovered about the customer, distribution channels, or markets that would drive the definition of the product and marketing program, and ultimately would drive market success.

A series of discussions led our design and development director to request permission to contact consultancies that could help us sort out the dilemma. After several passes, the field was narrowed to three. Prior to the first meeting with a consultancy, no one in marketing or senior management understood why the developers were so intransigent or what benefit qualitative research could possibly provide. A mixture of consultant assertiveness, humoring the developers, and a scheduling opportunity led to the first meeting between our management team and the consultants.

In his first meeting with Laerdal's senior managers, a representative from GVO, a product design company in Palo Alto, California, spent an hour trying to explain ethnography. We did not get it. At the end of the session, he issued a challenge. "Think of the impossible mission. What market is impenetrable? What goals are unattainable? Which of these impossible tasks will make the biggest difference?" After a short time, one of the board members said quietly that perhaps we should explore teaching cardiopulmonary resuscitation (CPR) in public schools. In hindsight, all agreed that the project was obvious. However, it took another hour of discussion before our glazed eyes gave way to excitement.

We created a multidisciplinary team to figure out why CPR training was not already in schools, and then to figure out how we might encourage it. The project involved three ethnographers and ten representatives from a client organization with which we were partnering. To succeed, the ethnographers had to learn about Laerdal, CPR, and our partners. Much of the work that Laerdal, the American Heart Association, the American Red Cross, and others have done over the last forty years emphasized universal CPR. CPR is one of several therapies used in combination with one another to reverse sudden cardiac death. The other therapies are early defibrillation and early advanced cardiac life support. Together with early recognition of signs and symptoms and activation of 911 (early access), these are known as the "chain of survival." Out-of-hospital studies have shown that with strong chain-of-survival, patient survival rates from sudden cardiac death can be elevated from around 1 percent to as much as 40 percent.

One of the pioneering emergency medical systems, Seattle's Medic One, began an outreach to the community about thirty years ago. The result is that every graduate of Seattle high schools completes a course in CPR. Seattle now enjoys the highest rate of citizen CPR in the world, which has led some to observe that it is safer to have a heart attack in the streets of Seattle than in the lobby of most U.S. hospitals. Given Seattle's success, one would think that every U.S. high school student learns CPR as part of his or her curriculum. Not so. Despite the best and continuing efforts of the American Heart Association, American Red Cross, Citizens CPR Foundation, National Parent Teacher's Association, state legislatures, local EMS agencies, and local school districts, CPR was far from universal. Clearly, something was missing.

The team's goal, then, was to figure out why CPR wasn't taught in all schools, and to recommend ways to boost its appeal. The team and ethnographers developed a strong bond, partly because they had to rely on each other's skill sets to succeed. The program led to a jovial rapport and healthy professional respect for one another's professions and unique contributions. The team reviewed the literature on education, CPR training, and teens before heading out to conduct interviews with educators and students across the country. We learned that any educational program mandated from the top downward, whether by legislatures or boards, is bound to fail unless it has a built-in, internal constituency. CPR education must be so compelling for students and teachers alike that *they* institutionalize it. Otherwise, any mandatory CPR program, worthy as it may be, will lose the battle for funding and attention against the competing priorities of academics, sports, and extracurricular activities.

This insight eluded some of the best health, education, scientific, and business minds in the world for more than thirty years. This insight further led the team to identify a way to boost CPR education nationwide. I use the term "identify" because the researchers uncovered the fact that a successful method of institutionalizing CPR education had evolved independently in schools spread throughout the United States. None of the organizers from the independent programs knew each other. Having learned how and why we needed to institutionalize CPR programs, we declared the project a success. Laerdal and its partner are now undertaking a pilot program to institutionalize CPR programs.

The project taught the Laerdal team several lessons about consumer-driven product development. First, seemingly impossible problems make good projects because there is general agreement that a problem exists.

Table 7.2
Twelve Business Risk Factors

Market	Customer Preferences	Customer Positioning
Category	Corporate Competition	Sales Skills
Product Regulations	Product Benefits	Promotional Campaigns
Product	Distribution Channels	Price Points

Second, problems may be market *or* product oriented. That is, companies should not concentrate just on product development. In some circumstances, companies may find that market programs may actually be more effective than products. We also learned that the lessons the team learns may be counterintuitive from everybody's point of view. In many cases, not even the ethnographers can predict their findings or the resulting product and market programs.

WHY SHOULD BUSINESSES EMBRACE SOCIAL SCIENTISTS?

As you might have gathered from the case study, social scientists can certainly contribute by discovering consumer needs, perceptions, and motivations, and offering alternative ways to approach a tough problem. So, to answer the question "Why would businesses embrace social scientists?" the answer is, to increase profit and/or reduce risk.

Risk implies a tension between the likely costs and benefits among alternatives. In general, risk is defined as the degree to which one may not be able to predict, let alone control, events. All product development projects carry a certain amount of risk for the companies and the professionals who participate. Some risks are related to business, others to individual team members. Some risks are measured quantitatively, others qualitatively. Different kinds of risk factors can be measured in either qualitative or quantitative terms (see Table 7.2).

In general, the more one knows about each risk factor, the better one is able to generate alternative options and to predict their outcome. It follows that companies that focus on their existing competencies and "known" variables minimize the uncertainty, and thus, the risk of product development. Those that venture into unfamiliar situations increase their risk.

There are many ways to think about the degree of product innovation. For our purposes, the simplest distinction is the most effective. Breakthrough products are new kinds of things, usually the first of their kind. Derivatives are simply copies or next year's model. By definition derivatives descend from other, similar products. Breakthroughs tend to inspire competitors to develop close copies that are in fact derivatives in their own right. For example, the first Xerox photocopier and Apple personal computers were breakthrough products. They established new product categories and had no direct competitors when they first appeared. They entered the American marketplace and lexicon. Now copiers and PCs are both commonplace and their companies face stiff competition throughout the world.

There is a simple, direct relationship between risk and innovation. The more innovative something is, the riskier the investment. The reason is that innovative risks involve higher costs of development in highly uncertain, often unprecedented markets and/or product categories. Breakthrough products are essentially high risk because they involve both high costs and uncertainty. In contrast, derivative products mean lower costs and uncertainty. For example, think of a pharmaceutical company that tinkers with the taste of children's aspirin. Presumably, the company already knows what children like. Sweet is in. Sour, unless it is grotesquely sour, is out. The company's product development team already knows parents' price sensitivity. And they have well-established distribution channels into grocery stores, department stores, and pharmacies. Since they know and control all of these risk factors, the changes pose little risk to either the company or the individual project team members. Little ventured, little gained. In comparison, imagine that same company developing and commercializing the world's first genetically engineered vaccine against influenza. That is far more innovative and far riskier. The company would have to create and market an unknown product, offer a new set of benefits, establish a new customer base (doctors, not parents), create new distribution channels in hospitals and clinical trials, and set new price points. It also brings significantly increased regulatory risk, the added time of clinical tests, and the possibility that governments will nationalize the formula with little or no compensation. Like any breakthrough product, it is bound to have higher development costs and demand a longer time between the day the vaccine was first imagined and the day it was released in the market. In addition, it is bound to have a much slower, nonlinear adoption rate in the market. Its high costs and drawn-out revenue schedule may not justify the investment.

All things being equal, the less risk the better. In stable markets, it is usually safer for managers to make minor changes to existing products and release them at new price points. However, all things are rarely equal and markets are almost never stable. That is certainly the case now. Technology and consumer needs are incredibly dynamic. Companies sweep in and out of markets with unprecedented speed. Communication is virtually instantaneous. Executives assume their competitors are on their heels or ahead of them. And consumers are incessantly shopping for the best deals; brand loyalty, though still a factor, has never been weaker. Therefore, everybody in business today is compelled to take greater product development risks than they might have twenty years ago. Under today's economic conditions, companies that do not innovate don't last long.

Given this relationship between innovation and risk, it should be no surprise that product development managers ask a number of risk-related questions at the beginning of every project.

• What is the chance the project will fail?
• What is the chance it will succeed?
• If it succeeds, what is the chance we can implement the consumer research findings?
• If it fails, what is the chance of a "career-limiting event"?

They also ask some pointed return-on-investment oriented questions such as

• What is the most likely return on investment?
• Can we use the results to make money?
• Will the findings provide a competitive advantage?
• What career enhancing results (for the manager and team members) are likely?

Team members who ask these risk assessment questions should not be thought of as uncaring or alienated. If anything, they strive to outdo themselves. Being consumers themselves, product developers and marketers truly admire exceptional products and services. Indeed, they are probably even more sensitive to quality than other consumers. It should be no surprise that team members feel heartbroken and personally rejected when "their" products and services "fail" or are criticized.

Marketing literature often call products that don't sell "product failures." I disagree with the term. Products do not fail. They cannot; they are inanimate, and therefore, cannot think or act for themselves. It is far more likely that the project teams fail to devise a solution compelling enough to motivate senior managers, manufacturers, vendors, and/or consumers. Although market failures may still occur for external, and often, unpredictable reasons such as changes in technology or laws, teams that do their homework are far more likely to see their products succeed than those that do not.

Managers and project team members do two things to set an acceptable level of risk and to define an appropriate direction for product development. First, because some risk factors are more important than others, the team can select which "unknowns" to target. Second, they convert those "unknowns" into 'knowns." Teams tend to achieve the greatest reductions in the overall risk of their projects while leaving opportunities for innovation by tightly focusing on the most important risk factors.

Both tasks are important. Together, they can mean the difference between launching a derivative product and launching a new company. Introducing an existing product into a new channel of distribution or a new product into an existing channel is less risky than doing both on the same project. Let me give you an example. Several years ago, Laerdal Medical Corp. finished developing two products that it "inherited" in an acquisition. The products were clearly breakthroughs; we had the clinical tests and peer-design awards to prove it. But customers didn't buy them. We conducted an internal project assessment and found that the products did not sell because they did not fit Laerdal's established strategy channels. The products did not fail. We failed to realize that we had to modify our distribution channels to launch the breakthrough products. Once we learned this lesson, our teams incorporated "channel-matching" tasks into their product development projects. Over the course of several projects, we learned that launching a breakthrough product and developing a new distribution channel were not mistakes in and of themselves. The mistake was inadvertently doing both at the same time. That is tantamount to launching a new company. The lesson is clear. If you launch the equivalent of a new company, plan accordingly. Project managers minimize these mistakes by carefully matching the risk level to corporate strategy and then focusing on the most important risk factors.

Companies usually hire ethnographers when their managers are compelled to assume greater degrees of risk in search of higher returns from breakthrough products. Consequently, ethnographers are most likely to participate in projects when the team members are most uncomfortable. Everybody faces relatively high risks and uncertainty. Therefore, the principal decision makers must clearly communicate that high risk/high payoff is the strategy, and then everyone must resist the urge to minimize personal and corporate risk by limiting the scope of innovation. Fortunately, the high-risk conditions also mean that team members might be more willing to experiment by working with ethnographers.

By its very nature, ethnographic research compels the entire project team to consider the perspectives of each team member as well as those of consumers. Ethnographers help the team define exactly what is and is not known. Then, together with the other team members, they go on to discover tangible customer needs, some of which may be unarticulated, and communicate them in a way that all the team members can understand. At that point, marketers can evaluate research results and

Figure 7.1
Project Schema

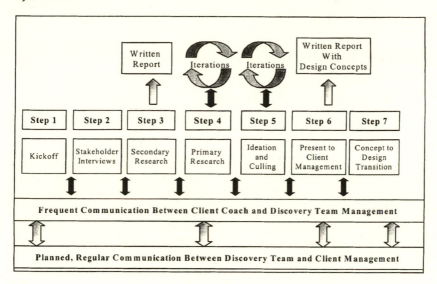

help define the direction of a product. The developers work with the marketers to set that direction, and then go on to turn product development directions into viable product designs. The entire team reconvenes at specific points to reassess the projects. At each point, they can either stop or proceed to the next phase.

In a sense, by incorporating ethnographers into the process, the team circumvents the polar cultural conflict between marketers and developers. By reframing what both perceive as reality, they help marketers and developers communicate and develop products based on a stronger understanding of the intended consumers and the problems they wish to address. This simple change in the team's internal dynamics turns the multiple points of view from a disadvantage to an advantage. It fosters rather than stifles innovation while muting risk. However, a caveat is in order. The ethnographers have to be very careful about how *they* interact with the team members because they bring in their own goals and biases.

ANATOMY OF CLIENT ENGAGEMENT PROJECTS

Over the past few years, Laerdal's product development teams and GVO devised a project procedure with seven project steps plus a project preparation on the front end and a postproject review on the back (see Figure 7.1). The seven project steps are (1) kickoff, (2) stakeholder interviews, (3) secondary research, (4) primary research, (5) ideation and culling, (6) presentation, and (7) transition to a subsequent phase in product development. Obviously, there are many alternative ways to outline the first phase of product development programs. Each company's processes will probably follow a slightly different path.

Preproject Preparation

Projects don't just happen. They are defined and planned. Corporations and the consultancies they might work with must address five issues in every project: (1) project leadership, (2) team building, (3) goals and expectations, (4) communications, and (5) resources. All of these affect the level of risk. Project managers must confront all of these interdependent issues simultaneously. For example, project managers must develop project teams that can handle the increased risk that innovation demands. Some professionals thrive in risky, highly uncertain conditions, whereas others wither. Some like the big picture, whereas others concentrate on the details. Some are comfortable with their current positions, whereas others are striving to advance through the ranks. Ideally, the team members will balance each other's strengths and weaknesses and points of view.

Every project requires a champion, preferably a senior executive. The champion is the link between the internal project team members, an internal reference group of senior executives, and the consultants, if any. The champion represents the project team (including consultants) to a reference group that has oversight authority. The group should include representatives from all the corporate divisions that the project team must engage to bring the product into development. Ideally, there should be at least one vice president representing manufacturing, sales, and marketing divisions as well as an expert from the field sales organization. The champion mentors the team members so as to help them avoid political mistakes.

Additionally, the champion acts as a coach, mentor, or advocate for the consultancy. The champion begins by working directly with consultants of equal or higher decision-making authority. Thus, a vice president or a product manager from the client organization negotiates, organizes, oversees, and reviews projects with the principals or project managers from the consultancy. Each is responsible for their respective employees and organizations. Together they define the client's goals and set the project objectives. That should enable them to create explicit criteria to evaluate the project. The consultancies use those discussions to formulate a proposal that the champion can evaluate, often against those submitted by competing consultancies. The proposals should clearly create solid expectations about team member skills, work process, schedules, methods, tools, deliverables (even their formats), locations, and resources. The proposal clearly outlines mutual expectations between the client and consultancy, measures of quality, and the criteria for determining successful completion of each step.

The project proposal often sets the parameters for the team's creative efforts. Most people bridle against constraints, believing that these limit creativity. I have found just the opposite to be true, but only when the constraints set direction or screening criteria. In other words, if you want to challenge creative people, put constraints on their options, and within those constraints provide complete creative freedom. For example, in one of Laerdal's programs with GVO, the project managers and champion imposed five constraints to establish the parameters, scope, and goals of the product team. These were as follows:

1. The product must save lives: the more, the better.
2. It must represent a new, discontinuous product category. (In other words, it had to include new patentable technology and new applications for existing technologies. Moreover, it had to be sufficiently novel that Laerdal would be recognized as the first-to-market in a new product category).
3. The product must fit tightly enough into our core product set and market channels that sellers can simply include it in their existing sales calls and presentations.
4. The product must perform a specific lifesaving function.
5. The product must meet explicit financial criteria.

The multidisciplinary team composed of Laerdal and GVO employees had to work within these constraints. There were four industrial designers and three marketers from Laerdal. Although GVO's team members varied by phase, an engineer and ethnographer largely handled the earliest phases. When an entire team goes through the process described below, the project is more likely to be successful. In fact, the team generated more than forty ideas that we could pursue and many more that we could not. At this writing, several product initiatives are under way that promise to be significant contributions to Laerdal's mission of helping to save lives. The trick we learned was to provide enough direction so the team could succeed without having to propose a new business, establish a different distribution channel, or require massive marketing efforts.

Step One: Kickoff Meeting

Kickoff meetings initiate projects. Their purpose is to introduce the team members, review the project goals and schedule, and allocate work. Since, to some extent, the risk tolerances for the company have already been determined by the time the project is planned, project leaders must explain to the assembled audience why the group seeks breakthrough products rather than derivatives. Managers who are just introducing the ethnographic approach of consumer-driven research and product development should take the opportunity to carefully explain the entire process to everyone. They must explain what consumer-driven research is. It follows that they have to explain how and why they will use research techniques more closely identified with traditional community ethnography (interviews, participant observation, etc.) than with traditional business and quantitative market methods (focus groups, telephone surveys, market segmentation reports). Many team members will be uncomfortable leaving the relative familiarity and safety of the conference room for the field and shifting from statistical analyses toward more qualitative analyses. I've found that it helps to explain that qualitative field research is a great way to figure out which questions to ask. Quantitative survey techniques are great to answer just how prevalent something is. Lastly, the project managers should make sure that the team members understand that the consultants need the insights and skills of the company employees. Consultants may have ethnographic and social science training, but it is unreasonable to expect that they know everything about the business and market.

Step Two: Stakeholder Interviews and Analysis

The stakeholder interviews and analysis is vital because it helps the team achieve several critical objectives. By interviewing all the project participants and some of the other executives (principally from the reference group), consultants can (1) build a common understanding and set of expectations, (2) become more knowledgeable about the client's corporate culture, market, and product category, (3) establish trust and project buy-in, (4) spot risk factors and establish tolerances levels, and (5) create directions for market research and ideation. By fulfilling these objectives, stakeholder interviews and analyses can turn the unstable foundation I mentioned at the beginning of this chapter into a solid platform for innovation.

My own appreciation of the stakeholder interviews and analyses comes through personal experience. We did a stakeholder interview and analysis with GVO in our first project. Some of the team members and most managers initially criticized the confidential interviews as a waste of time and money. After all, the objective was to be sure that we were "all on the same page." Senior managers claimed that everything everyone needed to know was in the project proposal. Middle managers thought it might be interesting, nothing more. Team members were suspicious and, fearing the interviewers might have ulterior motives, often asked to speak off the record.

To everybody's surprise, the stakeholder analysis demonstrated that no one was "on the same page." In some cases, we were not even reading from the same book! Everyone had a different perspective on the project's challenge and its likely outcome. Ironically, in a group where professional differences might present insurmountable cultural differences, the divergent perspectives became the team's greatest source of creative strength. By documenting the client team members' perspectives in a nonthreatening way, the consultants helped our own product developers, marketers, and senior executives come to consensus about the project's goals, means, and evaluative standards.

Just as importantly, the analysis revealed some of the critical questions that product developers and marketers ask that might otherwise have gone unanswered. As I learned later, some of the product developers wanted to learn more about how the contexts in which consumers live and work shape their use of existing products; in other words, they wanted to know more about the customer's use models. In contrast, marketers were especially interested in the process by which customers made purchase decisions. That information, often omitted in traditional research reports, could help the marketers create effective distribution channels, or at least make sure the existing distribution channels were compatible with the eventual breakthrough products. Together, questions like these represent some of the critical issues that both product developers and marketers have to attend to if they are to collaborate effectively.

Although it was not really the initial purpose, the stakeholder analysis also helped us establish a benchmark of our existing knowledge of the risk factors, formulate theories, and allocate work responsibilities. The stakeholder analyses revealed a wide array of observations and ideas. They essentially identified the risk factors that the team considered important. Those findings immediately reduced the risk of product development by finding out what the individual team members knew that might not be common knowledge. They also provided the objective basis for a knowledge baseline: anything not included in the stakeholder analyses but found in the literature and field constituted "new" findings. Both the "knowns" and the questions helped the team formulate tentative, competing theories about the market and consumers. Those theories naturally suggested ways we could adjust our original research design and schedule. In the process, we discovered new strengths and professional ambitions among our own team members. We considered those when allocating work responsibilities so that the project became an opportunity for personal and professional growth.

The stakeholder analysis clarified some obscure points about the communication and decision-making processes that we would use to move the project along. For example, we clarified the communication process between the client and consulting team members. One of the reasons the stakeholder analysis was successful was that the consultants previewed their findings with the project champion before releasing it to the rest of the team or the reference group. That simple step helped keep the analysis on track. The champion helped the consultants minimize political blunders, breaches of etiquette, and confusing statements. Meanwhile, the consultants demonstrated that they could be trusted with sensitive information; they were not going to betray the company or the team members.

Step Three: Secondary Research

Secondary research is bound to vary across industries. In the medical devices industry, secondary research must include literature searches and expert interviews. The research might include market segmentation reports, product competition benchmarking, patent searches, and interviews with medical researchers and physicians about best practices and controversies. The investigations help reduce risk by gathering and organizing existing information about risk factors. Again, the end product of the secondary research step is a concise document that spells out what we learned and what it implies for the team's ultimate aim, a breakthrough product. Again, the champion should preview and edit a draft or two before releasing it to the entire group. The group then discusses it and decides upon the course of action.

Often, the secondary research constitutes the first chance to test the theories that the team members formulated during the kickoff meeting and stakeholder analysis. It is really not too important that a specific theory be supported. It's more important that the team thoroughly understands and prioritizes risk factors so the team can improve on ideas that will be put to the test during the next stage of research.

Step Four: Primary Research

Project teams are far more likely to create breakthrough products if they make new discoveries about risk factors. Thus they should carefully reconsider customer market segments, product lines, distribution channels, and price points as well as their relationships. If the purpose of secondary research is to reconsider existing knowledge, then the purpose of primary research is to make new discoveries.

Ideally, the project team will design the primary research based on lessons drawn in the previous steps because those findings will help determine the most appropriate qualitative and quantitative techniques for data collection, management, and analysis. Normally, however, project plans cannot be so open ended. The project goals, schedule, budget, and the skill base of the client and consultant teams have to be considered. Typically, design firms and client companies think of ethnography as being a process of qualitative research that emphasizes contextual interviews, participant observation, guided tours, and videographic documentation.

The field teams themselves should be multidisciplinary and include individuals from both the client and consulting firms. The reason, as is stressed throughout this book, is that the team leverages the talents of the individuals and firms. The consultants provide clients with a fresh perspective, and perhaps research and design skills that are not available internally. Meanwhile, the clients provide the in-depth industry knowledge and skills that the consultancy might lack. The individuals from both organizations conduct the fieldwork precisely because they will lend their own perspectives to situations and people (especially consumers). The lessons they glean from their work with consumers and their own conversations throughout the period inevitably identify consumer needs, marketing tactics, and design approaches for later development.

Several other benefits grow out of the collaboration of individuals across corporate boundaries. First, the client team members who participate are more likely to understand the project process and feel more responsible for the lessons they learn. In other words, they take the work personally. Second, by doing multidisciplinary field research, the team members are more likely to develop a common understanding of the methodology and results. They should be able to explain and defend the work to skeptics. A third benefit is that the team members can draw upon their own experiences during the creative and culling phases of the project. They will all have insights into particular aspects of the research. Fourth, all of these benefits make it possible to reduce the amount of documentation. Since the project teams participated, they should not require an extensive written report. The comprehensive report itself is nearly impossible to create under the constraints (time and money) in which businesses typically operate. It is too time consuming, expensive, and potentially so unwieldy that it would lose its meaning. As the saying goes, "There is no substitute for being there." Proper context enables clients to more fully understand recommendations and more intelligently select from alternatives. Clients can also add their perspective to ideation sessions and stimulate more and better ideas. Ultimately, the team's work will be much easier if all of the individuals participate in the research, ideation, and culling because they will share the background, motivation, and sense of responsibility for the project.

Step Five: Ideation and Culling

Ideation and culling are, respectively, the most enjoyable and painful activities in the entire project. Ideation is essentially the process of generating a lot of ideas about products. Culling is the process of selectively eliminating ideas based on qualitative and quantitative business and development criteria.

Ideation sessions are structured. If the team has conducted some research, then the researchers should develop a model highlighting various risk factors and lessons which, when combined through some compelling argument or story, serves as a springboard for discussion. The subsequent sessions are devoted to either structured or freewheeling brainstorming. Although the brainstorming sessions are fun, for some liberating, they have to be fairly focused on the stated project goals and the lessons derived from the research.

Keep in mind that ideation is frustrating for many people who prefer linear, quantitative work processes, if not outright formulas. Ideation is not linear. The group utilizes qualitative data, an oxymoron for linear or quantitative thinkers. Lessons and ideas are often represented as a set of seemingly unconnected data points such as photos, quotes, and researcher observations. The process of uncovering previously unrecognized relationships, paradigms, and insights moves at an inconsistent and often random pace.

As ideas begin to emerge, they are often as flashes of insight. In his book *Six Thinking Hats* (1999), Edward DeBono explores what he calls "green hat thinking." The objective is to create "movement" by exploring ideas in a nonadversarial manner. Exploration without destruction is one path to intuitive leaps. Remember that in ideation, there are no dumb ideas. In fact, the bridge to brilliance may be built with dumb ideas.

Toward the end of the session, ideas have to be culled. Often a hundred ideas are boiled down and/or selected until only ten remain. Obviously, culling is not nearly as fun as ideation because nobody enjoys seeing his or her own ideas criticized and dropped from the survivor's list.

The roles of team members change throughout the ideation and culling processes. Researchers lead during the investigative processes and the first part of ideation. Designers, engineers, and creative marketers lead during the ideation sessions. And the engineers, designers, and/or business analysts lead the culling process. The team members must constantly ask themselves, "Which ideas are we dropping?" "Is it for the right reasons?" "Can we implement those that remain?" The knowledge gained during the stakeholders' interviews will help them to answer the last two questions, especially if the team revisits the original assumptions as presented in the kickoff meeting. Has anything changed? Does everyone still agree? For example, is senior management still committed to a breakthrough product that may have large investments or a long adoption curve? Whatever happens, the team members must not let an idea that everyone agrees is dumb survive, especially for political reasons, because the team members may find themselves implementing it.

Step Six: Presentation to the Reference Group

Once the team has completed its own work, it must present its findings and options to the reference group that I mentioned earlier. This is another culling step and provides a quality control check for upper managers. The project manager will present three to six ideas with an assessment of business, market, and technical issues. Senior managers expect well-reasoned analysis of problems and recommendations. The presentation may either be accepted, rejected, or spark some efforts to refine concepts based on the perspectives of the managers and experts.

Most assignments result in recommendations to pursue a specific direction or activity. When the final report is presented, everyone who reads it will look for his or her "contribution." It may be an idea presented in the stakeholders' interview. It could be the selection of people interviewed. It may be the methodology selected, overheads presented, or structure of the report. The more people embrace the report, the greater the chances of acceptance, implementation, and follow-up business. When one's recommendation is pursued and provides positive results, one gains personal satisfaction, credibility, and stronger relationships.

Step Seven: Idea to Project Transition

Once product ideas have been culled and evaluated by the reference group, the company must enter into a new phase of development to transform the concept into a viable, tangible, deliverable, and usable product. Even here, there are opportunities in which research might actually aid the business planning.

For example, we conducted an entire project to evaluate the options available when planning derivative modules for our line of CPR manikins. Unfortunately, our marketing groups around the world each had a different "wish list." When the executive management team reached an impasse, we commissioned an additional round of customer research. But this time we selected an external consultant to conduct the research. We asked the researcher to answer the question, "Are we on the right track?" within thirty days. The question was specific enough to direct the researcher. It was flexible enough to avoid suggesting any right answer and allowed for options that had not already been considered. We briefed the researcher in the product area by providing much of our own background research and explaining the modules and features we wanted to prioritize.

Because time was tight, the project team conducted a couple of days of participant observation at training centers and held five customer meetings across the United States. Although the meetings resembled focus groups, their dynamics were more like informal group interviews and demonstration sessions. The customers considered themselves experts and we treated them as such. We did not employ video, one-way mirrors, or scripts. Although we set the initial direction of the discussions, the customers set the tone, and often redirected our inquiries. We encouraged the customers to "show" or "demonstrate" their points on the current line of products. The freewheeling discussions, tactile demonstrations, and on-the-spot prioritization of issues that concerned the customers helped us get their best input about existing products and hints about how to prioritize the development of the modules.

The results, which we presented to senior management and several board members, largely confirmed the basic direction. The project gave us the opportunity to rethink our assumptions about the customers and competitors. Once we compared the findings with our previous studies, we realized that our customers were more heterogeneous than we suspected, yet the needs of those in the United States did not differ from those in Europe as much as we thought. The top five to seven needs were the same everywhere; only the ranking differed. And those would not slow or derail the project since we would develop the modules together. Therefore, the wish lists were easily merged once the initial set of modules was expanded from three to seven.

The research also changed our views about our competitors. In fact, after a high-level dialogue, we found that one company's efforts were more complementary than competitive. We formalized an alliance that has benefited both organizations and our customers. In retrospect, the project taught us that ethnographic research can

- be used to evaluate the direction of product development efforts;
- be conducted quickly if methodological compromises are made;
- reframe a topic and stimulate new thinking;
- lead to worthwhile initiatives beyond the scope of the original project.

Postproject Reviews

As mentioned earlier, all projects, whether conducted internally or with a consultant, should be followed by a project review. A number of issues should be addressed in the postproject review. The review is meant to assess satisfaction on the project, suggest ways to improve the process, uncover future opportunities, and train individuals. The entrée is composed of two questions: "Were we on time?" and "Did we meet our specifications?" If the answer to both is "yes," congratulations. Otherwise we must explore what happened and why. Admittedly the reviews seem awkward at first, but they become easier after several projects.

Please note that the program review is a high-risk/return activity. If there was any dissatisfaction or failure to meet expectations, it should surface in the review. If the project was done with a consultant and done primarily for the consultant's benefit (process learning and securing new business), it should be offered *gratis* to clients. This will also help take the sting out of conflicts. Strong managers will address the issues and may be able to turn them into advantages. At the very least, the reviews can be used to remove the issue as a barrier to future projects. Ideally, the individuals and companies (if there are any) will emerge with a stronger relationship.

Just in case you think the final review is a waste of time, let me share an experience. I once reviewed a project initiated by my predecessor that needlessly led to the demise of a promising business alliance between Laerdal and a consultancy. Early in the need-finding process, the consultancy was engaged to provide, among other things, a market assessment and engineering services. As I sat in meetings, I noticed that in spite of the success of the product in the marketplace, my company's project manager was constantly pummeled for being over budget and over time. In my review of his project notes, I found out that the turnover of key personnel at the consultancy resulted in much if not most of the project delays. As you can imagine, there was no immediate repeat business for that consultancy. Approximately, two years later I found out, quite by accident, that all was not as it had originally seemed. During the project preparation, my company changed both the scope and direction of the project. This was communicated to our internal team members but not highlighted in the formal documentation for the consultancy. Thus, the entire project was hampered from the very beginning. Rather than review the project and fix the intercorporate working process, my company dropped the consultancy and changed its contracting process. The next three assignments were contracted on a fixed-fee basis and given to other consultancies.

In this instance two activities might have not only preserved, but also enhanced, the relationship. First, a postproject review with the project management and one level higher may have identified both the cause and result of preproject scope changes. This in turn may have led to better process control. Second, upon discovering that a new senior manager was in place, an introductory visit by the consultancy combined with an invitation for our management to visit their studio probably would have cemented the relationship and resulted in that consultancy's being given almost exclusive consideration for the next five assignments.

CAN ONE PROJECT AFFECT ANOTHER?

Yes. If the consultancy is successful, it will have taught clients something about how to do their own internal, ethnographically informed product development projects. Eventually, the clients should try to go it alone, especially on smaller projects, because it does not make sense to constantly hire a consultancy for an activity that they wish to gain long-term corporate acceptance. It also helps institutionalize the practice and paradigm of qualitative research and increases the likelihood of using a consultancy for major projects in the future.

By the time Laerdal and GVO had completed their fifth project, Laerdal began to independently apply a consumer-driven approach and the previously learned ethnographic findings about consumers. For example, we were considering purchasing intellectual property from an unsuccessful start-up. The company that had failed was founded in the early 1980s and had quickly established itself as a pioneer of multimedia education. The company's system consisted of software, course documents, and proprietary peripherals for CPR and advanced cardiac life support training. Essentially, the company put a training program on a PC–laser disk platform and later converted it to a Windows CD platform. The products' market size was significant and accessible. The industry regarded the products as breakthroughs. At its peak, the start-up company employed thirty people and generated several million dollars in annual revenues. So what went wrong? Perhaps a better question is, "Why did Laerdal purchase the property and enter a line-of-business in which others had lost millions?" Simply put, the start-up company's business model was wrong for the consumer culture. Laerdal was in a position to avoid the mistake.

The original company's products were sold on a capital-purchase model with an initial charge of $25,000 to $40,000. Traditional instructor-led classes ranged from $150 to $350 per student, and institutions commonly train 80 to 200 students per year. Given these parameters, any competent business undergraduate can quickly calculate acceptable financial returns. With a market demanding 10,000 placements over a five-year replacement cycle, it was an excellent opportunity.

We realized, based on our independent research among consumers, that the start-up failed to appreciate the implications of changing customer purchase and training practices on their business model. First, the culture of today's health care institutions is now largely dominated by "cost per" business models: cost per bed, cost per procedure, cost per admittance, or in HMOs, cost per patient per year. Revenue is treated in a similar fashion. Second, health care institutions use a lengthy capital budgeting process. It usually takes a year to purchase products that cost more than $500 because they are defined as "capital" expenditures that must go through the annual budgetary process. The process forces vendors to endure long sales cycles and high transaction costs. Finally, most health care institutions consider education to be an overhead expense. When budget cutting, one always looks to overhead first. Therefore, since this product used a capital-purchase business model, it created its own intolerable and wholly unnecessary dilemma. Sales took too long and cost too much. The revenue stream had significant spikes and valleys. Adoption rates were too slow. In the end, by using a capital-purchase business model, the venture created the seeds of its own demise.

After reviewing our findings, our CEO realized that the product could be commercially successful if Laerdal could make some minor changes to it, shift the target market slightly, and then match the business model with the customer and end-user buying habits. We renamed the product Heartcode™ and introduced it to the market along with a new pay-per-use business model. Heartcode™ became one of the first, if not the first, pay-per-use software products in the market. Rather than purchase the equipment outright, each customer essentially paid for each student taking the class: one student, one use, one payment. Moreover, our CEO recognized that Heartcode™ was positioned as a pay-per-use product, and thus, was ideally suited to convenience and retraining programs, not initial training programs. So he shifted the target market. Initial training is best performed in a group. However, those who are just trying to refresh their skills are not interested in struggling with expensive, time-consuming group learning sessions. They are more interested in refreshing their skills at their own convenience. For them, scheduling is tougher than learning. Thus, the pay-per-use business model supported individual scheduling flexibility and institutional budgeting practices.

Whether or not Heartcode™ is a "new venture" depends on your point of view. From Laerdal's perspective, though, this was a new venture. In all there were fourteen new changes. The only constant was that Laerdal sold peripheral manikin products.

For most of us associated with the project, Heartcode™ was an excellent venture, albeit peppered with considerable growth pains. We learned several important lessons about how we could understand our customers and apply the insights:

- Qualitative decision making is not restricted to social scientists.
- Occasionally, it is worth the risk to incorporate many changes in a "challenged" program.
- The business model is as important as the product.

Of course, the ultimate message is that organizations that institutionalize their own ethnographic research capacities won't need consultants.

A CLOSING WORD TO SOCIAL SCIENTISTS

Social scientists have to apply the tools of their trades to learn about business people and designers if they are to demonstrate how their skills help reduce the risks and increase the returns associated with product development of any kind. The benefits are far from obvious, especially since most businesspeople focus more on quantitative marketing reports than on the kind of ethnographic research and analysis described in this volume. Fortunately, the task is becoming easier because a few pioneers from the social sciences and business schools are creating interdisciplinary programs—or are at least advocating cross-disciplinary studies. An excellent example is Harvard University's executive education program called Product Development. The one-week executive seminar includes a significant section on "emphatic research." Another example is Rensselaer Polytechnic Institute's small but highly flexible business school, which encourages students to take classes "up the hill," in the sciences.

REFERENCES

DeBono, E. 1999. *Six Thinking Hats*. Little, Brown & Company.

Harvard University. 1998. Product Development. A week-long seminar taught at Harvard University. *www.exed.hbs.edu.*

Heiman, S.E., and D. Sanchez. 1998. *The New Strategic Selling*. New York: Warner Books.

Leonard, D., and J.F. Rayport. 1997. Spark Innovation Through Empathic Design. *Harvard Business Review*, (November/December): 102–113.

Management Roundtable. 1999. *Publications and Seminars. www.management roundtable.com.*

Product Development Management Association. 1999. *Publications and Seminars. www.pdma.com.*

Reis, J.T. 1999. *Marketing Warfare*. New York: McGraw-Hill.

8

Communicating with Clients

Rita Denny

This chapter focuses on communication. I will examine how anthropologists and businesses communicate and how that communication can be improved. My premise is that how we talk reflects assumptions about the way we think the consumer world works. I discuss both the language of business and the language of anthropology. I address the assumptions often made by business about both consumers and the research task, and offer strategies for mediating opposing sets of talk.

MY PERSPECTIVE

I am an anthropologist by training and market researcher by profession. I have studied communication systems of monkeys, fiddler crabs, and nursery school children at the University of Pennsylvania and linguistic and nonverbal systems structuring face-to-face encounters at the University of Chicago. The perspective I bring is grounded in inductive analysis of the rules, constructions, and signs that are implicit in consumer and producer (designer, marketer, brand manager, advertiser) behavior—linguistic or otherwise—and that together act as a framework for that behavior.

For the last fifteen years I have conducted market research for consumer products, advertising, financial, auto, and electric utility industries. The B/R/S Group is a small market research and consulting group, a rather unique firm of twenty-two partners in which each partner develops a particular business practice—high tech, new products, consumer branding, advertising development—according to their professional experience and proclivity. My work is in decoding the meanings of brands, bringing the consumers of products and services to life as cultural beings, and understanding the role of products, brands, or services in the context of everyday life, where meaning is produced and consumed. It is at heart a cultural analysis. If the task is successful then marketers or designers gain a renewed understanding of themselves as professionals, consumers, and cultural beings. In the end, I am an observer.

A BETTER MOUSETRAP

Anthropology, in the marketing world, is all too often embraced in the hope that it represents a better mousetrap. Brand managers, research directors, account planners, and marketing directors, in search of answers or insight, grasp new approaches or new techniques in an effort to gain market share, win an advertising account, create breakthrough advertising, or capitalize on shifting market dynamics. In the last decade, a shift to "understanding consumers" or desires to "get closer to consumers" has put a spotlight on anthropology and/or observational methods throughout the marketing world. For anthropologists interested in consumer culture, these can be good times (see Sherry 1995).

Postmodern Consumption

There is an increasing awareness on our clients' part that traditional ways of comprehending customers are inadequate. This is especially true of advertising agency clients whose task it is to create breakthrough communications. This sense of things is partially a result of changes observed in the marketplace. Markets are increasingly global, and growth for mature brands depends on new markets. Categories are being invented and redefined by technological change. For example, what is a phone today versus yesterday? Is a PC used for word processing or Internet access? Products in a category may be at parity functionally speaking, rendering traditional advertising messages (unique selling propositions) impossible. Consequently, there is rising reliance on "the brand" as the sole source of distinction among a competitive array.

Consumer behavior, as well, is seen to have changed. Gone is the loyalty of yesteryear. Products and brands are accessible to such a wide range of consumers that target audiences may be indistinguishable or so fragmented that they are unreachable by a single message. Whatever the motivating reasons, interest in anthropology and ethnography stems from a desire to grasp new models of consumer behavior or at least alternative ways for understanding.

Cova (1996), in an article addressed to business managers, suggests that the marketing field must view the consumer as postmodern. This means accepting that contradictory behavior in consumption is normal: "heterogeneity with uniformity, passive consumption with active customization, individualism with tribalism, fragmentation with globalization (1996: 16)." Fundamentally, the consumer must be seen as producer of experience. Cova (1996: 17) continues:

In postmodernity we are witnessing the emergence of the customizing consumer—the consumer who takes elements of market offerings and crafts a customized consumption experience out of them. . . . In modernity, consumers were increasingly divorced from their ability to control the objects or their lives; they ended up as stooges. In postmodernity, the consumer may be finding the potential to become a protagonist in the customization of his world.

In a more academic vein, Holt (1997) suggests that we must understand the everyday process of consuming—that it is in the process, and not in the objects of consumption (e.g., antiques, home computers, luxury cars), that distinctions of class, status, and culture are created and perpetuated. Whether or not business managers subscribe to the theory of postmodernism and its implications for consumption, practically speaking, business clients are forced to look more broadly at consumers when traditional models fail to provide predictability or fail to be useful in quickly changing markets. This means that consumers are given a stronger voice in describing their view of the world. From a client's perspective, the reality is "change" and thus, is the motivation for engaging anthropologists.

The Trap

Nonetheless, expectations of anthropological analysis are often misguided. Anthropology, at its best, offers clients a way to recast their understandings of consumers and the consumption process. This, however, is not the explicit client intent. Rather, the intentions are pragmatic, directed to a particular business issue, and seemingly concrete. For example, "I want to understand healthy lifestyles." "We need to uncover new learnings about . . ." "We want to understand the personality of our brand." "We need a distinctive positioning [in a category of parity products]." "We need to go beyond superficial responses to this new product idea." Or, my favorite, "What are the unmet needs?" By "getting close to consumers" and using anthropologists as the facilitators of that ex-

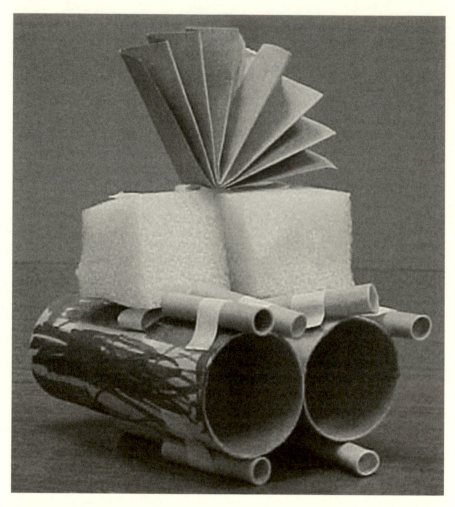

Photo 8.1. Business' view of anthropology: A bizarre, distinctive means for look-ing at customers. Photo by author.

perience, our clients hope that elusive facts become visible (see Photo 8.1).

Implicit in clients' intents, though, are beliefs about consumer behavior and an epistemology of knowing. I will highlight three assumptions that anthropologists would certainly view as cultural constructions.

The first assumption is that knowledge is concrete and layered. We simply need to have better tools, dig deeper, mine new areas, uncover new learnings, discover unmet needs. This is the pervasive language of business among designers, brand managers, or executives. Implicit is a modernist assumption that producers fulfill desires and needs of (passive) consumers.

The second assumption is that functional and symbolic arenas are separate. Thus corporations might view their reputation or image as distinct from its operational identity. An electric utility, for example, might charge its public relations department with building the image of the company through community service programs and not recognize that customer payment policies, meter-reading practices, and employee merit programs are equally important in sending a message about the company's priorities—its image. New product teams might separate technological function from the social or symbolic functions it enables (implicitly or not). Brand managers might separate tangible, functional features of their brand from the brand's less tangible equities, such as the values it stands for in consumers' lives, and concentrate only on the first—the easily measured, easily articulated functional properties. But, for example, should sport utility vehicle's functional four-wheel-drive performance ever be separated from the idea of freedom that such functionality symbolizes?

The third assumption is that actions speak louder than words. Behavior speaks for itself. Consumers, consciously or not, present themselves in a certain way. Their words are suspect, so managers, developers, or research directors try to get beyond any public posturing to real behavior. In a *Harvard Business Review* article Leonard and Rayport (1997) discuss the need for "empathic methods" (read "observation") for discovering consumer needs. From our standpoint, however, both words and actions are conventionally, culturally grounded, and neither is more real than the other. Focus group formats, and the typical methods of qualitative research they suggest, more narrowly constrain behavior than does a person's home, where multiple roles are being enacted almost simultaneously. It is not empathy as such that is required as much as recognizing the fundamental role of consumers who give meaning to the goods in the marketplace.

Within a worldview that is partially structured by such assumptions, anthropology is viewed as a potential tool by the business culture—it gives a new set of utterances or is instrumental in providing a behavioral view. Thus, researchers, marketers, or new products managers have a larger arena for witnessing what is there. At one extreme, anthropological ethnography is conflated with observation—just another word for "looking" at customers. Cited by Nardi (1998) is an "ethnographic" study of twenty to thirty people, all of whom were interviewed in one three-day period. Thus, thirty-minute interviews consisting of refrigerator or closet checks become "ethnography" in the marketing world. Consumers remain objects of study—their distance from us is preserved—and there is no shift in the presumed client-customer relationship.

At another extreme, anthropology is called on to speak to the human dimension of product innovation. Our expertise is called on to answer such questions as "Has technology gotten ahead of our humanity?" "How will a particular technology evolve in human communication?" "Who will adopt this technology?" "What will be the next minivan?" In these instances the most intensive look at a consumer's life would yield no predictive value.

Anthropological ethnography is not merely an observational method, and it falls somewhat short of an explanation of humanity. It is not a better mousetrap as constructed by the business culture. It represents a different way of knowing and requires clients to invoke a different set of assumptions about who consumers are and the relationship between consumers and producers. Participant observation recasts the relationship between researcher and subject—forcing both proximity and subjectivity. In contrast to client assumptions about the way the world works, it assumes that functional and symbolic arenas are inseparable. We also assume that language and behavior are grounded in social context and it is this contextualization that is crucial to understand when positioning brands or creating new products and services (Denny 1995). Ethnography is about "why." It offers explanation, new understanding, and often, new observational facts. These facts do not stand alone; they are embedded in a cultural matrix. It is not enough, for example, to observe the therapeutic use of herbs without a corresponding analysis of the shifting cultural definition of health. It is not enough to witness college students downloading music from the Internet without a corresponding focus on the roles technology plays in their everyday lives. And so anthropology offers a different worldview, often based on different assumptions about the way the world works.

The potential for misunderstanding between anthropologist and business client is great. Jargon, conceptual structures, and the routine shorthand of organizational speech makes talking past each other a very real possibility. I have given presentations that were disasters. Looking back, I realize that I failed to get my clients beyond their assumptions about consumers and their behavior. In a study of refrigerator use for a hard goods manufacturer, I tried to emphasize the symbolic importance of a full refrigerator (in the United States) and, by implication, the importance of customizing space. The ranking research manager kept asking, "But how do you know this is true—did consumers *say* that?" The lesson here is that if anthropologists are to form constructive partnerships with business, they must provide a way to mediate worldviews. Otherwise conversations occur but with no attendant understanding.

MEDIATING WORLDVIEWS

It is all too easy for the business culture to forget that consumers do not typically share the language of business and its accompanying implications for how the world works. Service representatives for credit card companies whose job is to get "delinquent cardholders" (are they customers or not?) to send in a "payment" might classify cardholders as "habitually late," "one-time offenders," "abusers," or "casually delinquent." If metaphors of drug addiction permeate conversation among service representatives, management, or customers—and they do—businesses constrain the nature of their conversations with customers. The language sets a tone, invoking an implicit oppositional, didactic, or patriarchal relationship. Language constrains what we experientially know. As an ethnographic observation in a research process, such metaphors speak to the implicit relationship between card issuer and cardholder and beg the strategic question of whether this sort of relationship is optimal, even viable, in today's marketplace of consumer finance.

The term "recovery," used by a multinational financial institution to refer to a consumer's reversal of a poor financial situation, suggests the notion of progress itself, that a consumer moved from one discrete state to another in goal-like fashion. It makes a cultural assumption about financial goals. But what if "recovery" is simply a reflection of taking a financial picture at a discrete moment? What if there is no intentional progress on the consumer's part, or what if there has always been such intention but no progress? Electric utilities, to use another example, have traditionally referred to their customers as "ratepayers," whereas consumers have thought of themselves as "customers." Customer descriptors such as these make tacit assumptions about values that may well obscure a consumer reality, as experienced. In turn, this provides a foundation for systematic misinterpretation of customer attitudes or behavior.

Consumer products companies are typically organized by brand and product offerings—each a fiefdom. Such organization is sometimes projected onto consumers, explicitly or implicitly. A manufacturer's brands may not be distinguishable in their use by consumers; functional difference may not be a relevant difference in the consumer's world. And so the separate domains of the corporate structure are not reflected in the consumer's world. Yet the corporate organization is often not questioned; indeed it is perpetuated in the research design and process, perpetuating notions of difference when none exists.

In part, anthropological studies bring such assumptions of business organizations to the forefront. This is a crucial step, a first lesson in the notion that we are all participants in the culture—conventionalized, social, and arbitrary. Mediating client and anthropological worldviews requires that clients question their own conventions, but the onus is on the anthropologist to make that task part of the research process. If we, as anthropological researcher and client, comprehend the task, then we are one step closer to the consumer's world.

Clients as Mediators

Mediating disparate ways of understanding consumers is not possible if clients are not part of the process. Clients who buy anthropological expertise are themselves mediators. Within advertising, our client is typically the research director or senior account planner. On the industry side, our client is typically a brand or research manager or director. In either case, our clients mediate several points of view—from research and development, to marketing, to creatives (on the agency side). Our clients have broader horizons—they might be looking at a broad array of brands, considering a global market, or actively planning the future.

Our clients recognize a more complex relationship between consumer and brand/product. They go beyond functional difference to question the relevance of the difference to consumption or to consumers' lives. They are comfortable talking about the "intangible" equities of a brand, product, service, or category—what we would term the "symbolic meanings." Their terms might be

- skills versus personality of a brand (following Aaker 1996) in which the tangible, functional properties (skills) are separated from intangible, symbolic properties (personality);
- tangible versus intangible properties of a category, including discussion of technical aspects of a cell phone design and the meaning of mobility in today's society;
- functional equities versus imagery or added-value equities (following Blackston 1992).

They are comfortable posing the question "What does this brand/product/category represent in consumers' lives?" as a means toward product and brand innovation.

Although our primary client on a project will be comfortable (if not in agreement) with an anthropological worldview, their internal clients will probably not. And so, our best clients are translators. They know their internal audiences—the language, constraints, and opportunities—better than we, as consultants, do. They also know their market better than we do. Research abounds: attitude and usage studies, market segmentations, market dynamics, consumer trends, brand equity studies, and so on. Often, these research paradigms are much more familiar to client organizations. Our clients, in the end, have to translate our findings, insights, and explanations into the language of the corporation. It might be a statement of "brand essence" or "soul." It might be the "key consumer insight." It might be a discussion about "platform strategy versus the base business." If new positioning ideas are the objective, then product concepts ready for consumer testing are the deliverable.

THE PROCESS OF PRODUCT DEVELOPMENT WORK

Our work occurs largely to aid discovery of new ideas for product or service development, brand positionings, or creative development (versus evaluating existing ideas). Research objectives include developing new product or service ideas (e.g., cleansers, banking services, electric utility communications programs, cat litters, personal communicating devices), policies (e.g., bank credit card programs), brand positionings, or brand extensions. Such goals are often articulated as discovering "unmet needs." Packed into this phrase is an unspoken assumption about the consumer-producer relationship: producers are conduits of objects and consumers are receivers. "Need" implies a concrete, objective, even deterministic reality—consumers constitute a puzzle with a unique solution. Not so.

Product design innovation walks a tightrope between what is possible, technically speaking, and what is relevant, symbolically speaking. This tightrope, implicit in all our projects, is most visible here. Perhaps this is because technological difference is so concrete. Perhaps because in a rationalistic world, we cling to the notion that innovation is about functionality—a new feature, a new design element. Whatever the case, strong research and development firms (high-tech or consumer products) cling to functional difference as the hallmark of innovation. In going to consumers, getting close to them, they are searching for implicit functional needs to which they can respond with a technical solution. From our anthropological standpoint, functionality is inseparable from symbolic meaning—the role of products/services/brands in everyday life and the meanings that *consumers* are generating through experience. In the United States, for example, biomedical advances in treating asthma have not resulted in better management of the illness by teenagers, the group hit hardest by the disease. In this case, technical breakthroughs in treatment do not sufficiently consider what a teenager's world is about and that technological function is mediated through subjective experience (Rich and Chalfen, forthcoming). These are young people who happen to have asthma, not the reverse—a crucial distinction to make. Although clients' questions are often grounded in the future, anthropology tends to predict the future by decoding the present (ideally obviating the need for prediction altogether). The process for balancing on that tightrope is outlined below.

Photos 8.2 and 8.3. Left: What is a phone? Right: What is a PC? Photos by Rita Denny.

Step 1: Reframe the Question

As noted earlier, the research questions posed by our clients are practical, focused, and in industry language (whatever the industry is). Our first and completely essential step is to reframe the question—first in conversation, then in a proposal. The reframing always makes questions of the cultural assumptions implicit in client research questions. For example:

"Will digital photography replace silver halide?" becomes "What is a photograph?" and "What is a camera?" as subjectively experienced by consumers. Another example: "What are the brands' equities?" would also include "What meanings does the category have for consumers?" "How have consumers integrated a set of products/a particular brand into everyday life?" "What meanings have consumers' created?" "How can we observe this in everyday living?"

"How is technology integrated into the home?" becomes "What is a telephone?" (See Photo 8.2.) "What is TV?' in the context of everyday living. And "What is home today?" We would also ask, "What are the values embodied by specific forms of technology?" "How does behavior perpetuate such values?" "Are there tensions or contradictions?"

Or consider a third example. "What are the unmet needs in spray 'trigger' cleansers?" becomes "What does clean mean today?" "What are the values of home that are embodied by cleaning habits, routines, and preferences?"

The process can be applied to every industry. "Will a particular portable information-capturing device have a mass market appeal?" becomes "What does technology symbolically do in everyday life?" "What strategies have consumers developed in their use of portable technology?" "How do these strategies fit with larger cultural values?" (See Photo 8.3.)

In these cases, the explicit intents of the research include explorations into the lives of consumers and, for us as anthropologists, into the cultural life of products, services, and brands. Whether we have persuaded buy-in on the basis of "intangible equities" or "behavioral data," we have permission to structure an ethnographic study.

Step 2: Embrace the Subjectivity of the Enterprise: Partnering with Consumers and Clients

Respondents in our studies often become analysts of themselves in the process. The methods we use (visual diaries, audio diaries) allow our subjects to observe themselves. Because our time with consumers is limited, these other forms of observation are highly valued.

Just as we engage consumers in a more participatory process, so we try to engage clients in a more participatory process. We invite them to be participant observers of the in-home (or in-office, in-store) experience. Although we limit the number of people who can accompany us (two maximum), client core team members will trade off with each so that each attends some of the interviews. There is an additional cost factor here, both financially and logistically. The investment is worthwhile. Each interview provides an opportunity to experience the complexity and coherence of consumption. It also provides opportunities for great insight. Several years ago we worked with an advertising agency that was trying to win the Domino's Pizza advertising account. In an effort to understand the dynamics of the category, we were asked to conduct a cultural analysis of pizza consumption. Business pitches are notorious for their time constraints, so we conducted a series of in-home interviews with people who frequently ate pizza and conducted the interviews on Friday and Saturday evenings, at dinnertime. One of the crucial findings of the project was that when we had the household members order pizza, we were expected (indeed culturally obligated) to share in its consumption. Our observational role was no longer permitted. This became a key ethnographic observation about the meaning of pizza.

We sometimes construct panels of consumers that meet periodically.

In these cases clients get to know the consumers in a much more visceral way. In a study we did for a large retailer, we created a panel of Christmas shoppers who met weekly from mid-November through early January. The goal of the study was to determine sales and advertising opportunities for the retailer during the Christmas season. Translated, our goal was to understand the meaning of Christmas, how women (in this case) shopped with the meaning of Christmas in mind, and then to explore the roles of advertising and sales in this overall context. Quite spontaneously, project participants offered to call me when they saw gifts I might want to buy, traded tips with each other, and brought their Christmas finds for others to see. It is hard to distance oneself as an observer through this process. Indeed, as a result of the participatory, engaged process, we all participated in crucial dimensions of what it meant to "shop Christmas."

Step 3: Interactive Reporting

Debriefing or report presentations are work sessions first among a core team. Observations, findings, and arguments are all presented with time for questions. Implications for the team are often part of that discussion and facilitated by our primary client. This is hugely beneficial. We can determine what part of the project remains confusing or unclear. We can also observe what findings and implications have the most effect on the business problem from their viewpoint.

Another form of process is to insert a brainstorming or ideation session into the mix. Our research findings, typically exploratory, provide the basis for a daylong ideation session that we facilitate. Clients, advertising creatives, and outside industry experts might all be included in this process.

IN THE END

An anthropological analysis must persuade and be persuasive with an audience beyond a core team. It must be a comprehensible cultural reading. It has to make sense to the primary client and in many cases has to be translated by them as well into terms and structures understood within the corporation. In projects we have undertaken, whether in the field of consumer technology, financial services, package goods, or automobiles, clients have remarked that they haven't learned new things as much as gained a new understanding of what is known. We recast what is known by placing it in a broader context, creating new understanding. We bring consumers to life so that their behavior shows coherence. We tell stories. We integrate video, pictures, or consumer constructions of themselves (such as collages and objects representing key values) into the body of the report. Finally, the implications of our work for the client problem are ideally set forth in the client's language because there is far greater chance of their implementing them if they can understand them in terms that resonate with their own cultural system. Thus, we often speak of "brand essence" or "product plus" or "financial recovery" rather than "glosses," "material culture," or "regained acquired status." Ultimately, we return to the client worldviews, knowing that the journey alters even these.

REFERENCES

Aaker, D. 1996. *Building Strong Brands*. New York: Free Press.

Blackston, M. 1992. Beyond Brand Personality: Building Brand Relationships. In *Researching the Power of Brands*, edited by M. Blackston. New York: Advertising Research Foundation.

Cova, B. 1996. The Postmodern Explained to Business Managers: Implications for Marketing. *Business Horizons* 39: 15–23.

Denny, R. 1995. Speaking to Customers: The Anthropology of Communications. In *Contemporary Marketing and Consumer Behavior*, edited by J. Sherry, Jr. Thousand Oaks, CA: Sage.

Holt, D. 1997. Poststructuralist Lifestyle Analysis: Conceptualizing the Social Patterning of Consumption in Post-modernity. *Journal of Consumer Research* 23: 326–350.

Leonard, D., and J. Rayport. 1997. Spark Innovation Through Empathic Design. *Harvard Business Review* (November): 102–113.

Nardi, B. 1998. Relevant Anthropology Viewed from Technology Studies. *Anthropology Newsletter* 39 (8): 22–24.

Rich, M., and M. Chalfen. Forthcoming. Showing and Telling Asthma: Children Teaching Physicians with Visual Narratives. *Visual Sociology*.

Sherry, J. Jr. 1995. Marketing and Consumer Behavior. In *Contemporary Marketing and Consumer Behavior*, edited by J. Sherry, Jr. Thousand Oaks, CA: Sage.

9

Anthropology and Industrial Design: A Voice from the Front Lines

Mark Dawson

We know from other chapters presented in this volume that anthropologists, designers, businesspeople, and engineers are something like different species. We each have our own lens on the world and a different set of philosophies about product development, and we use our own language to discuss them. Yet, within the environment of the product design firm, we have to develop working methods that bridge these interspecies gaps to communicate with each other. Beyond the internal communication, as a multidisciplinary group, anthropologists, engineers, and designers must eventually come to a final presentation and eventual product that speaks from a single voice and philosophy to the corporate client. The product "solution" must meet a number of conditions. It must at least (1) meet the emotional and functional needs of the user, (2) be manufacturable, (3) be affordable, and (4) be profitable for the company producing it.

This chapter illustrates an evolution in this communication process from the perspectives of two different design firms and three members of the two multidisciplinary product development teams. My perspective is based on the work from two successful collaborations at two different design firms between myself, a design anthropologist, an industrial designer (Peter Brandenburg), and an information designer/design strategist (Katie Minervino).

The purpose here is not to provide a theoretical perspective, guidance for—or methods of—analysis. Rather the object is to let the new design anthropologist, and those interested in the services of an anthropologist, know what sorts of activities and answers will be expected of them as part of a product development team. I will focus on how the anthropologists communicate with designers and then, how both communicate with their clients. In short, this is about understanding

- how to bring a true multidisciplinary team through the process;
- the important balance of validity and inspiration;
- that presentation is an additional form of validity; and
- that the collection and analysis of data is not the conclusion—the hard product is the conclusion.

There are a number of names for the work I do. Because each design firm in the industry needs to stand out from the crowd, they tend to use differing terms to describe similar activities. In some instances, these activities are part of the "branding" process, a normal part of business. In others, it can represent a true difference in philosophy toward user-centered design. "Design Anthropology," "Design Ethnography," "Discovery Process," "Design Research," and "User-Centered Design" are all terms that have been used at times by the author. For the sake of clarity, I will use "Discovery Process" and "Research" interchangeably. "Design Anthropology" or "Design Ethnography" is a part of the methodology, but not all of that is discovery process. It is useful to note that "research" is a word with which some who are involved in the product development process do not wish to be connected. There is some legitimate reason for this worry, as "researchers" are sometimes associated with individuals who are adept at the mechanical aspect of fieldwork and analysis, but not involved in the application of findings. This kind of researcher plans and executes the collection of data and brings analysis to a certain point, stopping short of the actual using of the results to make a hard "go/no go" decision. Do the research results inspire or otherwise add to the complex process of product innovation? The term "research" suffers when data is produced that the team cannot directly apply to a final product solution, or larger strategic product innovations.

THE PHASED APPROACH TO PRODUCT DEVELOPMENT

Please note that for the majority of my time in Design Anthropology, I have been on the beginning side of the product development process, rather than the latter stages. The product development process is usually approached in phases (zero to four or five or six, etc.), with phase zero usually being the "discovery" or research phase. Phase one is the "concept" phase, in which the industrial design (ID) staff (with research and engineering input), develop a number of possible product concepts that address the user needs and client's concerns. The next phase is refinement, in which the number of concepts is reduced. Those that make it to refinement may then be subject to further development and possibly through to engineering and manufacture. Although these phases are largely linear and sequential in the sense that you cannot (or should not) begin conceptualizing until you have a foundation of discovery, and conceptualization is followed by engineering, there is still a good deal of overlap between phases. In addition, each phase is constantly iterative within itself, creating ideas and frameworks, discarding them, and inspiring further refinement.

I am personally rarely in a position where I am conducting research intended to evaluate business viability or conducting large-scale testing of the developed concepts. This is not to suggest that it is an unimportant part of the process, and a number of anthropologists do just that as part of the market research community. If anything, the opportunity to evaluate concepts and products in the process does not get enough attention. Rather, in my case, I have usually been in the earliest phases of the process where no product exists, a new product or line is to be launched, or the client is looking to make some new technology functional for the public. For this reason this initial phase is often referred to as a discovery process. The objective is to uncover user needs: emotional, functional, financial, and so forth. It can also be argued (at some later date for a chapter on methods) that it is preferable for the discovery process and the evaluation process to be conducted by separate teams to help reduce potential bias.

COLLABORATION AND THE MYTH OF MULTIDISCIPLINARY TEAMS

A common refrain heard in the halls of business is the need to create "multidisciplinary teams" to foster innovative thinking by focusing differing professional perspectives on a problem or project. This approach is central to the process of collaborative work between social science and other disciplines in the product development effort. The difficulty in creating these teams and making them work together effectively is that companies do not teach them to communicate with each other. Each group has its own concerns, priorities, and issues that it is attempting to communicate, and often they speak in different languages as well. Some companies seem to expect that each discipline will develop a certain amount of empathy and spirit of compromise by being thrown together

Figure 9.1
Over the Wall Communication

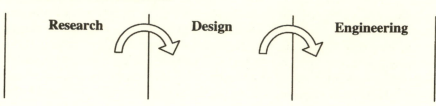

in the crush of a project. Ideally, collaboration should not be about compromise (to put a fine point on it: always reaching the average—mediocre—result), but about winnowing and refining ideas from multiple perspectives.

This desire to create multidisciplinary teams sometimes stems from a problem referred to as "throwing information over the wall." This refers to the difficulties of a linear development process in which a group finishes their portion of the task and hands it off to the next group. The "over the wall" problem continues to occur because the various groups are working to solve a specific problem in an isolated fashion. These groups do not have a common perspective. As a result, the task is handed off; the meanings and efficiencies are lost as the next group attempts to work on the next phase of the project from their new point of view (see Figure 9.1).

The potential problem with using this type of "team approach" is that each part of the team still cannot communicate effectively, and each goes off to its own corner to work on the part of the problem it understands best. Then the multidisciplinary team is in fact a group of individuals working on parts of the project, which are brought together with the other teams at a later date. The result is that the research and discovery teams (still multidisciplinary) continue to toss information over the wall when the zero phase is over.

Despite the dangers of the "over the wall" problem, the approach design anthropologists most often recommend and use is the multidisciplinary effort. Many design firms refer to it as their standard practice. As a multidisciplinary process, this means that each phase (discovery and directions, conceptualization, design, engineering) is led by a primary discipline, with the support of the other groups. In this case, I typically work at the beginning of the development process to help determine directions for potential products and the first part of design conceptualization. The key to success is in understanding that the end product of our research and collaboration is most often some hard object or related set of objects.

WHY IS THIS TEAM APPROACH SO IMPORTANT?

There are two primary objectives to the multiteam effort. One is to gain multiple points of view from diverse stakeholders. The second is to ensure that the individuals carrying the product to the conclusion (manufacturing, packaging, etc.) fully understand the field research and its implications.

We are seeking "research results" that are inspirational and generative, rather than evaluative. However, it is rare that a product as originally envisioned by the development team appears on the market unchanged. A host of other influences from cost of engineering and production, time to market, or a sudden shift in company strategy can exert pressures on the final output. During each of these phases, there must be someone who understands the nature of these constraints and is willing to negotiate these changes based on the directions from the discovery and conceptualization phase.

The idea of someone shepherding a product from discovery-based research through final production is an ideal and not always attainable. In the case of consultants, we are not always privy to larger company strategies that affect downstream development decisions. On the corporate level, the product has to go though numerous checkpoints and stakeholders, each of whom may influence the outcome or possibly terminate that product development path. Regardless of the likelihood of ever having an "ideal" project, the spirit behind it remains the same: for individuals to make the best use of research, they must internalize it to the extent that they can relate the findings directly to design and development issues with little or no referring to a written document.

By inviting nonresearch disciplines into the fieldwork and analysis process, we begin the process of internalizing these ethnographic findings across disciplines.

MULTIDISCIPLINARY APPROACH TO FIELDWORK AND ANALYSIS

The first way to try to prevent the "over the wall syndrome" in a multidisciplinary team is to be sure that all members of the development team are active participants in the research design process. This may seem an obvious first step, but I have worked in instances where research is considered a much less tangible part of the process, and is treated as a lower priority for participation by team members. Everyone who is included in the process of developing the research strategy receives a thorough grounding in both the benefits and limitations of what the research process will be able to offer. This "buy-in" is important, so the whole team can see the logical trail of understandings that lead to a

Figure 9.2
Dynamic Multidisciplinary Interaction during Three Project Phases

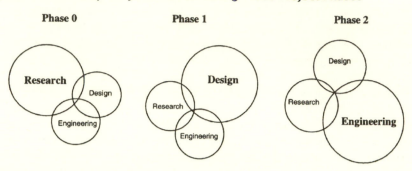

particular analysis and conclusion. By the same token it enables other team members to challenge the social scientist's worldview by offering an understanding of their own important questions. This is not to say that anthropologists expect other disciplines to develop sophisticated research and design and methodology. However they do have a unique view and understanding of issues that someone with a specialty in social science could miss. The multidisciplinary model this chapter advocates is one in which each discipline leads at different phases of the project, so that each discipline dynamically moves between the roles of project lead and support staff (see Figure 9.2).

THIS IS NOT TO SAY THAT COLLABORATION IS EASY...

Any time an anthropologist has to venture into the field for the first time with a new culture, he or she must learn the language, customs, and folkways of that new group. (See Agar 1980; Barrett 1996; Goffman 1996a, 1996b; Goodwin 1994; Jorgensen 1989; McCracken 1990; and Spradley 1979, 1980 for good introductions into relevant ethnographic methods.)

For the purposes of this chapter the "other" is the culture of industrial designers (ID), engineers, marketing managers, strategists, and others in the product development process. In order to be a true "team effort," all the members of the team must develop a working level of communication without access to a postgraduate understanding of the other disciplines. The objective of the work is to tell the external client a coherent story about users, the clients' business, and the role industrial design will play in meeting and leading these diverse needs. The core of this issue is the question of how to transfer this story, which includes ethnographic understanding, to those clients in a way that is meaningful to them.

ROLES WITHIN THE COMMUNICATION PROCESS

Anthropologists and designers typically take on two different overlapping functional roles. Anthropologists are trying to ensure that the *valid* voice of the consumer is driving the project. Designers are seeking inspiration for innovation so they can change the material world around us. If one catchphrase of cultural anthropology could be "cultural relativism," then the catchphrases of designers doing product development might be "change is good for you."

Communication between industrial design (ID) professionals and those trained in social sciences is affected by fundamental assumptions held by each discipline. As students, ID professionals are taught that the results of the practice of their profession could have a profound effect on the material culture of the world. At their core, industrial designers want to make the world a better place. The objects around us should somehow enhance our daily lives by being easy to use and functional, by providing an innovative use no one has considered before, or simply by bringing an extra source of beauty into our lives. ID students come to understand that in some ways they are the gatekeepers of the world's esthetic. Whereas the anthropologist is taught to seek the status quo of the material world around us, the industrial designer actively seeks ways to change and improve it, whether the target user realizes it needs improvement or not. The resulting objects reflect the designer or design team's solution to a problem or need as perceived by the ID professional.

LANGUAGE DIFFERENCES: TEXT VERSUS VISUAL

Interestingly, both designers and anthropologists work in the form of "sketches." In the course of a project, designers will create dozens or hundreds of sketches before they narrow down a series of design concepts. These sketches are a very physical and visual iterative process in which ideas are experimented with and discarded. This visual ability (and slowly, the ability to do this on a computer alone) is an important part of the designer's professional identity. Even something as mundane as signing a name or a caption to the sketch can reflect on the designer's visual and creative abilities. In turn, sketches provide a tool that allows the team to review, accept, or discard concepts in quick order. On a whiteboard, multiple people can interactively create a visual representation (the sketch) of a concept that incorporates elements of all the other sketches.

To go further into our generalizations, however, anthropologists are essentially text based, whereas designers are visually oriented in training. Since someone with a formal background in research may be perceived as being more rigorous, a number of designers are surprised to learn that sometimes the information they receive from us is in fact our version of "sketches." The conceptualization process can be quite analogous to qualitative analysis. We (social scientists) begin by sifting through the different forms of data we have in an attempt to find meaningful patterns that we can begin to construct into a framework. In our process of constructing the final framework (the social scientists' final concept) we will create and discard numerous other frameworks and models of understanding. Much like a sketch, these can't truly be tested them against the rest of the data until we articulate them and begin writing them down. As this cycle of developing and testing frameworks continues, we eventually come to our final concept.

Unfortunately, unlike a true sketch, text-based work is not as accessible in preconcept form. To be able to "brainstorm" around that analysis in the way designers can brainstorm around sketches, the semicomplete analysis has to be read and digested for further response. Our discipline is noted for a rigorous systematic approach, so when we allow other disciplines to observe and participate in this process, they are often frustrated when they are told that these initial frameworks are like sketches of things to come. Imagine the frustration of the industrial designer who, having learned that the future of the ID discipline is in user-based research, is confronted by a researcher who keeps saying, "Wait, you can't use this material yet, it's not quite right."

GOLDEN RULE OF COMMUNICATING WITH OTHER DISCIPLINES

The more you write, the less they read. This is not to say that members of the product development community object to reading, but more often than not, the in-depth material design ethnography uncovers is simply too much information to be absorbed and acted on in a timely manner. The "mountain guide" is an apt metaphor for the anthropologist's job in this field: be sure to point out were the dangerous cliffs are, help them find and navigate the best path(s), and provide illuminating anecdotes about the local flora and fauna. The objective is to provide the designers with a practical understanding of what it takes to get up the mountain with an appreciation of the variety of life on it without insisting on a detailed understanding of the mineral content of every rock. On the other hand, as the guide to these sociocultural phenomena, the anthropologist needs to be able to provide in-depth insight to the development team. In this way, the design anthropologist is something like a living document for the design team, and acts more fully as a participant in the product development process. The data and analysis is an important part of the process, but anthropologists and other formally trained researchers must remember that it is not the point of the project. Our work means little if it cannot be converted—interpreted into design and ultimately, products that can be manufactured.

Researchers must do more than persuade designers to read, absorb, and make useful commentary on their work. To reach product it is necessary to go beyond text. We are creating something physical and visual. The research results must be valid to correctly inform the design process, but to meaningfully contribute to that process, results must also inspire the designer and provide some criteria against which to test designs. A large part of the analysis process within product development is the discourse that occurs around the field artifacts and the artifacts created by the designers.

IMAGE BOARDS

A common research and inspirational technique used by designers is known as the "image board" and reflects a number of themes related to the project. These image boards are collections of images that can be from any number of sources, such as magazines or the Internet. Common themes might be competing products or artifacts the designers feel are representative of the target market. Other boards could be composed of images from nature, or unrelated objects providing inspiration for color and textures. These boards can often be used later to demonstrate to the client the thought process that went into design choices made during conceptualization. The process of creating the image board is not just an exercise in finding an image that is appropriate. In the process of choosing what images will appear, designers engage in strong conversation about the merits of a particular image in attempting to communicate the theme of the board. They may choose a series of images that they feel represent the look, language, and artifacts of country and western music.

In discussing what sort of imagery is appropriate, they build an understanding of that group, culture, or product line from their point of view. Through the image board, designers try to get to the country and western consumers' unspoken set of values and motivations, to begin developing concepts. The problems with this are obvious, although the intentions are good. This sort of image board is an example of designing on *behalf* of consumers, rather than true user-centered design. The images can show examples of form and function, and imply values or motivations that the creators of the board are ascribing to them, yet the "informants" related to the images have never been consulted. Be that as it may, anthropologists must accept that by collecting and organizing these images, designers begin to build an understanding that can then be translated into design elements for the product.

To follow through with a true "team" approach, data collection and analysis must be handled in a way that serves the needs for rigor, allows group participation, and catches the inspirational "ha's" that are some of the best outcomes of the group process. We know there are challenges between visual and textual ways of working, and our mission is to combine the two. Most often we have done this by a process that consists of a large group interaction, supported by a smaller core group that usually works though textual issues and provides feedback to the larger group. There are numerous ways to handle the situation, but I want to offer two short examples of bringing textual information to the level of inspiration.

ETHNOGRAPHIC IMAGE BOARDS

Industrial designer Peter Brandenburg and I modified the image board process by creating image boards from still photos that were taken during fieldwork on a day-to-day basis. In this case, they were the homes or offices of users of laptop and desktop computers. Using large sheets of foam core, we began to tape and pin up photos, creating a visual order of the chaos of data. The images addressed a variety of themes, including the related objects people carried in laptop cases, and wide shots that showed the contexts in which their computers resided, among others. As with the image boards, a great deal of the initial work of understanding the basic framework of the problems and issues occurred during the conversations between designers, researchers, engineers, and others. The photographs were initially grouped into simple categories; each informant might have his or her own set of pictures. Quickly, however, the images were arranged to represent other, deeper categories that pointed to new questions, in addition to merely providing visual clues.

This large group use of photos also aids the multidisciplinary fieldwork teams in debriefing their field experiences. The reality is that the designers and engineers will not write up field notes for you, and even if they do, it is our job to provide guidance in the effort of sifting the important from the unimportant. During the discourse about what is seen in the photos, an enriched conceptual "picture" of the informants begins to emerge and some of the biases of the research and design group may become apparent. A role of the professional researcher in this area is like that of the air traffic controller. During this discussion that we call a "debrief," I work in something like a secondary interview, where I ask questions of the team to help distinguish whether assumptions are facts or opinions. Since anthropologists are trained to seek out trends and patterns in behaviors and motivations, I can probe them to elaborate on a point: "When did she say that? What was she pointing at?" As these conversations progress, it brings very real field experiences to the front of each designer's understanding of the user, and they begin to identify patterns and gaps across their informants. "Really? She did that? Jimmy [another informant] did that too, but said he had a different reason." Allowing the designers access to the users in this way facilitates actual user-centered design.

As a side note, nonanthropologists become just as strong a set of advocates for "their" group as anthropologists do. Each field team will tend to fight for the opinions of their informants. A designer once asked me if it was okay to feel a small emotional attachment to "their" informant. Naturally it's okay. . . . That means you have rapport.

STRING ART

Not all of the research work done by design firms is primary fieldwork. Time, money, and appropriateness means that secondary research is all that is either available or needed. In one case Peter Brandenburg and I were dealing with a client that had already conducted considerable research. I had access to that data. Parts of what was sent were enormous MS-Excel files of survey data. The data covered a wall from floor to ceiling with row upon row of densely packed type. Given my limited skill at manipulating quantitative data electronically, extracting just the parts that were relevant would have taken more days than we had. The solution I found was a "string-art" method of drawing the data out. Using pushpins and bright colored yarn, I began making visual and physical connections between parts of data, adding sticky notes of the implications on the way. In some cases, the reader could follow the flow of the string to find data that contradicted itself, with my theory about why this could be. As I continued my secondary research with other articles, I would also pin them to the wall, again using the string to link important paragraphs to other data/articles (for example, see Turkle 1997). For this example, let's say we were doing work for a boating-related product: part of the data were typical demographics of sex, age, income, work, leisure, boating habits, and so on. I might find links between amount of boating by season among certain groups and the amount of time those groups actually spent out of the sight of land. I could then link this article to a printed database reporting Coast Guard rescues and the causes (e.g., navigational error and inexperience) of the incidents.

Peter and I discussed this data in a large-format way. Through the use of Post-it notes and string, we could pose questions and state assumptions, post them in an accessible way, and visually capture the passing conversation.

Both of these ways of working are simply tools to begin an iterative, frame-building process. It allows group access to the data and gives the anthropologist fast access to a diverse set of skills and point of view to bring to bear on the data.

BREAKTHROUGH PRODUCTS

It must be remembered that by trying to develop that "breakthrough product," the team is in essence attempting to create an object that *has never existed before*. That statement may be some hyperbole, but it grounds an important point. The primary role of team members with formal research training (not just anthropology) is to provide a disciplined and grounded point of view (POV) for the team. This POV is often about the current environment, activities, attitudes, and so forth of the target group or market as they relate to our project. In turn the development team as a whole must be able to incorporate this information to construct frameworks for understanding the deeper emotional, social, financial, and other motivations of the user. However, in product innovation, there is an inherent conflict in that to be truly innovative, you have to make a leap that goes beyond what the data and frameworks tell us. This is the business risk. Innovation occurs in that space "beyond data" where designers and researchers have to meet, collaborate, and take on some of each other's roles. At this point, designers are looking for inspiration that will allow them to connect these underlying consumer wants and needs to products that meet the needs of form, function, financial, and physical manufacturing issues.

The challenge for the product development team is to present a compelling case to themselves and the client to risk making the innovation. In phases zero and one (discovery and direction, conceptualization), the team has to tell a complete story about the people and the product. This story, in our case the presentation, must incorporate all the elements—background, process, and directions—needed to commit to that innovative leap. As a metaphor, think of the design team as a group of people trooping across a vast plain. That forward motion is the research and discovery process. Suddenly (but expectedly) the team reaches a vast chasm, on the other side of which is the land of innovation. We know we cannot build a bridge all the way across, but we can use our research knowledge to build a solid foundation of knowledge that informs us which way to jump. The client must be able to read in the text and hear in the explanation that the basis for making these decisions is sound. The job of research is never to eliminate risk, but to mitigate it. As researchers, we tend to believe that a presentation that communicates the validity of our research process and findings is sufficient. What researchers tend to miss is that the presentation must communicate the validity of our findings and clearly show the ability of the design firm to on those findings. In order to show the holistic validity of our development process, the development team must demonstrate the ability to balance rigorous method with intuitive and inspirational visual skills. This balance is representative of the balance that occurs between teams' visual and textual ways of working.

THE ALL-IMPORTANT CAVEAT

Many large organizations have become interested in the value of ethnographic studies as we can see from the other chapters presented here. I recently went through a job search and one of the statements made to me after an interview was that we as anthropologists have to start demonstrating the effect we have had on products and companies. We need to able to specifically tie our particular type of research to the change and innovations we help bring to the companies we work for. Our obligation to demonstrate the direct effect of our work, most often product or product strategy, is not limited to the client's upper management. In order to develop and maintain credibility with the other members of the interdisciplinary teams with whom we work, we also must demonstrate to them that we transform their process and are not merely sources of extraneous data.

NOTE

Although this chapter reflects personal experience and opinion, I have been influenced by a number of individuals in the course of my career. First and foremost are Peter Brandenberg, Hauser Design, and Katie Minervino, formerly of Design Continuum. Through projects, dinners, and inspiring volatile debates, they have shaped my career and thoughts. I wish to thank Monica Peters (a graduate school colleague) and Jean Canavan (Motorola) for providing invaluable comments and proofreading this chapter. And thanks to the editors, Sue Squires and Bryan Byrne, for many conversations and much encouragement.

REFERENCES

Agar, M.H. 1980. *The Professional Stranger: An Informal Introduction to Ethnography.* San Diego: Academic Press.

Barrett, S.R. 1996. *Anthropology: A Student's Guide to Theory and Method.* Toronto: University of Toronto Press.

Goffman, E. 1996a. *The Presentation of Self in Everyday Life.* Garden City, NY: Doubleday.

———. 1996b. *Asylums: Essays on the Social Situation of Mental Patients and Other Inmates.* Garden City, NY: Doubleday.

Goodwin, C. 1994. Professional Vision. *American Anthropologist* 96 (3): 606–633.

Jorgensen, D.L. 1989. *Participant Observation: A Methodology for Human Studies.* Newbury Park, CA: Sage.

McCracken, G. 1990. *Culture and Consumption: New Approaches to the Symbolic*

Character of Consumer Goods and Activities. Bloomington: Indiana University Press.

Spradley, J.P. 1979. *The Ethnographic Interview*. New York: Harcourt Brace Jovanovich.

———. 1980. *Participant Observation*. New York: Holt, Rinehart and Winston.

Turkle, S. 1997. *Life on the Screen: Identity in the Age of the Internet*. New York: Touchstone.

10

Semiotics as Common Ground: Connecting the Cultures of Analysis and Creation

Heiko Sacher

Personal computing is becoming a ubiquitous activity in North American culture. Other cultures are following quickly. In a few years, many experts predict, the majority of products and services will be created, advertised, sold, or delivered to customers with and through the Internet.

The fact that those customers' interactions need to be designed to compete successfully in the digital marketplace represents a huge opportunity for the design business. This is a dimension of creation and consumption that the relatively young product design discipline has never experienced before. Taking advantage of the Internet's design opportunities, however, is not as easy as it looked at first glance.

An essential part of user-interface design practice is the involvement with individuals from a wide variety of backgrounds such as graphic design, industrial design, computer science, software development, psychology, human factors, and social science. Although individual backgrounds are diverse, the conventions that evolved from design practice have shaped two core cultures that coexist in this community. In the following I will call them "analyzers" and "creators." Amongst the analyzers one will encounter mainly psychologists, anthropologists, sociologists, and human factors experts. The creators typically consist of graphic designers, industrial designers, and software developers. This model just describes a trend—there are many crossover types and multifaceted personalities—but it is certainly applicable for the overall picture of how user-interface design gets done in practice.

Because of my background and other reasons I would put myself into the creator category. I was trained in Germany. The German name of the discipline I graduated in is *Gestaltung*—giving things a Gestalt. Because of my preference for giving digital, electronic, interactive things a Gestalt, I am usually called an interface designer, interaction designer, or user-experience designer. Most ideas presented here are directly linked to experiencing life as an interaction designer in a large computer corporation as well as in a small design consultancy. A chain of lucky coincidences gave me the opportunity to live and design with mainstream computer users from China, Singapore, and Japan. An important lesson from that experience was that there is not so much difference between understanding a scientist in a North American lab and employees in a Chinese office. A sense for the interdependence of language, culture, and interaction design that I developed through this experience is certainly an important ingredient of the approaches I talk about here.

Back to the two cultures living in the interface design world. Analyzers focus on understanding how users and interfaces perform in the real world. Their initial focus is on user needs. They make predictions about what a user might understand and might not. Later on they study how user interfaces or prototypes perform. Analyzers are wizards in observing how users and interfaces cope with each other. The outcome of analyzers' work is typically a set of insights along with a recommendation. This might be a report, a statistic, or a documentary video communicating statements such as "Seventy-seven percent of the subjects initially did not understand what XYZ button does. The label and icon must be more explicit."

Creators focus on producing "stuff"—visual designs, interaction protocols, information architecture, navigational structures. Creators' work is based on more or less concise requirements from technology, markets, or users. They create designs that address the user requirements within a given schedule and budget. The desired outcome may be a product concept, an interface design, or even a functioning prototype of either of those. The closer it is to the real thing, the better—that's the premise of creation.

The two cultural groups—analyzers and creators—are dependent on each other in the user-interface design process. For both groups the Internet brings changes that make things more complicated. Motivated by their distinct roles and backgrounds, analyzers and creators react to those challenges with different perspectives and strategies.

For the analyzers, capturing the complex relationships unfolding on the scale of the Internet becomes increasingly difficult. The desktop meta-

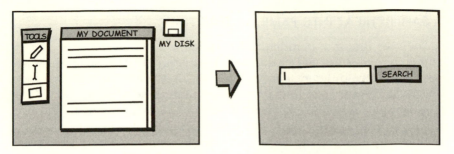

Figure 10.1. The user interface paradigm shift of the Internet: From simulated tools toward asking questions and getting answers.

phor did a good job of constraining things. There was a user, a desktop, documents, tools, and a set of tasks. The analyzers' job was to identify the right tool for the task. Graphically presented and consistent with the overall metaphor, things would more or less fall into place. This was the formula under which great word processors, desktop publishing programs, and image-processing tools were created. Today, analysis has expanded to include enterprisewide collaboration, huge knowledge databases, distributed systems, mobile access, intelligent agents, and so forth. The activities unfolding on the scope of Internet computing are complex and diverse. The safe ground of the desktop metaphor seems lost. Things are getting fuzzier.

The Internet is equally challenging for the creators. The known techniques for designing user interfaces have mainly evolved in the context of graphical user interfaces. Not surprisingly most creators have a background in some form of visual design. The desktop metaphor utilizes users' spatial thinking and organizes files by associating them with a specific place. Creators are experts in designing visual simulations with meaningful relationships between objects, spaces, and behaviors. The Internet, however, has a virtually infinite navigation space that changes dynamically. Lacking a spatial organization principle, users usually interact with the Internet by asking questions. While document icon, tool palette, and hard-drive icon constitute the desktop interface paradigm, the query box is the interface paradigm of the Internet. Creators are confronted with a shift from creating visual metaphors to designing protocols of asking and answering questions (see Figure 10.1).

To overcome the challenges of the Internet and take advantage of its opportunities, both analyzers and creators are forced to rethink and adapt their approaches: most importantly, their interdependency and the need to collaborate more closely increases. However, there are indications that the opposite occurs in the design practice.

A SAFE RETREAT INTO FAMILIAR TERRITORY

The user interface paradigm shift of the Internet absorbs the full attention of analyzers and creators. Not surprisingly, the two groups approach it from different perspectives, seeking solutions with the tools and techniques unique to their cultures: analysis or creation.

Individuals from the analyzer culture such as social scientists and psychologists often have a more academic background. They approach the problem by developing more scientifically elaborated and formalized analysis methods. Recently analyzers have developed more sophisticated approaches for contextual analysis, usability engineering, and system modeling. These methods capture and describe the increasing complexity of interactions across network systems. The creators—mostly designers by training—are equally ambitious in applying and improving their techniques to the new challenges. They do so by focusing on areas of the Internet where visual presentation plays a pivotal role such as online entertainment, education, promotional Web sites, and multimedia content. These are all in areas that benefit directly from creators' skills of producing compelling visual user experiences.

This polarizing trend is reflected in the landscape of the design industry. Interface design takes place primarily in two types of organizations:

• Small product design firms, which integrated interface design to their services or specialize in multimedia and Internet.

• Usability and user-interface departments of large computer or software corporations.

Creators seem to be concentrating in design firms, which focus on visual content for multimedia products and Web sites. Those firms are centered more around the core skills of creators. Furthermore, the work culture in a small, creative design firm is more consistent with the preferences most creators have toward professional culture. In contrast, analyzers can usually be found in the design departments of computer and software corporations. Large corporations can offer the long-term schedules and budgets required to support large-scale scientific research. Many analyzers find that corporate research and development is closer to the culture of academic research that they are used to working in. The cultures of analysis and creation seem to prefer different organizational models in the design industry. This can even be observed in the way software corporations and design firms communicate their services differently in the market (see Photos 10.1 and 10.2).

Photos 10.1 and 10.2 showcase a computer corporation versus a design firm. IBM sends a behavioral scientist into the ring. Frogdesign provides

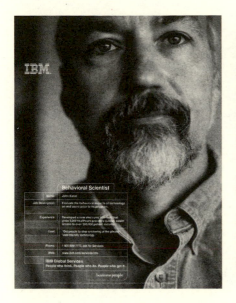 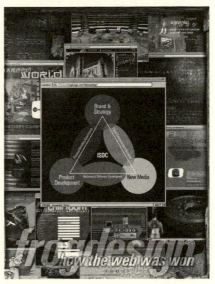

Photos 10.1 and 10.2. Advertising for user interface design services. Photos reprinted by permission from International Business Machines Corporation. © 1999 IBM Corp. (left) and (right) frogdesign.

a box full of visually elaborated creations. It is obvious where analyzers and where creators are being showcased.

This trend is worrisome. Within their distinct cultures the creators and analyzers have made significant achievements. But this process has polarized the two cultural groups. They seem to drift away from each other. In the day-to-day practice, this trend may be indicated by some common collaboration conflicts. The creators may have difficulties understanding the outcomes of increasingly sophisticated methods applied by analyzers. That is not because creators cannot appreciate analyzers' findings. The right user insight might be there, but spotting it and addressing it in the creation of products is often not easy for the creators. Gaps resulting from those misunderstandings force creators to improvise in order to deliver their "stuff." Research insights might be lost in this process. The analyzers obviously have a different perspective on this. They become suspicious whenever creators start improvising. Designs that are created with no solid scientific basis frustrate them. Then what is science good for? Conflict often emerges because analyzers feel their findings are being ignored. Improvisation, intuition, and heuristic methods are traditional key techniques for designers—but deeply suspicious to most analyzers. Additionally, analyzers have to deal with the fast pace of the Internet business, an environment with no time for long-term re-

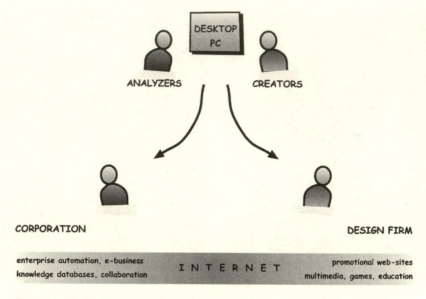

Figure 10.2. Drifting away from the shared focus of the desktop PC: The scope of the Internet makes the two cultures move into areas in which they feel most comfortable and effective.

search. A product idea that initiated a study might be gone before the study can be completed.

For both cultures—creators and analyzers—the concept of a task, an application, a user, and a PC used to be a handy way to guide the design activities. The desktop PC served as a point of focus. With the Internet and its broad scope, this point of focus seems to disappear. Creators and analyzers give their best to tackle the challenges of the Internet. They do it in aspects of the Internet where they could have the most influence. But even though they both advance their individual disciplines, they seem to move away from each other. This trend could become a major impediment to collaboration between creators and analyzers (see Figure 10.2).

WHAT COULD BRING THE CULTURES OF ANALYZERS AND CREATORS CLOSER TOGETHER?

A common ground for analysis and creation is a recurring theme—somewhat of a Holy Grail—in the user-interface community. Sometimes it is approached explicitly in cross-disciplinary experiments. On other occasions it unfolds implicitly in the daily disputes between creators and analyzers in the work context. Although sometimes unpleasant for the participants, those discussions are an excellent opportunity to observe the different perspectives of the two cultures. Those discussions give valuable hints for finding the connections between them. A shared approach must be equally useful for analysis and creation. It must have relevance—or if possible, a tradition in both cultures. And to be instrumental in practice a shared approach must be able to address the emerging issues of the Internet.

In the context of practicing design and seeking solutions to those questions, the team at GVO—a design firm in Palo Alto, California—discovered semiotics as a potential shared framework. Semiotics emerged as a solution to practical needs the team encountered while executing a range of commercial user-interface design projects. Semiotics has some essential characteristics that made it attractive for the problem at hand.

First, semiotics can be applied across different kinds of systems: spoken dialogues, social rituals, literature, movies, visual art, or even the navigational structure of a database. Thus semiotic structures from the physical world (e.g., user behavior) and semiotic structures of a software interface can be compared within the same framework.

Second, user interfaces are communication media. They communicate to users the status, options, and informational content of a software product. In his *Theory of Computer Semiotics* P.B. Anderson discusses in detail how software can be understood as a semiotic system:

Although in many respects computer systems can be conceived as tools in analogy with typewriters, pencils, brushes, and filing cabinets, they differ from these tools by not primarily existing or being used as physical objects, but as signs. The pencil of the drawing program is no real pencil that can be used to chew on, it merely stands for a pencil, represented by a collection of pixels on the screen. Computer systems resemble other media by primarily acting as carriers of meaning. (Anderson 1997: 1)

One implication of this is the fact that utility and perceived value of a software product depends on how well the underlying functionality is communicated to users through the interface. Anything that is not communicated does, from the users' point of view, not exist. This might sound obvious, but it emphasizes the crucial role of language and communication in interface design, particularly when compared with traditional product design (see Figure 10.3).

Because of physical properties, the "I-am-no-chair" message of a beanbag does not prevent users from sitting in it. Miscommunication of the utility of a software leaves users with a screen that is meaningless and useless to them.

Furthermore, the Internet shifts toward a conversational paradigm. Instead of visual metaphors, asking questions is the key interaction technique for large knowledge databases. The design challenge here is to

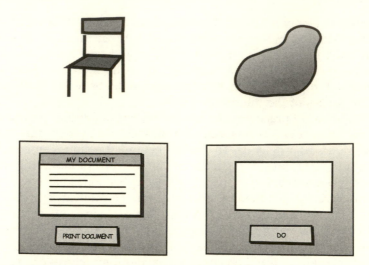

Figure 10.3. Communicating utility to users through the interface is crucial for software products.

define meaningful and efficient conversations that bring the user to the
desired information. Semiotics is perfect for understanding and defining
conversational structures.

Finally and most important: semiotics has a tradition in both cultures—analysis and creation. Language-based approaches exist in the
social sciences and in design theory, a common ground that needs to be
rediscovered.

SEMIOTICS IN THE TRADITIONS OF ANALYZERS AND CREATORS

The study of language or linguistics is a core element of social sciences.
The language of a society is not only a means of communication, but
also reflects its members' view of reality. Shared beliefs, rules, and rituals
are embedded in the language a culture speaks. Social scientists have
been using forms of language analysis as a key to deeply understanding
cultures. Michael Agar highlights the potential of language for cultural
analysis in his book *Language Shock*:

Cultures are different, no question about it. But if you just get a handle on a few
of the words out there in the space between you, you can start into the concepts
that travel with them. Everyone uses words—they're human similarity. The
words will lead the way into the differences. Culture is a conceptual system
whose surface appears in the words of people's language. (Agar 1994: 79–80)

In customer research social scientists—or analyzers in general—use semiotics for their prime objective: analysis. It enables them to discover the mental models, perceptions, and expectations shared by individuals within a customer group. Customer researchers apply semiotic techniques, such as conversation analysis, to understand what Michael Agar calls the ethnographic semantics: "semantics because it deals with word meanings, ethnographic because the point of studying meaning isn't to write a dictionary for second-language learners, but rather to learn about the view of the world that some group of people has" (Agar 1994: 79–80).

The role of semiotics in the design disciplines is less commonly known. In the context of the critique of functionalism, semiotics was part of a major paradigm shift in design and architecture. In the 1970s, the awareness of an ecology crisis and the social consequences of modern urban planning led many designers to profoundly rethink their approach. What they realized was a huge disconnect between the social and psychological reality of consumers and what modern designers had envisioned for them. In that context, the semiotic perspective provided a way to bring culturally meaningful content back into the products. Inspired by the writings of, for example, Roland Barthes, Jean Baudrillard, and Umberto Eco, designers started thinking about the stories their products tell rather than merely their practical functions. Beginning in the late '70s, design groups emerged that practiced design based on those—postmodern—ideas. Most famous for their "radical design" approach were the Italian groups Alchimia and Memphis. They created furniture, interiors, and objects that were humorous, ironic, absurd—sometimes seemingly useless. Their designs promoted a provocative, antithetic attitude toward the functionalism school that was predominant at that time. The style connected to this design approach became popular with designers and consumers in the '80s. This trend evolved with groups such as Kunstflug that put less emphasis on the antifunctionalism message, but continued to explore the potential of connecting design to contemporary cultural rituals. They embodied symbolic themes into furniture and household goods that let consumers experience common objects in new ways (see Photos 10.3 and 10.4).

A tree with an integrated coffeemaker serves as a center of tribe gatherings in the office. In combination with a gas burner, an otherwise normal-looking table turns into a "desktop fireplace."

The success of this design approach—also referred to as "product semantics"—marked the peak of a shift away from Louis H. Sullivan's famous slogan of "form follows function." Designers—or creators—used semiotics for what they were good at: creating objects. Practically, this approach could be described as a hermeneutic cycle in which designers create a sketch or an object and then interpret its possible cultural mean-

Photos 10.3 and 10.4. Designs that reflect cultural symbols of use rather than technology or functionality. Right: Kaffeebaum (coffee-tree) Design: Kunstflug 1981. Left: Feuertisch (fire-table) Design: Kunstflug 1983. Photos copyright by Kunstflug.

ings. Based on this insight, designers use an iterative process until the envisioned meaning appears. This approach was particularly popular for the design of microelectronic products, where the technology behind a function is invisible. Unlike a bicycle, for example, where the actual technology (sprockets, chain, etc.) serves as a sign for what a bicycle is and does, the hidden microchip does not signify anything. Avoiding putting chips into ambiguous boxes, designers created metaphorical sculptures to communicate what the chip inside does. This ultimately helps customers understand and use unfamiliar technologies used in digital products (see Photos 10.5 and 10.6). The shape of this event information terminal refers to a paper scroll hanging from the ceiling in a very literal way. To convey the essence of this portable TV the designer applied a more abstract composition of visual symbols associated with sending, transmitting, flickering, and so on.

 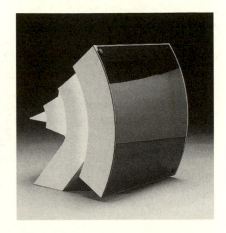

Photos 10.5 and 10.6. Metaphors make the functions of hidden microelec-
tronic technology tangible. Left: Public event information terminal by Raab,
Schupach, Sulzbach, and Bürdek, 1988 (photo courtesy of Bernhard E. Bürdek).
Right: Television by Kurt Becker, 1988 (photo courtesy of Kurt Becker).

Today most designers look at both the functionality and the meaning
of products. They try to create an appropriate composition incorporating
both. However, defining what exactly the meaning of a product should
be requires insights into the meanings that are out there in customers'
culture. In cases where the designer is not a potential user or is not well
informed, finding and communicating the right meaning through a product can be difficult.

CONNECTING THE SEMIOTIC TRADITIONS OF ANALYZERS
AND CREATORS

Both the analyzers and the creators have a tradition of semiotics. Both
cultures use it exactly for what they are passionate about. Analyzers use
semiotics to learn about a culture. Creators use semiotics to create culturally meaningful designs. The benefit of connecting those two
traditions seems obvious. In the following I will describe a process
framework in which semiotics integrates user analysis and design generation. This framework has been used for commercial design projects
at GVO. We call this approach semiotic modeling of user interfaces.

To computer scientists the term "semiotic modeling" is probably not
new. Semiotics has been applied for the creation of complex, intelligent
systems. The linguistic theories and concepts used in that context are
similar to the ones referred to here. However, the scope and application
of semiotic modeling of user interfaces are quite different. The aim of
semiotic modeling on a system level is typically the creation of entire

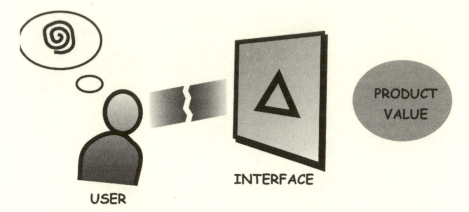

Figure 10.4. A user interface that does not speak the user's language can't communicate the underlying product value.

systems that feature learning, reasoning, artificial intelligence, and so forth. The focus of semiotic modeling of user interfaces is the understanding of the user-product interaction. It is tailored for the practice of designing a representation of a system that connects to users—not to specify an entire system architecture based on linguistic concepts.

SEMIOTIC MODELING AS A SHARED FRAMEWORK FOR ANALYSIS AND CREATION

Like languages, user interfaces consist of rules and elements. Using those rules and elements, a software or Internet product needs to communicate how it fulfills users' goals. Usability issues, inefficient use, or misunderstanding of product benefits often indicate a communication breakdown between user and interface. If the interface fails to connect to the user, the whole product becomes valueless, whether valuable functionality or information is there or not (Figure 10.4).

The product not only becomes difficult to use from the users' point of view but also loses its value. Semiotic modeling focuses on the communication between user and interface. It makes tangible the language that is used—or attempted to be used—by both parties. It reveals the roots of usability symptoms and extracts the language that users understand. The user interface can then be adapted to reflect the language of the user, which makes it more understandable, intuitive, and ultimately easier to use. In practice the three steps of semiotic interface modeling look like this (see Figure 10.5):

1. *Collect*: User language is collected. Users are encouraged to talk about their work, tools, strategies, and goals. Although this may also include problems

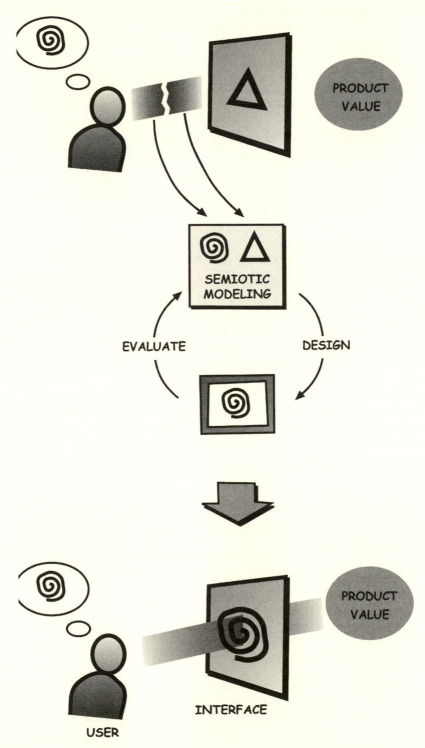

Figure 10.5. Semiotic modeling of a user interface. Language of user and interface are analyzed.

with existing products, an existing system or its application does not define the scope.

2. *Model and Compare*: The rules and elements of users' language and existing interface are analyzed. Both models are compared to identify similarities and differences. The discrepancies of the two models point to the roots of usability issues.

3. *Create*: A design is created that reflects users' language. The rules are implemented in interface design, navigation, dialogue structures, and so on.

Comparison reveals similarities and differences. An interface design is created and evaluated that embodies the semiotic model of the user.

AN EXAMPLE FROM PRACTICE: SCIENTIFIC WEB DATABASE

This example for the application of semiotic modeling is based on a commercial design project done by GVO for an industrial client. It involved team members from GVO as well as from the client side and took about three months. The team consisted of analyzers and creators: two social scientists, one designer, and two software developers. The challenge was the user interface for a database with more than 4 million items that supports scientists with experimental work in the lab. The interface to use this Web database was provided on HTML pages accessed by a standard Web browser. Each item in this database had distinct features and could be of interest to the scientist. The scientists use this information to complement their experimental research work. The performance and usability of the user interface directly affected the likelihood of a significant scientific discovery.

The existing user interface for this application followed the standards of Web design. The scientists queried the database for information. The information was structured using hyperlinked pages that allowed users to jump to other information about an item. This was a typical example of interaction with information on the Internet, as we know from Web sites and Internet services. Even though most scientists were familiar with the World Wide Web, they did not feel comfortable with this interface design. They avoided using large parts of the system, even though they could provide significant utility. The scientists had difficulty understanding how the system could support their work. On the other hand, all scientists thought that the actual data in the database could be of great value to them.

As soon as the team started with the project, it became obvious that using a straightforward, "conventional" approach would be difficult. Feedback collected from users on the usability of the interface was limited to broad expressions of inappropriateness, such as "It doesn't seem efficient," "It is clumsy," and "I don't like it—don't ask me why." The attempt to do a task analysis did not lead to useful results either. The interviews and observations showed that the scientists shared a set of simple, generic tools and processes. But how those tools would be applied to research work was strongly driven by diverse individual strategies. The scientists believed that their personal strategies were pivotal for successful findings and even for individual careers. In fact, in discussions scientists consistently rejected the notion of a task-driven approach to the design of their tools. An interface that implied a certain way of use was considered to be inappropriate. Understanding the task and then tailoring a tool for it—one of the paradigms of user-centered design—did not seem applicable to this user culture.

The solution to those problems came with the semiotic modeling approach. It allowed the team to establish a thorough understanding of this seemingly hard-to-tackle user culture by revealing a consistent set of rules and elements in scientists' language. Inherent in the descriptions of their database use, lab work, and the larger context of their research projects was this recurring story: "I [scientist] go out there, gather things, and bring them back. I look at the things, keep the good, and dump the others. Then I go out again." Some examples:

"I **go to** the database X and I **go to** database Z and I read about it **there**."

"I wanna know what's **out there**, what **others** have done."

"I **take** the hits from the search . . . **pick** a few . . . **go back** and **look** at those analysis results . . . Then from **there** I might **take** those and search again . . . then I'll **get** the items themselves and **take** that . . ."

"I **get** the information and then try to **store** this information and then I **go back**."

For easier internal communication and because of its obvious analogies, the design team gave the scientists' mental model the name "Hunting and Gathering." A visual map for this semiotic model was also created (see Figure 10.6).

The language elements observed in the semiotic analysis followed consistent core themes: distinct places, concentric navigation, spatial logic (here versus out there), and collection of items. Although the individual scientists used different terms, they described the same underlying rules and elements (Table 10.1).

Based on this hypothesis, the team validated whether this model is truly unique to the scientists. Language was collected from users who use the software, work in the same context, but with a different role and background (i.e., software development). This group did not engage in any lab work, but focused on customized or advanced database searches. The finding was that their language had a significantly different model,

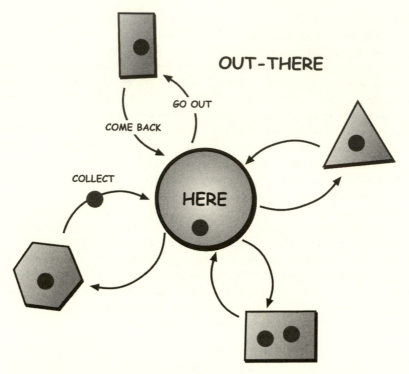

Figure 10.6. Semiotic model inherent in scientists' language: Hunting and Gathering.

even when they described exactly the same activities as the scientists. Their story was, "I modify data. I receive a report and review it." The semiotic model underlying their language did not feature the notion of distinct spaces, gathering, or active navigation.

Finally, a semiotic analysis of the existing user interface was conducted. Not surprisingly it revealed a structure rooted in the hypertext or World Wide Web paradigm. This made sense, because this interface paradigm was adopted implicitly with World Wide Web technology.

In an ambiguous constellation of places linked by paths that take users from one place to one or more other places, users may jump from place to place in a process without explicit beginning or end. Consequently the resulting semiotic model was called "Dungeons and Dragons" by the team (see Figure 10.7).

The comparison of the Hunting and Gathering and the Dungeons and Dragons models highlights the causes for the usability issues and the

Table 10.1
Components (Top Row) of Scientists' Mental Model and Expressions Used (Columns)

Home	Move around	Out there	Hunt	Gather	Investigate
my	leave	places	troll	get	put together
we	go back	outside	go through	take	collate
us	back home	over at	shop around	pull out	play around
ours	go there	external	look around	capture	prioritize
internal	come here	somewhere	see	pick	decide
inside		theirs	find	select	analyze
within		somebody's	discover	a snapshot	understand
		beyond	a close look		eliminate
		unsecured	find details		dump
		gray area	right place		compare

general discomfort the scientists had encountered when using this product (see Table 10.2).

In other contexts like Web surfing or catalog browsing, the Dungeons and Dragons model may be very appealing. We all know the excitement connected to drifting around on the Web and discovering unexpected places. However, for the scientists this model clearly clashes with their mental model of doing research work. The scientists actually described how they perceived the dungeons. Their language revealed the fact that they can't follow the rules of Hunting and Gathering with the existing user interface.

> "You can **go deeper** in one question and if you have another question you're **thrown off**. You have to **walk all the way back**, that's a real problem."
> "There's **no way to get to it directly**; you have to do all this **indirect** . . . you have to go into a URL and then **have it come back** and **go backward**."
> "There is **no way to get to it directly**. You **have to follow a few paths**."
> "Want to go to the next search and try to save the findings before I **must go down**."

The team's comparison of both semiotic models led to a deep and shared understanding about the causes of usability and acceptance issue

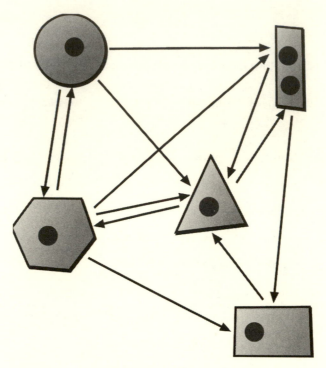

Figure 10.7. Semiotic model of the user interface with usability issues: Dungeons and Dragons.

Table 10.2
Comparison of the Two Semiotic Models Revealing Discrepancies and Roots of Usability and Acceptance Issues

Hunting and Gathering	Dungeons and Dragons
Concentric navigation	Maze
Here versus out there	Arbitrary places
Choices where to go	Given paths
Gathering	Things stay in place
Collating things	One thing per place

that had been observed in the beginning of the project. In terms of analysis this was great success. And even better, the semiotic modeling had led to some really juicy content for the creators: the rule and elements of the scientists' Hunting and Gathering mental model. The creators just went ahead and started working on simple interface prototypes that followed the Hunting and Gathering rules. They embodied the semantics of Hunting and Gathering into the navigational structure, interaction design, and visual representations on screen. The semiotic model identified in the scientists' language was translated into a semiotic concept of a user-interface design. The prototypes allowed the team to validate whether scientists recognize their model in the user interface—and in fact they did. The scientists perceived the design as being more intuitive and easier to use. They displayed more willingness to use the database for their research work. Ultimately, this leads to an increased likelihood of scientific findings being made with this database—an important aspect for the perceived value for this kind of product.

By using semiotic modeling as a collaborative framework, both analyzer and creators had succeeded in this project. Both cultures contributed what they do best. The analyzers identified the Hunting and Gathering model. The creators translated the rules and elements of Hunting and Gathering into an appropriate interface structure. The semiotic models—Hunting and Gathering and Dungeons and Dragons—served as powerful shared concepts throughout the design process. The semiotic models were meaningful and practically useful for analyzers and creators (Figure 10.8).

WHAT'S NEXT?

The use of semiotics for the creation of user interfaces is not common in the practice of product design. However, the GVO team's experience with this approach in several commercial design projects for Internet and Intranet applications was very promising. As a shared thinking tool, semiotic modeling established common ground for analyzers and creators. The team members perceived an important benefit in a positive effect on the speed and productivity in the design process—a key requirement for being competitive in the Internet age.

Language-driven approaches to user-interface design will also become more important as we move toward more conversational interaction techniques, such as phone dialogue systems, speech input, query-based interaction, intelligent agents, and so forth. In such systems the language spoken within the target customers' culture is the basis for establishing a successful dialogue through the interface. Analyzing real world conversations and transforming their logic and protocols into interfaces is

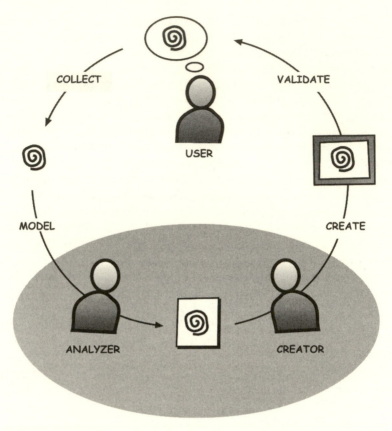

Figure 10.8. The semiotic model Hunting and Gathering served as a continuous thread throughout analysis and creation phases.

the key to making such product-customer interactions truly conversational.

Another benefit of the semiotic approach is rooted in the rule-based nature of language. The fact that with language the same content can be expressed in various ways as long the rules—or grammar—are followed has interesting aspects for interfaces. Customers increasingly access the networked information with a diverse range of devices such as PCs, phones, handheld devices, and TVs. The interface points to such a system can no longer be defined with a single, graphical representation. Semiotic approaches can help establish a design grammar that allows an interface to communicate consistently in changing contexts and with diverse appearances.

Finally, today's design firms and corporate design groups are forced to continually rethink their organization, management, processes, and skill set in order to keep up with the rapidly growing demand for the design of Internet products and services. Semiotic modeling has the ability to foster integration of the core skills—analysis and creation—required to tackle major interface challenges in that area. This could make it a core competence of a new type of design organization that is not only keeping up, but also explicitly addressing the emerging opportunities of the Internet for the design business.

REFERENCES

Agar, M. 1994. *Language Shock*. New York: William Morrow and Company.
Anderson, P.B. 1997. *A Theory of Computer Semiotics*. Cambridge: Cambridge University Press.

PART IV

CONCLUSION: THE FUTURE OF DESIGN

Professor Ken Friedman suggests that the shift to a global, information-based economy is forcing fundamental changes in design as a profession. Design is shifting from a crafts-oriented discipline that emphasizes individual creativity and commerce, into a more robust multidisciplinary profession devoted to the conceptualization, configuration, and implementation of meaningful living environments, products, services, systems, and brands. Successful "design" will have to merge crafts-oriented and interpretive ways of knowing with scientific knowledge about people, information, and material systems.

11

Conclusion: Toward an Integrative Design Discipline

Ken Friedman

This book is based on a simple premise. Corporate competition in evolving global markets requires an interdisciplinary partnership between design and consumer research. For this partnership to work, professionals in design and consumer research must understand each other's professions. They must adapt their working concepts to work effectively in multidisciplinary teams. They must renew their commitment to the idea of design as service to customers, consumers, and end users.

Social scientists must become more familiar with the principles guiding design: industrial design, graphic design, interaction design, and software design. Similarly, designers must become more familiar with the principles of social science, not as scholars in the field, but as professionals whose work should be informed by the needs of those for whom they design. Many of the previous chapters have touched on efforts to create effective organizations, communicative processes, and research methods.

In this chapter, I will argue that this process is causing fundamental changes in the very definition of design, the domains of knowledge and skills that comprise it, and the balance between art and science. Students who wish to become designers in the postindustrial knowledge economy will enter an inherently multidisciplinary profession. This profession involves a wide variety of professionals, including scientists (physical, biological, and social), engineers (industrial, civil, biological, genetic, electrical, and software), and managers, as well as the many kinds of artists and artisans now called designers. I suspect that in the coming years, the distinctions between analyzers and creators or between researchers and designers will fade substantially. Everybody engaged in the process of defining, planning, and configuring artifacts and systems will be considered "designers."

Since its origins in the 1960s, this transformation has promoted the emergence of an interdisciplinary design science (Fuller 1964, 1965, 1967, 1969, 1981; Fuller and Dil 1983). That discipline is attempting to create the general knowledge and practices that underlie attempts to move from thought to action. Without a richer scientific foundation, none of the people in the design process who have responsibility for product and service outcomes will be prepared to work within the teams that manage a complete design.

REDEFINING DESIGN FOR A POSTINDUSTRIAL ERA

As professions go, design is relatively young. But the practice of design predates all professions. In fact, the practice of design—making things with a useful goal in mind—predates the human race. On the one hand, design helped to make us human. On the other, the act of designing has in some way been so closely linked to human culture that we haven't always given it the thought it deserves.

The verb "design" describes a process of thought and planning. This meaning takes precedence over all other meanings of the term. "Design" as a verb had a place in the English language by the early 1500s. The first written citation of the verb "design" dates from the year 1548. The 1993 edition of Merriam-Webster defines "design" as "to conceive and plan out in the mind; to have as a specific purpose; to devise for a specific function or end." Related to these is the act of drawing, with an emphasis on the nature of the drawing as a plan or map, as well as "to draw plans for; to create, fashion, execute or construct according to plan."

Half a century later, in 1588, the word began to be used as a noun describing "a particular purpose held in view by an individual or group; deliberate, purposive planning; a mental project or scheme in which means to an end are laid down" (Merriam-Webster 1993). Here too, purpose and planning toward desired outcomes are central.

Although the word "design" refers first and foremost to process rather than product, it has become popular shorthand for designed artifacts. This shorthand covers meaningful artifacts as well as the merely fashionable or trendy. As I see it, design is a process. I will not use the word "design" to designate the outcome of the design process. The outcome of the design process may be a product or a service but the outcome itself is not "design."

"Design" as a verb or a process description noun frames design as a dynamic process (Friedman 1993). This means that design can be used to structure an activity framework. Design as an activity framework translates utilitarian, symbolic, and psychological needs into functions. The design function translates needs and wants into ideas, and it translates these ideas into the structural descriptions entities to produce required functions that satisfy needs (Gero 1999).

DESIGN DOMAINS IN A POSTINDUSTRIAL SOCIETY

The nature of design as an integrative discipline places it at the intersection of several large fields. In one dimension, design is a field of thinking and pure research. In another, it is a field of practice and applied research. When applications are used to solve specific problems in a specific setting, it is a field of clinical research.

I propose a generic model of design as a field of theory, practice, and application composed of six domains. Three theory domains (natural sciences, humanities and liberal arts, and social and behavioral sciences) are interrelated with three domains of practice and application (human professions and services, creative and applied arts, and technology and engineering). Design may involve any or all of these domains, in differing aspect and proportion, depending on the nature of the project at hand or the problem to be solved.

Design professionals must be able to work with a far wider range of issues than any one discipline can master. In my seminars on strategic design at Oslo Business School (Friedman 1992, 1995c, 1997) and later at the Norwegian School of Management (Friedman 2000a, 2000b), I developed a schema of design skill and knowledge domains based on field research, personal experience, and an emerging theory of design practice (see Table 11.1). The taxonomy identifies four bodies of knowledge with which design professionals must eventually acquaint themselves. The first domain involves skills for learning and leading. The second is the human world. The third is the artifact. The fourth embraces the environment. Each requires a broad range of skills, knowledge, and awareness. Although these are necessary domains of design knowledge, no one design professional can be expected to master all these areas of knowledge and skill.

The issues in these four domains go far beyond the image of designers as artists who configure artifacts. If these taxa stipulate the kinds of issues that design professionals will probably encounter during their careers, and if no individual can possibly master all of them, the natural question arises, "What core knowledge do designers need and how can they develop it?" The question raises a host of philosophical issues suggesting that the design field straddles art and science. Design in the post-

Table 11.1
A Taxonomy of Design Knowledge Domains

Learning and Leading	The Human World	The Artifact	The Environment
Problem solving	The human being	Product development	Natural environment
	--Human behavior	--Methodology	--Ecology
Interaction method	--Information semantics	--Market research	--Evolution
	--Knowledge creation	--Innovation research	--Environment
Coaching	--Physiology and ergonomics	--Problematics	--Impact
	--Research and methodology	--Product generation	
Mind mapping		----Creating new products	Built environment
	The company	----Transforming old products	--Cityscape
Research skills	--Organizational management and behavior	--Product regeneration	--Economy
	--Business economics	----Correcting problems	--Social web
Analysis	--Company culture	----Improving products	--Infrastructure
	--Leadership	----Positioning	--Traffic
Rhetoric	----Administration	----Re-engineering (lean production)	
	----Future planning		Telecommunication
Logic	----Process management	Design	--Airports
	----Change management	--Product design	--Food distribution
Mathematics	----Process skills	--Ergonomics	--Human ecology
	--Company functions	----Product semantics	
Language	----Governance	----Product graphics	Architecture
	----Logistics	----Functionality	--Informated buildings
Editing	----Production	--Graphic design	--Usage
	----Marketing	----Visual ergonomics	--Architecture as idea
Writing	----Finance	----Typography	--Architecture as corporate identity
		--Corporate design	--Profile architecture
Presentation skills	Society	--Behavioral design	
--Public speaking	--Trends	--Information design	Interior
--Small group	--Legal issues	----Knowledge design	--Furniture
--Information graphics	--Media	--Process design	--Interior as corporate identity
	--Social economics		--Psychology
	--Communication	Manufacturing	--Function
		--Technology	--Social structure
	The world	--Operations	--The shape of work
	--World trade: European Union, USA, Asia	--Statistical quality control	--The shape of play
	--Cross-cultural Issues	--Logistics	--The shape of private life
	--Political economics	--Process management	
			Installation
	Theory Basics		--Philosophy of space
	--Culture theory		--Culture theory
	--Sociology of knowledge		--Art ideas
	--Reception theory		--Inquiry
	--History of design		
	--Sociology of taste		
	--Content analysis		
	--World history		
	--Paradigm analysis		
	--Models		

industrial era is becoming an inherently multidisciplinary profession that admits and goes beyond the secular divisions between many of the individual disciplines.

Systemic thinking gives perspective to the models of design offered here. The design process has no center. It is a network of linked events. Systemic thinking makes the nature of networked events clear. No one person succeeds unless an entire team succeeds in meeting its goals.

THE FOUNDATION OF DESIGN KNOWLEDGE

From the time of the first stone artifacts to the era of batons with appreciable symbols, the design of cultural artifacts precedes symbolization by just under two-and-a-half million years. Tool making is more deeply integrated into our behavior and our culture than symbolization or philosophical inquiry. Symbolization and philosophy give us the power to inquire about the relationship between our tool making and the world around us.

At first glance, one might imagine design an unsuitable forum for philosophical inquiry. In its older incarnation as craft, this would certainly be so. Originally the distinction between theory-driven knowledge and skill-driven practice was simply a distinction between kinds of activity.

Skill-driven practice was rooted and situated. Although it may have been possible to explain some aspects of skill, skill essentially involved what we term "tacit knowledge."

The world depends on both, but the kind of thinking represented by each is foreign to the other. Precisely because the mysteries of the craft can't be put into words, one cannot imagine a philosophy of craft. If design is craft, there can, by definition, be no philosophy of design, and there need not be. This may change in the future with the development of craft-based industries. Although inspired by and rooted in craft, these forms of design develop into knowledge-intensive configurations of professional practice. The tacit knowledge of the inarticulate craft tradition needs no philosophy.

As we have seen elsewhere in this volume, design has begun to take a new form in the knowledge economy. The need for designers to consider their work as an integrated process flowing through and embedded in the entire process of conceptualizing, planning, and realizing products and services means that design is now both a philosophy and a technology. The larger frame of general thinking and planning also establishes several senses in which design may be examined in the philosophical perspective.

The philosophy appropriate to design may also be a new kind of philosophy that blurs prior distinctions. The knowledge economy is blurring the boundaries between product and service, material and immaterial, hardware and software. In this context, nearly every design practice has immaterial dimensions along with the material. Design as defined here is an act of conceptualization linked to the managerial concept of governance and the industrial concept of control.

DESIGN: AN EMERGING DISCIPLINE, FIELD, AND SCIENCE

Design scholars are still debating whether the arena of design knowledge constitutes a discipline, a field, or a science. My view is that it is, in some measure, all of these.

One aspect of the debate is current because design has entered the university curriculum during the past half century. This development has taken different courses in different nations. In North America, for example, design courses began to enter colleges and universities with art programs. Most of these began in the late 1940s and afterward. Many—perhaps most—university-level programs with a specific focus on design are innovations of the past two decades, as contrasted with the occasional design courses available in larger and somewhat older art programs. In other nations, design programs grew within and then grew out from architecture schools or technical colleges. In the United Kingdom, design entered the university when the colleges of art and design that had become polytechnics were merged into the new universities.

These changes were rooted in economic and educational transformations. Placing design in the university also rendered visible the design profession as an important service profession in the postindustrial knowledge economy. Design entered the university in a time of economic transition. The years between 1950 and 2000 were the years in which the economy shifted from an industrial economy to a postindustrial economy to an information society and a knowledge economy. Contemporary design takes place in this new economy—including the process of shaping artifacts through industrial design and product design.

The new location of design education in the university clarified the nature of design as a professional practice rather than a vocation or a trade, but design was integrated into the university in a way that confused as much as it clarified. Art and design came into the university through arts and crafts schools or professional schools, but the educational foundation these schools offered was not the basic philosophical foundation offered for admission to the other professional schools. It was often a combination of vocational training and preprofessional education.

However well the development of university-level design programs clarified the importance of design as a profession, it began to make clear the gaps in our understanding of design knowledge. The emergence of a new professional training was not accompanied by the deeper understandings of ontology and epistemology that serve as the foundation of other fields.

As a result, the field of design is built on contradictory bases for its traditions of knowledge. On the one hand, the design profession is anchored in the trades, vocations, and crafts. These have never been defined in philosophical terms because they have had no basis in the work of explicit definition. Instead, they are rooted in unspoken assumptions anchored in the inarticulate nature of a practice going back beyond prehistory to our prehuman development. On the other hand, the design profession is a contemporary field growing within the university.

With few historical roots in a philosophical tradition—few that go deeper than the past few decades—we have yet to shape a clear understanding of the nature of design. We do not agree, therefore, on whether the practice of design constitutes a trade, a vocation, a profession, an art, or a discipline. Neither have we decided whether design knowledge constitutes a discipline, a field, or a science. Perhaps design practice fits under more than one of these rubrics. Perhaps design knowledge meets the criteria of two or even all three. In different ways and at different levels of practice, it seems that design practice fits the standards of all five kinds of practice. In much the same way, design knowledge involves all three kinds of knowledge, as it must.

DESIGN SCIENCE

One way to move the design profession into the knowledge economy is by adopting a design science approach. The term "design science" is adapted from Buckminster Fuller's (1964, 1969) usage and from Herbert Simon's (1982) landmark book *The Sciences of the Artificial*. In using the term, however, I do not adopt or use all of Simon's ideas or Fuller's. I use the term "science" to describe a broad, systemic design practice anchored in a generalizable, theoretical approach that functions for all the design professions. Design sciences are technical or social sciences that focus on how to do things to accomplish goals.

According to Simon, design sciences emerge when skills-based professions move from traditional rules of thumb or trial-and-error methods to the use of theory and scientific method. Many forms of design are at this point now, including graphic design, industrial design, information design, and design management.

The growth of a design science is implicit in the ongoing transition from an arts-and-crafts approach to a theory-based design. The design science challenge is to shape an effective process of design that yields effective outcomes. This must be an inquiry-based process, a problem-solving process linked to effective methods for design development. This, in turn, requires the use of systemic thinking, a scientific approach.

As it stands now, there remains a great deal of resistance to design science among academic and studio designers. The general tendency among students in art schools and in the craft schools that aspire to their status is not to read, but rather to look at pictures. The little reading that does take place often focuses on the current interests of trendy critics and connoisseurs. There are exceptions, but they are as notable as they are few. In general, arts and crafts-based design schools have not been centers of reading or theory building.

This is understandable. Faculty members shape schools and their culture, and design faculty members generally come from an arts and crafts tradition. Reading and research have not been prized in the arts and crafts tradition. The tradition of research, writing, and professional dialogue on which scientific progress depends has been, for the most part, absent. Those who oppose the scientific tradition of design theory dismiss it as mere "book learning." Some state openly that "real designers" do not use words. Rather, they say that "real designers use their hands" to make things, artifacts that will speak for themselves and for their makers.

Outstanding design artifacts do speak for themselves and for their makers. Nevertheless, artifacts do not articulate or clarify the design process. This is where the problem lies. The key difference between design and craft is not in the crafting or the beauty or the esthetic quality of the artifact. These may be the same. It is a question of process. The design process begins above all with inquiry. Jens Bernsen (1986: 10) describes design as "translating a purpose into a physical form or tool."

Designed artifacts and natural artifacts have much in common, but designed artifacts are, finally, the result of a conscious process of evolution. Bernsen describes solutions in nature and design that "vary in purpose and are adapted to different environments." He writes that we use many of the same kinds of terms to describe the results of design and evolution, including purpose, economy of manufacturing and construction, beauty, interaction with the user, and relationship to the environment. "The fact that the designs of nature and the designs of man can be analyzed according to a common set of criteria," writes Bernsen (1986: 10) "stems from the fact that they have a basic property in common: they are solutions to a problem."

The title of Bernsen's book suggests a frame for the design inquiry: the problem comes first. The artistic approach all too often involves a solution looking for a problem. This means a look, a style, or an answer waiting to be settled on an unsuspecting client. The solution may be beautiful and the results may be artistic. The results may even evolve to fulfill a need. But unless the process is a conscious problem-solving process, it is not design.

The definition of design science distinguishes the search for knowledge as science from the productive application of knowledge in art or technology. Design requires both. The art and technology of design practice for the knowledge economy requires a general base. This must be established on a science of design, a broad, systematic field incorporating all the disciplines and practices of design, building on and contributing to basic research, applied research, and clinical research.

The science of design does not mimic natural science. Design sciences are technical or social sciences concerned with how to do things to accomplish goals. Design sciences emerge when skills-based professions move from rules of thumb based on trial and error to instructions based on scientific method. The design professions are at this point now.

It should also be clear that the scientific approach to design does not contradict the artistic aspect of design. Successful design artifacts have esthetic values and qualities, sensual and engaged. All designed objects, tactile, mechanical, visual, and auditory, are mediated through the physical senses. Sensory quality is a central issue for articulate objects that work in a physical world. The purpose of this chapter is to consider the design process and the education designers need to carry out the process successfully, so I will not focus on sensation or esthetics. It is, however, vital to note the importance of the esthetic dimensions of design.

A robust design process embraces the esthetic as well as the scientific. The central difference between the scientific approach and the artistic approach is that one must start with the parameters of the problem rather than look and feel. Look and feel, tone, feeling, and flavor emerge in the solution phase once the parameters of the problem establish the basic requirements of a solution. The most successful design artifacts join science, art, and commerce as effectively as they were combined in the life of a good medieval workshop.

Given our evolutionary history, it is clear that a good artifact may evolve without a conscious problem-solving process. We cannot know what goes on in the mind of a designer. We cannot, therefore, know whether an artifact emerges through the process of scientific discovery or through the process of evolution and selection, justified afterward by clever language. The questions of intuition and multiple languages make this even more difficult to distinguish in practice than in theory. Intuition plays a role in every science. Intuition often involves nonverbal and—at first—inarticulate thinking. The many ways in which people represent ideas and express their work also mean that there are many possible languages of articulate inquiry.

Entirely distinct from the issue of many forms of articulation and the role of intuition, it is possible for a designer to stumble upon the design of an artifact or muddle through to a solution without conscious effort. Without conscious problem solving, however, including the proper use of intuition, we are not talking about design but evolution. The work of the unconscious designer is no more and no less a product of evolution than the tools evolved by Homo habilis in 2,500,000 B.C. The evolved artifact may have a fancy package and a trademarked name, a snappy look and a good effect, but unless it is the result of a proper design process, the individual who produced it has not yet learned to walk upright as a designer.

It's clear that we may stumble on appropriate designs by randomly generating hundreds of ideas and filtering them through conscious criteria. Much like the process of evolution in natural, random development and selection work effectively at a high price in failed developments and extinct lines. The evidence of new product failure is clear. One study suggested that of new product ideas that move beyond the proposal stage, 57 percent achieve technical objectives, 31 percent enter full-scale marketing, and only 12 percent earn a profit (Mansfield et al. 1971: 57). According to some experts, more than 80 percent of all new products fail when they are launched, and another 10 percent fail within five years (Edwards 1999; Lukas 1998; McMath 1998). Planning and study can never yield perfect results. Even so, I assert the need to foster the development of a design science for the design professions.

Some leading designers now enhance their success rate by using scientific method and an articulated problem-solving process. A growing number of designers, scholars, and scholar-practitioners are active in the field of design research. A few outstanding design schools teach theory, research, and problem solving, and these schools require a heavy diet of reading and writing along with the exercises and projects that most design schools require. These efforts are laudable and should be encouraged.

But science and the scientific method should not be equated with positivism. Although many contemporary designers and even some anthropologists believe that science means positivism, it does not. There are many valid approaches to science. Many can be usefully applied to design and design research (Alvesson and Sköldberg 1994; Argyris, Putnam, and Smith 1985; Feyerabend 1962, 1974, 1977, 1978, 1987; Galtung 1967; Gleick 1987; Kuhn 1970, 1977; Lewin 1993; Lincoln and Guba 1985; Newton-Smith 1981; Olaisen 1996; Robson 1993; Rock 1979; Scheffler 1982; Stegmeuller 1979; Suppe 1969, 1977, 1978; Waldrop 1992).

The appropriate selection of method depends on the problem at hand. My own approach is far from positivistic, but positivistic science also offers valid methods for certain fields of design research. Science and scientific methods involve a rich relationship between theory and practice, between conceptualization of the world and the world itself, between tacit understanding and the ability to articulate tacit understanding as conscious knowledge. This conscious knowledge is science, the understanding of how things are and how they work based on fundamental principles.

When considered as a union of art and science, the comprehensive design process is a rich, complex integration of the scientific and the sensual, the intellectual and the intuitive. The effective designer has as much in common with Isaac Newton as with Picasso, and more in common with either than with Philippe Starck. The outstanding designer has as much in common with Hokusai as Marie Curie, and more in common with both than with the latest design star.

DEVELOPING A THEORY-RICH DESIGN DISCIPLINE

A comprehensive design approach and successful design requires explanatory principles, models, and paradigms. Thus far, the design profession has developed few of these. Achieving desired change requires a conception of preferred situations in comparison with other possible situations and an understanding of the actions that lead from a current situation to a preferred one. This demands a foundation in theory. General principles are required to predict and measure the outcome of decisions. This is what W. Edwards Deming (1993: 94–118) terms "profound knowledge," composed of "four parts, all related to each other: appreciation for a system; knowledge about variation; theory of knowledge; psychology" (Deming 1993: 96).

To develop this theoretical framework, a community of researchers must identify themselves and enter into dialogue. This process has only recently begun for the field of design research. In the development of a professional research community, "discussion about the scope and content of a young field of research helps to form the identity of its scientific community. Internal organization and boundary definitions are central means for the social institutionalization of a specialty. The exchange of opinions and even disputes concerning the nature and limits of a field help to construct identity and thus become bases for social cohesion" (Vakkari 1996: 169).

In this context,

conceptions of the structure and scope of a discipline are social constructs that include certain objects within that domain and exclude others. Depending on the level of articulation, the outline of a discipline dictates what the central objects of inquiry are, how they should be conceptualized, what the most important problems are, and how they should be studied. It also suggests what kinds of solutions are fruitful. Although articulation is usually general, it shapes the solutions to specific research projects. This general frame is the toolbox from which researchers pick solutions without necessarily knowing they are doing so. (Vakkari 1996: 169)

The concept of profound knowledge establishes prerequisites for a design science toolbox that permits broad understanding linked to reasonably predictable results. Design is not physics, not even biology. Results can never be predictable in the sense that physics or astronomy allows prediction. A science of design is unavoidably linked to contingent, historical, and path-dependent issues. Design remains an art in practice— as medicine, cooking, and even engineering remain arts. At the same time, effective design is based on general principles as medicine and engineering are. One distinction between culinary genius and culinary disaster is a rich understanding of kitchen physics and stovetop chemistry. These relations parallel the relationships between the arts and sciences of design.

Designers who locate their discourse solely in the practice of a fine art of design are unable to move beyond craft skill and vocational knowledge to professional knowledge. The design process must integrate field-specific knowledge with a larger understanding of the human beings for whom design is made, the social circumstances in which the act of design takes place, and the human context in which designed artifacts are used. This requires knowledge across domains, linked to a general knowledge of industries and businesses within which design operates. A broad platform enables designers to focus on problems in a rich, scientific way to achieve desired change.

TRAINING FOR DESIGN SCIENCE

The challenge designers face is the transition from crafting things to understanding things. One must act to achieve results, but the classic distinction faced by practitioners of a design science is the distinction between "doing things right" and "doing the right thing." Doing the right thing requires a decision on what to do. That requires a design decision before technical facilitation.

To prepare design professionals intellectually for today's needs, design education and training require broad, scientific values and profound knowledge. To prepare designers to produce artifacts, design education requires experience rooted in the physical craft of design. These forms of education and training are in some ways at odds. In equally important ways, they can combine to great effect.

Solid foundations in material culture and physical technique can be combined with a thorough scientific understanding. A dynamic world requires dynamic concepts. Artifacts that function in this dynamic world rest on an effective understanding of the world itself. Traditional artifacts worked well enough in a more static world. Simple artifacts such as chairs, spoons, or tents work well because they fill static roles. Even so, it is possible to compare static and dynamic concepts by comparing the performance of traditional artifacts with the same artifacts designed and reengineered using a scientific approach.

Effective design requires appropriate methods and rooted understanding. Design in the industrial world is handicapped by outdated methods. The symptoms are rigid design thinking, the confusion of artistic solutions with design solutions, or—just as bad—the failure to understand the need for the union of grace and function in optimal design (Friedman 1991: 737). Although traditional training can lead to tacit knowledge, it represents the virtues as well as the vices of habit. To be useful, habitual knowledge must possess critical comprehension along with behavioral roots.

CHALLENGES FOR DESIGN PROFESSIONALS

In 1992, the Scandinavian Design Council published a manifesto addressing the broad interactive complex of nature, ecology, and human needs. The manifesto proposed a discourse rooted in a natural economics, an awareness of nature, an awareness of human dimensions, and an economical way of life. The manifesto called for design in a healthy society "based on sound ethical values; a framework for new ways of life, ecologically and economically sound; built on education; engaged design [that can] visualize, emphasize and realize a powerful message based on ethical principle, ecological balance and economic intelligence . . . to influence decisions in private business and in public life; [with] cooperation between designers, producers and users; between invention, industry and the customers they serve" (Scandinavian Design Council 1992).

Meeting these challenges with design as defined by Simon requires a design discipline that fosters the generation and application of scientific knowledge about change management, problem solving, creativity, and transforming information into knowledge. This demands a flexible, principle approach to design.

As a theoretical, scientific discipline, design will have to pay far more attention to the domains of human interaction and culture theory than to the technological issues with which it has thus far been engaged. The new discipline required for design is as much a branch of the human sciences as a branch of physical science or applied engineering. This new discipline is also a looming shadow behind the design professions as they are practiced today.

As a practice, design faces ten major challenges today: three performance challenges, four substantive challenges, and three contextual challenges. The performance challenges of design are to

1. act on the physical world;
2. address human needs; and
3. generate the built environment.

These challenges require frameworks of theory and research to address contemporary professional problems and solve individual cases. The professional problems of design involve four substantive challenges:

1. increasingly ambiguous boundaries between artifact, structure, and process;
2. increasingly large-scale social, economic, and industrial frames;
3. an increasingly complex environment of needs, requirements, and constraints; and
4. information content that often exceeds the value of physical substance.

In an integrated knowledge economy, design also involves three contextual challenges. These are

1. a complex environment in which many projects or products cross the boundaries of several organizations, stakeholder, producer, and user groups;
2. projects or products that must meet the expectations of many organizations, stakeholders, producers, and users; and
3. demands at every level of production, distribution, reception, and control.

These ten challenges require a qualitatively different approach to professional practice than was needed in earlier times. Past environments were simpler. They made simpler demands. Individual experience and personal development were sufficient for depth and substance in professional practice. Experience and development are still necessary, but they are no longer sufficient. Most of today's design challenges require analytic and synthetic planning skills that can't be developed through the practice of contemporary design professions alone.

Professional design practice today involves advanced multidisciplinary knowledge that presupposes interdisciplinary collaboration and a fundamental change in design education. This knowledge isn't simply a higher level of professional education and practice. It is a qualitatively different form of professional practice. It is emerging in response to the demands of the information society and the knowledge economy to which it gives rise.

REFERENCES

Alvesson, M. and K. Sköldberg. 1994. *Tolkning och refleksjon: Vetenskapsfilosofi och kvalitiv metode*. Lund, Sweden: Studentliteratur.

Argyris, C.R. Putnam, and D. McLain Smith. 1985. *Action Science*. New York: Jossey-Bass Publishers.

Bernsen, J. 1986. *Design. The Problem Comes First*. Copenhagen: Danish Design Council.

Deming, W.E. 1993. *The New Economics for Industry, Government, Education*. Cambridge, MA: Massachusetts Institute of Technology, Center for Advanced Engineering Study.

Edwards, C. 1999. *Many Products Have Gone the Way of the Edsel*. Johnson City, TN: Johnson City Press, May 23, 28, 30.

Feyerabend, P.K. 1962. *Explanation, Reduction and Empiricism*. Minnesota Studies in the Philosophy of Science, Vol. III. Minneapolis: University of Minnesota Press.

———. 1974. *Against Method*. London: Verso.

———. 1977. Changing Patterns of Reconstruction. *British Journal of the Philosophy of Science* 28: 351–369.

———. 1978. *Science in a Free Society*. London: NLB.

———. 1987. *Farewell to Reason*. London: Verso.

Friedman, K. 1991. Benktzon and Juhlin: Tablewares for the Disabled, in *Contem-*

porary Masterworks, edited by N. Colin. Chicago and London: St. James Press.

————. 1992. *Strategic Design Taxonomy*. Oslo: Oslo Business School.

————. 1993. *Introducing Strategic Design*. Oslo: Oslo Marketing Symposium.

————. 1995c. A Taxonomy of Design Domains. *Oslo Marketing Symposium 1995. Symposium Proceedings*. Oslo: Norwegian School of Management School of Marketing.

————. 1997. Design Science and Design Education. In *The Challenge of Complexity*, edited by P. McGrory. Helsinki, Finland: University of Art and Design, Helsinki, UIAH.

————. 2000a. Design Education in the University. Professional Studies for the Knowledge Economy. In Conference Proceedings. *Re-inventing Design Education in the University*. International Conference on Design Education, Perth, Australia, 11–13. December 2000, Curtin University of Technology. Edited by C. Swann and E. Young.

————. 2000b. Design Knowledge: Context, Content and Continuity. In *Doctoral Education in Design. Foundations for the Future. Proceedings of the La Clusaz Conference, July 8–12, 2000*. Edited by D. Durling and K. Friedman. Staffordshire, UK: Staffordshire University Press.

Fuller, B. 1964. *World Design Science Decade 1965–1975. Phase I (1964) Document 2: The Design Initiative*. Carbondale, IL: World Resource Inventory, Southern Illinois University.

————. 1965. *World Design Science Decade 1965–1975. Phase I (1965) Document 3: Comprehensive Thinking*. Carbondale, IL: World Resource Inventory, Southern Illinois University.

————. 1967. *World Design Science Decade 1965–1975. Document 5: Comprehensive Design Strategy*. Carbondale, IL: World Resource Inventory, Southern Illinois University.

————. 1969. *Utopia or Oblivion: The Prospects for Humanity*. New York: Bantam Books.

————. 1981. *Critical Path*. New York: St. Martin's Press.

Fuller, B., and A. Dil. 1983. *Humans in Universe*. New York: Mouton.

Galtung, J. 1967. *Theory and Methods of Social Research*. Oslo: Universitetsforlaget.

Gero, J. 1999. Understanding Design. Design as an Activity. *Seminar notes, March 3*. Key Center of Design Computing. University of Sydney.

Gleick, J. 1987. *Chaos. The Making of a New Science*. London: Sphere Books.

Johannessen, J.A., J. Olaisen and K. Friedman. 1997. *Clarified Subjectivity. Contributions to a Philosophy of Science for Information Science*. Syllabus for the Nordic Research Course in philosophy of science for library and information science. Copenhagen, Gothenburg, and Oslo: the Royal Danish School of Library Science, Gothenburg University School of Library and Information Science, and the Norwegian School of Management.

Kuhn, T. 1970. *The Structure of Scientific Revolutions*. 2d eds., enlarged. Chicago: University of Chicago Press.

————. 1977. *The Essential Tension. Selected Studies in Scientific Tradition and Change*. Chicago: University of Chicago Press.

Lewin, R. 1993. *Complexity. Life at the Edge of Chaos*. London: J.M. Dent.

Lincoln, Y., and E. Guba. 1985. *Naturalistic Inquiry*. Newbury Park, CA: Sage.

Lukas, P. 1998. The Ghastliest Product Launches. *Fortune*, March 16, 44.

Mansfield, E., J. Rapaport, J. Schnee, S. Wagner, and M. Hamburger. 1971. *Research and Innovation in Modern Corporations*. New York: Norton.

McMath, R. 1998. *What Were They Thinking? Marketing Lessons I've Learned from Over 80,000 New Product Innovations and Idiocies*. New York: Times Business.

Newton-Smith, W. 1981. *The Rationality of Science*. London: Routledge and Kegan Paul.

Olaisen, J. 1996. "Pluralism or Positivistic Trivialism. Criteria for a Clarified Subjectivism." In *Information Science. From the Development of the Discipline to Social Interaction*, edited by J. Olaisen, E. Munch-Pedersen, and P. Wilson. Oslo: Scandinavian University Press.

Robson, C. 1993. *Real World Research. A Resource for Social Scientists and Practitioner-Researchers*. Oxford, England: Blackwell.

Rock, P.E. 1979. *The Making of Symbolic Interactionism*. London: Routledge and Kegan Paul.

Scandinavian Design Council. 1992. Nature, Ecology and Human Needs. Design for the Future. A Scandinavian Design Council Manifesto, in *Norway's New Design*. by K. Friedman and J.B. Ofstad. Oslo: Norsk Form.

Scheffler, I. 1982. *Science and Subjectivity*. Indianapolis: Hackett.

Simon, H. 1982. *The Sciences of the Artificial*. 2d ed. Cambridge, MA: MIT Press.

Stegmeuller, W. 1979. *The Structuralist View of Theories: A Possible Analogue of the Bourbaki Programme in Physical Science*. Berlin: Springer.

Suppe, F. 1969. *Studies in the Methodology and Foundation of Science*. Dordrecht: Reidel.

———. 1977. *The Structure of Scientific Discovery*. Urbana: University of Illinois Press.

———. ed. 1978. *The Structure of Scientific Theories*. Urbana: University of Illinois Press.

Vakkari, P. 1996. Library and Information Science: Content and Scope. In *Information Science: From the Development of the Discipline to Social Interaction*, edited by J. Olaisen, E. Munch-Pedersen, and P. Wilson. Oslo: Scandinavian University Press.

Waldrop, M.M. 1992. *Complexity. The Emerging Science at the Edge of Order and Chaos*. New York: Simon and Schuster.

Postscript: Designing Ethnography

Eric J. Arnould

To paraphrase my favorite comic character Calvin, in this volume, "Ethnography Goes 'Boink!" (Waterson 1991). "Boink" is what happens when the creative mind, heedless of all the reasons something can't or shouldn't be done, goes ahead anyway. Calvin pushes the button on his cardboard duplicator and . . . boink! In this case, the ethnographic mindset is turned loose on the creative/destructive context—in Schumpeter's (1989) vision—of the corporate design world. And like Calvin's boinking duplicator, design ethnography opens up a Pandora's box of exciting possibilities. Whereas the duplicator created endless copies of Calvin, design ethnography provides a new vehicle for providing images and meanings to designers that can result in products that add real value to customers' lives. At the same time, as with Calvin's duplicator, successful design ethnography may unleash some unintended side effects. One danger, not much discussed here, is that turning the full power of design ethnography loose may provoke an unwanted level of intrusion into consumers' lives.

The articles in this collection are self-explanatory and self-revelatory. By this I mean that authors eagerly explain what design ethnographers do or to prescribe what they could and should do as well. In addition, they explain how other members of new product development teams may communicate with design ethnographers and vice versa more effectively.

Thanks to their self-revelatory quality, the parallels between this work and the development anthropology of the 1980s struck me forcefully (Horowitz and Painter 1986). Both projects are undertaken in a collaborative spirit. The chapters in this book as in the earlier volume offer sometimes wry commentary on the problems associated with communicating ethnographic insight to sometimes uncomprehending colleagues. Some of the lessons I've learned from successful collaborative development activities are also on display here, such as the necessity for a five-year time frame to develop effective partnerships as discussed in the articles on E-Lab, the desirability of transparency in the work processes (an elusive but valuable ideal), and above all, the importance of incorporating the interests of multiple stakeholders in the development process (Arnould 1990). But in the Horowitz and Painter volume, the voices of collaborators from the field, the farmers, herders, and local authorities with whom the anthropologists worked, were largely occulted by the authorial voice of the anthropologist. By contrast, those other voices are more fully present here, and as a result, the reader gets a good sense of how untidy, passionate, and rewarding ethnographic collaboration can be. It's an iterative bow-tie looping process, as Wasson shows. And as in the earlier volume, the disappointments that stem from ethnographers' roles as advisers and consultants rather than decision makers is also evident.

Some of the lessons here are similar to the lessons anthropologists have learned from their experiences working on multidisciplinary teams in economic development or health-related consultancies, for example. Design ethnographers work faster and more collaboratively than traditional ethnographers who do rapid appraisal work for program design (Arnould 1990). Often as Rita Denny and George Wall in their respective contributions insist, anthropologists need to attend to process: simultaneously to educate other professionals about the value of anthropology by providing concrete value-added guidance, and to learn from other professionals enough of their language and concerns to develop a shared working language. The shared semiotic language discussed by Sacher is one example of the payoffs of attention to process, but more generally, anthropologists who work in business have to become familiar with the prevailing buzzwords and business fads that provide the metaphorical language of practice in the corporate world.

An additional lesson is that working as consultants places the design anthropologist in a relatively weak role in determining outcomes. As Applin suggests, processes extraneous to the project and over which the design anthropologist has little control often determine outcomes. Cultural norms apportion responsibilities in design as in every cultural context, and stakeholders resist change. Any anthropologist who has worked in development has surely encountered situations when projects were funded or not funded irrespective of their merit because of considerations such as the "internal company problems" Applin describes that remain outside of their control. The limited solution to this problem is for design ethnographers like development anthropologists to co-opt those political processes to achieve outcomes, which their research tells them are in the best interest of their primary clients and other key stakeholders. What this means in turn is another double or triple job for the design anthropologist. Design ethnography plays a classic culture broker function.

Design anthropologists must do the ethnographic work necessary to produce simultaneously the deliverable required by the client, the translation work between team members, and sometimes, the insight into client processes needed to influence the client to actually do what they judge to be in the client's best interests. And as suggested, sometimes other forces subvert these interests.

This book is awash in a degree of reflexivity that the contributors to the classic Clifford and Marcus (1986) volume should applaud, although their sights were still set on the classic populations of ethnographic interest. We have designers and managers communicating with ethnographers about ethnographic practice, as well as ethnographers describing the practice of managers and designers. Communication and translation are key watchwords as in Dawson's discussion, which pinpoints mechanisms for fruitful dialogue. As a result of the experience of and with ethnographic practice, one has the sense that participants in the design process are more aware of their own practice and that of their colleagues, the culture of the organization is more available to scrutiny, and "formative evaluation," as Susan Squires suggests in her contribution, is more the order of the day than ever before.

One of my favorite insights is found in Heiko Sacher's contribution where he talks about the emergence of the Internet as a key site and vehicle for new product design. The Internet shifts the frame of reference of design work from a linear one to a more conversational paradigm. This point has been made in the context of marketing generally. The Internet is seen as a place where advertising must shift toward a more demand-driven phenomena. In the context of advertising production and content delivery, the Internet is seen as a mechanism that facilitates and indeed mandates mass customization. To be successful, mass customization or demand-driven advertising requires that marketers move to a conversational paradigm with their customers. To the extent that all these things are descriptive of some lived reality, readers will already have discerned that I mean to say that they place a premium on an ethnographic cast of mind. For although it often depends on the "revelatory incident" that arises from just hanging around long enough (Fernandez 1986), ethnography is also the most conversational of analytic procedures as a number of contributions to the present volume emphasize to varying degrees. Of course, as George Walls points out in his tutorial on speaking of ethnography to clients, there is no guarantee that designers or managers will respond to ethnographic insight without successful identification of common languages and shared practices. Sacher like Dawson describes shared languages and practices that may make it more likely that the ethnographic conversation will be joined. Collaborative exchange models of research, design, and delivery rely for their power, of course, on the gift so famously discussed by Mauss (1967) and Sahlins (1976).

Christina Wasson observes, as did leading actors in development anthropology, that the enduring power of ethnographic methods reside in the training ethnographers receive in social theory, in fieldwork experiences that enables them to master a variety of research methods, and in an apprenticeship that enables them to learn how to interpret observations, conversations, interviews, and artifacts. Early leaders in the field of design ethnography as Reese points out are also committed to the holistic contextual approach to practical problem solving that characterizes applied anthropology generally. Although perhaps not fully realized in design ethnography, it is clear that the core virtues of cultural anthropological tradition are alive and well in this newly energized realm of application. Byrne and Sands and Wasson suggest some reasons for the fit between ethnography and design. Both design and ethnography require creativity, intuition, self-reflexivity, and an inductive work process. Researchers and designers may be divided by their primarily verbal and visual orientations respectively, but they are natural partners in these other ways.

Thanks to the contribution of William Reese, this volume avoids a pernicious problem that often afflicts "hot" topical areas and emerging fields, ignoring history. In addition to artfully profiling the trajectories that have impelled some of the pioneers in design ethnography into mostly successful and sometimes spectacularly successful applications, Reese doesn't neglect the anthropological ancestors of the field. There is much to be learned from the rise and decline of first-generation "industrial" anthropology, but that story is beyond the scope of this comment. Susan Squires also refers us to the rapid appraisal work pioneered by development anthropologists in response to the urgency of development work and the impatience of their natural science colleagues (Beebe 1995; Manerson and Aaby 1992).

A further issue of history emerges obliquely in this volume. Reese documents cases of personal dissatisfaction with existing work processes in design, engineering, and marketing research that led to design ethnography. Viewed paradigmatically or institutionally, in both the dissatisfaction and the solution, I detect the ongoing reverberations of the interpretive turn that has driven not only the basic social sciences (Geertz 1983), but marketing and other business fields in turn (Sherry 1991). Horowitz and Painter (1986) pointed out that a space for development anthropology opened as a result of a crisis in earlier economic development policy based on discredited "growth-and-modernization" paradigms. Similarly, I think the crisis in demand brought about by the satiation and fragmentation of traditional consumer markets in North America, Europe, and Japan, and dissatisfaction with modernist scientific and business practice (Brown 1995) has helped open a space for design ethnography.

To invite further discussion, I mention some issues not developed here that I think could do much to fan the flames of future designer ethnographers' passion. For example, the authors say little about methodological innovation. Design ethnographers surely have something to contribute to visual anthropology, given their emphasis on videotaping naturally occurring observations, but little discussion of these techniques is revealed here.

Although Christina Wasson mentions it, the authors say little about the value of their comparative ethnological frame of reference and the cultural relativism that is near to the heart of the field of anthropology, and, as I take it, design as well.

Finally, the authors have said little either about the nature of consumer culture as they see it, or the culture of customers for the design work provided by design ethnographers and their design colleagues.

Let me conclude. Design ethnography shows that the subversive science of ethnography remains restless and viable as we enter a new millennium charting new horizons and entertaining new problems. Design ethnography shows once again the practical relevance of ethnographic method. The contributions to this volume remind us that the hallmarks of anthropological training—a comparative mind-set, methodological eclecticism, and a thorough grounding in social theory—pay out rich returns in insight and understanding.

REFERENCES

Arnould, E.J. 1990. Changing the Terms of Rural Development: Collaborative Research in Cultural Ecology in the Sahel. *Human Organization* 49 (4): 339–354.

Beebe, J. 1995. Basic Concepts and Techniques of Rapid Appraisal. *Human Organization*, 54 (1): 42–51.

Brown, S. 1995. *Postmodern Marketing*. London: Routledge.

Clifford, J., and G.E. Marcus, eds. 1986. *Writing Culture: The Poetics and Politics of Ethnography*. Berkeley: University of California Press.

Fernandez, J.W. 1986. *Persuasions and Performances: The Play of Tropes in Culture*. Bloomington, IN: University of Indiana.

Geertz, C. 1983. Blurred Genres: The Refiguration of Social Thought. In *Local Knowledge: Further Essays in Interpretive Anthropology*, New York: Basic Books.

Horowitz, M.M., and T.M. Painter, eds. 1986. *Anthropology and Rural Development in West Africa*. Boulder: Westview Press.

Mauss, M. 1967. *The Gift: Forms and Functions of Exchange in Archaic Societies*. New York: Norton and Co.

Manerson, L., and B. Aaby. 1992. An Epidemic in the Field? Rapid Assessment Procedures and Health Research. *Social Science and Medicine* 35 (7): 839–850.

Sahlins, M. 1976. *Culture and Practical Reason*. Chicago: University of Chicago Press.

Schumpeter, J.A. 1989. *Essays: On Entrepreneurs, Innovations, Business Cycles, and the Evolution of Capitalism*. New Brunswick, NJ: Transaction Publishers.

Sherry, J.F. Jr. 1991. Postmodern Alternatives: The Interpretive Turn in Consumer Research, *Handbook of Consumer Research*, edited by T.S. Robertson and H.H. Kassarjian. Englewood Cliffs, NJ: Prentice Hall.

Waterson, B. 1991. *Scientific Progress Goes "Boink."* Kansas City, KS: Andres and McMeel.

Index

Contributors

SALLY ANN APPLIN has been designing interfaces for science museums, software, and products for the past eleven years and now works as an independent research and interaction design consultant. She has designed interfaces for museums, software, and products for clients representing the software, entertainment, telecommunications, and e-commerce industries. Ms. Applin was one of the principal designers for Apple Computer Inc.'s landmark QuickTime™ project, The Virtual Museum. Ms. Applin has lectured at the College Art Association and the Graduate Architecture Department at Yale. She received a master's degree from New York University's Tisch School of the Arts Interactive Tele-communications Program, where she was awarded the departmental prize for Excellence in Design Aesthetics. Her artwork has also been featured in "California Copy Art," at Xerox PARC, Palo Alto, CA.

ERIC J. ARNOULD is professor of marketing at the University of Nebraska-Lincoln and holds a Ph.D. in cultural anthropology from the University of Arizona. From 1975 to 1989, he worked on economic development in more than a dozen West African nations. His recent research investigates consumer ritual, household consumption behaviors, postmodern motivation, magical consumption, service relationships, West African marketing channels, and the uses of qualitative data. His work appears in major marketing journals and many other social science periodicals and books. He is associate editor of the *Journal of Consumer Research* and deputy editor of the *Journal of Contemporary Ethnography*. Dr. Arnould speaks French and Hausa.

BRYAN BYRNE is an anthropologist who specializes in consumer research, strategic product development, and corporate development. He has conducted applied consumer research and product development for companies including the American Heart Association, Belkin, GVO, Hauser, Hitachi, Hewlett-Packard, Johnson Controls International, and Laerdal Medical Corp. He is also a cofounder of Baffin, Inc., a company that develops automated chemical processes to treat industrial wastewater. Most of his basic research concentrates on globalization, labor patterns, kinship, racial and ethnic identity, and the evolution of water-related organizations and law.

MARK DAWSON is senior design anthropologist at Eastman Kodak Corp., where he has been working exclusively in design anthropology since the mid-1990s. His emphasis is on consumer-based product inspiration and generation working in small multidisciplinary teams. As an anthropologist with some of the top design firms in the United States, his clients have included Fujitsu, Sega of America, Hitachi, Sunbeam, and NEC, among others. Past anthropological research work has ranged from the social networks of first-time prison inmates to the nature of "social gaming" among video gamers.

RITA DENNY is a partner and general manager of The B/R/S Group, Inc.'s Chicago office. She specializes in American consumer culture, focusing on culturally based meanings of products and services in everyday life for clients such as Apple Computer, Inc., the Boeing Company, Citicorp, guild.com, and SC Johnson Wax. She applies these findings to advertising positioning, new product and brand development, and corporate communication strategies.

KEN FRIEDMAN is associate professor of leadership and strategic design at the Norwegian School of Management Department of Knowledge Management, and visiting professor at the Advanced Research Institute of Staffordshire University School of Art and Design. Mr. Friedman's research on the foundations of design seeks to develop a philosophy and theory of design that anchor robust practice. Mr. Friedman has published books and articles on management, information science, philosophy, and art. He serves on the Editorial Advisory Board of ARTbibliographies Modern. As a practicing artist and designer, he was active in the international laboratory of experimental artists, architects, composers, and designers known as Fluxus. His work has recently been exhibited at the Tate Modern, the Whitney Museum of American Art, and in a major solo exhibition at the University of Iowa Museum of Art. He recently edited a book on knowledge management with Johan Olaisen and a special issue of the journal *Built Environment*. With David Durling, he co-chaired the La Clusaz conference on Doctoral Education in Design.

CHARLES LEINBACH is a professor and industrial designer who prefers and teaches the broader product development approach to design. He spent twelve years at Fitch as a product designer, vice president of design strategy, and vice president of market strategies. There he worked on the 1980s Human Factors/Industrial Design Strategy with Xerox, and on projects for GE, Rubbermaid, 3M, Boeing, Whirlpool, Polaroid, Ciba, Kodak, Owens Corning, Herman Miller, Square D, and many others. Mr. Leinbach earned a bachelor's degree in fine arts, a master's in industrial design, an MBA, and a doctorate in jurisprudence. He is a licensed practicing attorney, and was admitted to the U.S. Patent bar in 1977. Mr. Leinbach is a member of the McCulley Group, a San Diego–based strategy company.

WILLIAM REESE is a senior associate at the Philadelphia design research firm of Design Science, where he conducts behavioral research to help companies develop new commercial and consumer products. He earned his Ph.D. in cultural anthropology from the University of California, San Diego, where he was a winner of the NABC Award for his dissertation research, and a Fellow of the Institute on Global Conflict and Cooperation. Interested in the relationship between individual needs and social institutions, Dr. Reese has conducted extensive research in India, as well as design research in the United States, Europe, and Japan. His client portfolio includes, among others, GE, GlaxoSmithKline, and Motorola.

HEIKO SACHER is director of interaction services at GVO Inc. in Palo Alto, California, where he has applied his expertise in customer research and in human computer interaction to understand and address the needs of specific consumer cultures such as Asian users, teenagers, and scientists. Before joining GVO, Inc., Mr. Sacher was at Apple's Advanced Technology Group Research Center in Singapore, where he drove efforts to integrate advanced Asian language technologies, such as handwriting recognition and speech recognition, to create the world's first speech-pen interface solution for Chinese. Heiko Sacher earned a master's degree in product design from Hochschule für Gestaltung Offenbach, Germany, and was later awarded a Fulbright Scholarship for further study. Mr. Sacher has received many awards for his research and product designs, including Gold and Silver awards from IDSA/*BusinessWeek* and a Best of Category award from *I.D. Magazine*.

ED SANDS began his formal training in economics at Cornell University and then began to develop his extensive marketing and sales background while working in manufactured and consumer products at Bethlehem Steel and Corning, Inc. Since 1984, Mr. Sands has been actively consulting in industrial design, where he has concentrated on new client development and professional services for product innovation and marketing. Mr. Sands' client portfolio includes Boeing, Johnson Controls, Cybex, Square D, and the Coca-Cola Company.

SUSAN SQUIRES holds a Ph.D. in cultural anthropology from Boston University and has specialized in understanding how observed behaviors and communication patterns are reflective of, and influenced by, cultural beliefs and values. Her fifteen years of professional experience range from corporations and government agencies to nonprofit organizations. Her work has been applied to a broad range of clients, including Sun Microsystems, ENRON, General Mills, Xerox, Intel, Sprint, the *San Jose Mercury News*, Laerdal Medical Corp., SC Johnson, and the American Heart Association. During her work at GVO, Inc. she developed her skills in interaction media conducting ethnographic research on projects from telecommunications to Web site interaction for "start-ups" and established clients such as Sharp, Sun, and Ericsson. Dr. Squires is president of the National Association of Practicing Anthropologists, and her work has been featured in *Fast Company* magazine ("Anthropologists Go Native in the Corporate Village" and "How to Globalize Yourself") as well as the *New York Times, USA Today, Le Nouvel Observateur, Christian Science Monitor* and the *San Francisco Chronicle*.

GEORGE WALLS has twenty years' experience in technology and medical devices with Fortune 500, small business, private, and venture capital-based start-up companies. As a generalist, Mr. Walls works to bridge various disciplines into cohesive teams by combining diversity of thought and training with vision. As the founder of QualStone, a Silicon Valley research and marketing services company, he has combined research and content management into a unique service that helps technology companies manage customer-based content. Among the most notable is an effort with Palm and Price Waterhouse Coopers to develop the Palm Solutions Marketplace, which helps enterprise customers find solution providers. Many of his contributions are a result of his prior experience at Laerdal Medical Corp. Although he rose through sales and marketing, Mr. Walls ultimately became director of product innovation at Laerdal. In this position, he fused product developers and product managers into a cohesive business unit responsible for new medical devices and software products from concept to launch. During his tenure, Laerdal released more new products than at any previous time. In addition to achieving commercial success, several products won prestigious awards from the Industrial Designers Society of America and the Medical Device Manufacturer's Association. He holds an MBA from University of Houston's executive program, a bachelor of arts and bachelor of science degree in management and finance from the University of Dayton, and is certified as a New Product Development Professional by the Product Development Management Association. Mr. Walls resides in Morgan Hill, CA.

CHRISTINA WASSON has conducted applied anthropology in the private sector since 1992. She has consulted in the areas of both design and organizational change management. Clients have primarily been in the high-technology sector, but span the range from packaged foods to office furnishings. Dr. Wasson teaches anthropology at DePaul University. With her classes, she is conducting a long-term study of visitor experiences at the Field Museum of Natural History. Dr. Wasson's overview article, "Ethnography in the Field of Design," is appearing in *Human Organization*.